WAYS
OF
WALKING

Essays

Edited by Ann de Forest

NEW DOOR BOOKS
Philadelphia 2022

New Door Books
An imprint of P. M. Gordon Associates, Inc.
2115 Wallace Street
Philadelphia, Pennsylvania 19130
U.S.A.

Second printing, 2022

Cover design by Miriam Seidel

Library of Congress Control Number: 2021953536
ISBN 978-1-7355585-2-3 (paperback)
ISBN 978-1-7355585-3-0 (e-book)

For Joe Farrell

Contents

Pilgrimages, Routes, and Rituals

The Walkable City

The Body Resistant

A Subtle Magnetism in Nature

Lost and Found

Preface

AN ARCHAEOLOGIST FOLLOWS the traces of an ancient road through the heel and heart of Italy. An artist walks 100 miles of radial roads in Chicago, along native paths usurped and repurposed by European settlers. An American ex-pat takes a medieval pilgrimage route through modern Geneva, her adopted hometown. A traveler lands at LAX and decides to walk the seven miles home. A boy gets lost in the woods. An aging trail runner breaks his leg and slowly learns how to walk again. A Syrian refugee spends a month walking along the Jordanian border trying to find a way across to reach his family on the other side.

These are just some of the ways of walking collected in the pages of this anthology. The writers assembled here, myself included, count ourselves bipedal descendants of some early hominid, our common ancestor who first rose up straight on two sturdy, stalk-like legs and— presumably wobbling and swaying like any toddler—lifted a foot, swung a hip, bent a knee to plant that foot on solid ground, and then set off, moving through the world. But though walking may be our shared inheritance, we don't all walk the same way. In the 26 essays that follow, you'll find writers who amble, who zip, who stride, who stumble, who march in protest—toward freedom or in solidarity with others—who walk slant and walk slow, who consider themselves hikers or *flâneurs* or pilgrims. Some walk with assurance, others with assistance, depending on walkers or wheelchairs. Gender, skin color, the frailty or heft of their bodies, age, injuries and infirmities, the losses sustained and witnessed in the course of a life and throughout human history, all influence the way they walk.

The "ways" of the title has two meanings, of course. There are the ways that we move and the ways or paths we walk upon. Some of the ways followed in this book were carefully chosen, specific routes that might lead to discovery and insight: Liana Brent's trek along the Via Appia Antica; Paula Read's tracing of the Via Jacobi, a branch of the Camino de Santiago de Compostela, in western Switzerland; Adrienne Mackey's and J.J. Tiziou's circumnavigation of the Philadelphia border; Nathaniel Popkin's penitential re-enactment of the notorious Walking Purchase; JeeYeun Lee's methodical 100 miles through Chicagoland. Others find revelations in walking the streets and sidewalks and park paths of their own everyday environs: Kathryn Hellerstein gains intimacy with her neighborhood through a weekly practice of walking on Shabbes; Rahul Mehta, on a commute via underground concourses, is alert to those people for whom that transitway is shelter; Dwight Dunston reminisces with his late father about what's changed on the streets they once walked together and what, for Black men walking through the city, hasn't changed; and Mickey Herr views her own celebrated "walkable city" in a new light as her mother's mobility declines.

As in Herr's essay, not all the ways of walking presented here are comfortable or easy. Lena Popkin, accompanying her father and brother on a nocturnal stroll, is enraged by their obliviousness to the men who casually harass her as they pass. Hannah Judd stumbles aimlessly along the Chicago waterfront, grieving her father's sudden death. Victoria Farmer finds her yearning to follow the free-wheeling footsteps of Virginia Woolf through London thwarted by her own physical limitations, while Kabria Rogers' simple desire for a refreshing stroll to a nearby river is hampered (humorously) by a trifecta of heat, heaviness, and a global pandemic. Yasser Allaham tells a harrowing tale of escaping his native Syria, and Jay Heinrichs learns the virtues of slowness the hard way, by severely fracturing his leg.

Yet these essays celebrate walking's joys as well. Ruth Knafo Setton passes a dreamy summer walking with her father as he nears the end of his life, their conversations meandering from the present to his Moroccan boyhood. Kalela Williams celebrates the Black men and women, enslaved and free, who built her city, fought for freedom, marched against injustice; she delights in following their footsteps and revealing their paths to others. Even those, like Justin Coffin, who walked feeling hopelessly lost find enlightenment—and ultimately direction—in their disorientation. " [I]n the two kinds of great journeys," he writes, "we are either Theseus escaping the labyrinth or Odysseus trying to get home."

As fundamental and ordinary as walking can be, these essays reveal how, in an age that prizes speed and efficiency, walking has become a subversive act. For a long time, the working title of this collection was "Slow Going," to acknowledge that the deliberate pace of walking runs counter to society's drive to produce, accomplish—arrive. That necessary slowness also sharpens perceptions and heightens attention to one's surroundings, to small delights and gross injustices, as well as to the particular mechanics of one's own body. Among the rebellious walkers featured here, David Sanders muses on his tendency to walk "slant," against his city's grid; my own essay reflects on growing up in a place and time where walking was denounced as aberrant behavior; and Tom Zoellner describes his own eccentric practice of departing from airports on foot. Most renegade of all is Mark Geanuleas, who walks everywhere, forgoing all other forms of transportation no matter how distant his destination.

That commitment—for Geanuleas, a necessity not a choice—has affinities with an earlier walker philosopher and writer. Henry David Thoreau's spirit hovers over many of these essays, particularly in Christine Nelson's reflections on her own long relationship with Thoreau as keeper of his notebooks at the Morgan Library and in Sharon White's personal responses, not always genial, to his famous essay "Walking." But Thoreau is not walking's only acolyte or theorist. Nancy Brokaw introduces readers to a panoply of poets, painters, philosophers, and provocateurs like Wordsworth, Keats, Baudelaire, Robert Louis Stevenson, and Guy Debord, for all of whom walking was both a source of artistic inspiration and a key to living a fully engaged, active, present life.

In her essay, Brokaw quotes Robert Louis Stevenson: "The great affair is to move; to feel the needs and hitches of our life more clearly; to come down off this feather-bed of civilization." But coming down from that comfortable feather-bed means confronting the often discomfiting here and now. As Geanuleas writes about his own walking practice: "Between here and there *everything is more important than you*, everything must be faced, no mile, no mosquito, no neighborhood can be avoided."

The particular urgencies of our time demand such close witness and scrutiny. Yet there's a paradox in embracing walking as a means toward social and environmental redemption. As JeeYeun Lee observed when she and I were corresponding about her essay: "Climate collapse requires us to act with urgency, but in order to do so, we need to slow down enough to notice and connect to our environment and the people around us, and feel the histories that have shaped us. How do we do both at the same time?"

The essays in *Ways of Walking* invite you to ponder questions like these. Read them at a leisurely pace, then open your door, leave the confines of your screens and the enticements of the metaverse behind, and join in the long parade of humanity, past, present, and future, moving forward one step at a time on a calming, invigorating, eye-opening, heart-widening walk.

Ann de Forest

The Art of Walking

The Hiker and the *Flâneur*

Nancy Brokaw

Not to find one's way in a city may well be uninteresting and banal. It
requires ignorance—nothing more. But to lose oneself in a city—as
one loses oneself in a forest—that calls for quite a different schooling.
Then signboards and street names, passersby, roofs, kiosks, or bars
must speak to the wanderer like a cracking twig under his feet, like
the startling call of a bittern in the distance, like the sudden stillness
of a clearing with a lily standing erect at its center.
—Walter Benjamin

THE PATH INTO the woods led up a modest hill, past a modest stand
of East Coast trees—red oaks and tulip poplars, sugar maples, and
the stray dogwood. At the top of that rise lay a shallow pond. Not all
that much bigger than a big puddle, it nonetheless brought forth frog
spawn in the spring. I must have been nine or ten at the time, but I still
remember the first time someone—Bobby Quigley? one of the James
kids?—pointed out the egg mass; we returned week after week to watch
the pollywogs. A few weeks later, we'd hear the adults croaking as we
climbed up the trail.

The pond lay in a little declivity, and on the far side, the hill led to
another stretch of woodland where a pencil-thin brook ran through a
dip in the land. Reaching that tract meant crossing a long driveway that
led to a low-slung house that we knew belonged to rich people; from a
distance, the house wasn't all that imposing, but the land surrounding
sure was.

To cross that road meant I was most surely trespassing. Stepping on the macadam and scooting across the drive delivered a little frisson, a faint whiff of doing something forbidden. So I'd slip quickly down into that small patch of wildness and just ramble away the rest of the day. I remember: the November tulip trees stripped bare and beeches clinging to their paper-thin leaves; the spring flowering of May apple, trillium, jack-in-the-pulpit, sometimes even a lady's slipper; the sound and flash of white tail as a deer crashed through the undergrowth.

Beyond that stand of wood lay meadows, land that I assumed had once been farmed but, now in the hands of some more rich people, had gone to seed: sedge and Queen Anne's lace, milkweed and black-eyed Susans, blackberry bushes and joe-pye weed. I'd bushwhack my way through those meadows to Rahway Road—and then turn reluctantly back home.

It was my go-to playground where I'd ramble for hours, a classroom where I learned basic identifications of local flora, a laboratory where I first experimented with photography, an escape room where I fantasized about living rough like Sam in *My Side of the Mountain* or Karana in *Island of the Blue Dolphins*.

It's gone now, that landscape where I spent long hours of childhood and youth. The developers have developed land that seemed perfect in its undeveloped state. I haven't had the heart to return, but I have checked it out on street view. From the look of it, it's been given over to a cul-de-sac of pleasant suburban houses, generous backyards, and not a pedestrian in sight—even on a beautiful summer's day.

WHEN DID PEOPLE decide that walking was fun? I'm no historian, but I suspect that the emergence of walking-as-pastime is a relative latecomer to the species. For most of our history, we walked with a purpose: following after the flocks in pasturage, invading the neighboring kingdom, making the pilgrimage to Canterbury. So it's worth noting that the word *hike*, in the meaning of *a walk in the country*, didn't emerge until sometime in the early nineteenth century, just in time to be recruited by people unnerved by industrialization and its sidekick urbanization.

The English Romantic poets were notorious walkers. Chief among them was William Wordsworth, who famously wandered lonely as a cloud through the Lake District and less famously joined with a college friend on a Continental trek that clocked more than 2,400 miles. Like most hikers since, Wordsworth was in it for pleasure: these weren't pilgrimages or forced marches but rather, as John Muir would later put it, the urge to "get as near the heart of the world as [he could]."

The idea had legs.

It took off in 1818, when Keats walked from Cumbria to Scotland as "a sort of Prologue to the Life I intend to pursue," an occasion to "learn poetry," and Caspar David Friedrich headed out to the mountains outside Dresden for a sketching session. Back in the studio, he imagined what may be the iconic painting of the Romantic era, *Wanderer above the Sea of Fog.*

Later down the century, Thoreau's 1851 essay *Walking* set a high standard: "If you are ready to leave father and mother, and brother and sister, and wife and child and friends," he wrote, "and never see them again—if you have paid your debts, and made your will, and settled all your affairs, and are a free man—then you are ready for a walk." In 1878, a young Robert Louis Stevenson soloed through the Cévennes mountains of southern France. "For my part, I travel not to go anywhere, but to go. I travel for travel's sake. The great affair is to move; to feel the needs and hitches of our life more clearly; to come down off this feather-bed of civilization."

In October 1921, an article, "The Appalachian Trail: A Project in Regional Planning," appeared in the *Journal of the American Institute of Architects.* The author, Benton MacKaye, proposed that a trail be created along the Appalachian skyline to provide recreational escape—and something a bit more utopian: the trail would serve as a base for small, self-owning community camps—"and not a real-estate venture"—supported by larger communities of food and farm camps.

The trail, he argued, would address "the problem of living"—a problem he defined as being "at bottom an economic one." MacKaye was a Progressive who envisioned a new, better way of being: "The camp community is a sanctuary and a refuge from the scramble of every-day worldly commercial life," he wrote. "It is in essence a retreat from profit. Cooperation replaces antagonism, trust replaces suspicion, emulation replaces competition."

Underlying MacKaye's vision is the idea that a good walk in the woods—a hike—will save us. "In wildness is the preservation of the world," said Thoreau. "Civilization needs pure wildness," wrote Muir. Gary Snyder had "a vision of a great rucksack revolution, thousands or even millions of young Americans wandering around with rucksacks, going up to mountains to pray."

A DECADE OR SO after my woods wandering, I was living in Manhattan and still walking. Every day, I commuted to and from work, by foot, through Central Park—about three miles each way. On the weekends I'd take myself over the George Washington Bridge to the Palisades or to Staten Island or to Jamaica Bay. Or, camera in hand, I'd hunt photographs in my Upper West Side neighborhood.

But the walk that remains most vivid to me is the one from Riverside Park south down along the Hudson River. The park back then wasn't quite as spiffy as it is now—the Rotunda at the 79th Street Boat Basin was a crumbling mess—but the Hudson was beautiful, and I loved the idea that New Yorkers were living on houseboats.

The real adventure began below the park. I'd make my way past the abandoned pier that nude sunbathers had taken over—this was the early '80s—and hit my stride as I proceeded south under the West Side Highway and past the occasional ocean liner, the *Intrepid*, and the shuttered Midtown Ferry Terminal. On Sundays, when I took these walks, the street below the elevated was emptied out, but even during the week, this was a mangy place. And when the day was particularly beckoning, I'd walk the whole length down to what is now Battery Park City, where the conceptual artist Agnes Denes had planted a wheatfield.

Manhattan makes it easy to forget that you're living in a port city. But underneath the elevated, you remembered. The warehouses, factories, and slaughterhouses may have been vacant, or nearly so, the ferry terminal abandoned, and the piers rotting, but they spoke to a muscular history of industry, commercial shipping, and manufacturing. That history couldn't survive the transformation of the shipping industry (think containerization) or of transportation (the airplane and the automobile).

Unlike my woods ramblings, all these walks were solitary, my only companion my old Konica SLR. It seemed to me that, with the camera in my hands, I saw more and more intensely—as though it were leading the way. As I recall—the photographs themselves are long lost—what my camera found were the flotsam and jetsam of the old life that had transpired there. I remember images of gone-to-seed signs, color fields issuing from the sides of dumpsters, discarded oddments of rusted metals and rotting scraps of paper.

Although different in character from my woods rambling, that route, too, provided a kind of reverie that took me outside of myself, a glimpse into a different, older life. The image was a phantasm, to be sure, and a Romantic one at that. I'd think about all those old noir films—underneath the el, the scene was all chiaroscuro—and feel, stupidly, the thrilling possibility of New York, as though high-stakes drama was waiting just around the corner.

That landscape, too, is gone. It's been all spiffed up by the developers with efficient streets and blank-eyed buildings—the Javits Center, Trump Place, the Hudson Yards.

CITIES CAN GET a bad rap. Thomas Jefferson didn't much care for "the mobs of great cities"; Thoreau called city life "millions of people being lonesome together"; and as far back as the sixth century BCE, Aesop gave the country mouse the upper hand over his city cousin.

Yet, for all the defects of urban life—the overcrowding, the crime, the pollution—cities persist and even thrive. In her love letter to her Greenwich Village neighborhood (and evisceration of urban planning, Robert Moses–style), Jane Jacobs offers up what may be the best description of their enduring allure: "By its nature, the metropolis provides what otherwise could be given only by traveling; namely, the strange."

It's curiosity that attracts us to the metropolis and that gets us exploring its streets.

In 1722, Daniel Defoe published *A Journal of the Plague Year*, an imaginative recreation of London during the Great Plague of 1665. The book, like its unnamed protagonist, wanders through the streets, as in a fever dream, where it, and he, witness a ghost city, its "streets which were usually so thronged now grown desolate." His confession of just *why* he chooses to roam plague-ravaged streets—"My curiosity led, or rather drove me"—offers as good a description as any to capture a certain way of walking a city. We're driven to it, pandemic or no.

But the emblematic urban wanderer—the *flâneur*—emerged in nineteenth-century Paris. Balzac called *flânerie* "gastronomy of the eye," and Charles Baudelaire famously contributed this description: "For the perfect *flâneur*, the passionate spectator, it is an immense joy to set up house in the heart of the multitude, amid the ebb and flow of movement, in the midst of the fugitive and the infinite. To be away from home and yet to feel oneself everywhere at home; to see the world, to be at the center of the world, and yet to remain hidden from the world."

Flânerie covers a lot of territory: the compulsive pursuit of the crowd in Edgar Allan Poe's "The Man of the Crowd," the night ramblings of Robert Louis Stevenson's *Dr. Jekyll and Mr. Hyde*, any number of Walt Whitman's poems, virtually anything by Charles Dickens.

It also inspired a lot of theorizing. Walter Benjamin turned to the idea in his critique of modernity, urban life, and commodity capitalism: "The *flâneur* seeks refuge in the crowd," he wrote in *The Arcades Project*. "The crowd is the veil through which the familiar city is transformed for the *flâneur* into phantasmagoria. This phantasmagoria, in which the city appears now as a landscape, now as a room, seems later to have inspired the decor of department stores, which thus put *flânerie* to work for profit."

And then there's Guy Debord.

Debord was the leading member of the Situationist International, a mid-twentieth-century group of artists and thinkers with the modest aim of abolishing capitalism through the simple expedient of revolutionizing everyday life. Among the ideas they adopted to that end was psychogeography, defined by Debord as "the study of the precise laws and specific effects of the geographical environment, consciously organized or not, on the emotions and behavior of individuals."

The major methodology in conducting such a study was the *dérive*. As Debord explains, "In a *dérive* one or more persons during a certain period drop their usual motives for movement and action, their relations, their work and leisure activities, and let themselves be drawn by the attractions of the terrain and the encounters they find there."

Although looking suspiciously like *flânerie*, the *dérive* is, at heart, a political act: *dériveurs* were charged with careful documentation of the "psychogeographical effects" they observed—that is, what attracted and repelled them—and the data they collected would then be deployed in reconstructing a city where human, rather than corporate, values prevailed.

Would it were that simple.

I LIVE IN Philadelphia now, in one of the city's oldest neighborhoods, just north of where Swedes first huddled along the Delaware River. I still have itchy feet so I get out of the house as much as I can—walking to most destinations and doing occasional runs along the river.

The path I take on those runs leads through an edgescape, a little strip of fallow urban land between the river itself and the shabby boulevard built to serve the docks and, now, the big box stores. Snaking behind the Sheet Metal Workers offices, a Comcast facility, and the Walmart, the trail skirts a scrubby stretch of land where the athletically inclined bike and run, kids fish off the old piers, a handful of homeless people have pitched tents, and birds and animals still live.

Mallards dabble politely at the water's surface for food, while Canada geese and ring-billed gulls—their scientific name, *Larus delawarensis*, a nod to the river—colonize the Walmart parking lot. You know that spring has arrived when the red-winged blackbirds start croaking, and you nearly trip over garter snakes sunning themselves on the macadam path.

A few months before our own pandemic broke out, I decided to take a late afternoon run along the river. As I neared the path's end, I was stopped dead in my tracks by a sight that has given me a strange comfort ever since. A red fox, with a hawk giving chase, scooted across the path and disappeared into the tract of scrub land, overgrown in brush and waiting for the developer's hand.

Necessity and Choice

Mark Geanuleas

DESCENDING THROUGH a neighborhood toward the center of town, I caught sight of a branch of my bank and stepped in. What business the town had to conduct must have already been transacted, for the low-ceilinged lobby was empty; and slipping past the cordoned-off line I walked up to the teller, informing her, in response to her greeting, that I'd like to make a withdrawal.

"How much do you need?" she asked me mechanically. It was early fall, and I had just arrived in little Red Wing, Minnesota, on my way to St. Paul for the winter. Throughout the trip I'd regularly withdrawn a hundred dollars at a time in order to help pace my expenditures. But that seemed excessive at this juncture: twenty dollars a day had been my average, but surely I wasn't five days away?

"How far is it to St. Paul?" I asked her, vaguely wondering if the question had ever been asked in the bank before.

Her eyebrows drew together almost imperceptibly as if in confirmation of the supposition that it had not. A faint crease marked her forehead. "About fifty miles," she answered, puzzled and yet clearly trying to be accurate.

My eyes glazed over as I made a quick calculation: to reach my goal tomorrow would mean walking into the city later in the day, but I preferred an early entrance into a big city and the hours of daylight which that afforded. It was already two o'clock, and I still needed to eat lunch, maybe striking up a little conversation with an obliging local to rejuvenate myself for the final stretch. Therefore let me loiter a bit today, I told myself, take my time tomorrow, stopping where I would, and plan on a morning arrival the day after. "Two days," I mumbled softly, not quite aware of just how quiet the bank was.

The young woman smiled amiably yet ironically, giving a slight laugh. "What do you mean? You'll be there in an hour," she corrected me. Was I playing around with her?

Once, I might have tried to remain concealed, but I'd long since lost that kind of reticence, and anyway, my half-conscious mumbling had let the cat out of the bag. "Oh, well, I'm walking," I answered her, smiling myself now in anticipation of what this fateful revelation always brought in its train.

Her face went completely blank, and her eyes fixed on me challengingly. "You're *walking* to St. Paul?"

Surely it is no sin to take a little pleasure from such a confession and such bewilderment? I'd met with this many times before, and enjoyed the opportunity to allay the doubts and misgivings inevitable in my interlocutors. "It isn't really that far. I've already come a long way. If you—"

"Where did you start?" she interrupted me, her eyes still intent upon my face.

"Pittsburgh," I replied; and with that charming Midwestern abruptness of welcome, that ability to open the door to a stranger if the stranger should deserve it, she lost all of her confusion and suspicion and waved away the fifty miles she'd just allotted me.

"Ha! You're almost there! You'll be there by tomorrow!"

She was right. The next morning, rising in the dark, I wended my way up from the Cannon River and the little crossroads of Welch where I'd spent the night, and ascended toward the plains. It was October 1 and cold, and as I crested the slope I saw to my right the crescent moon facing down an incipient dawn. Lifting my hand for a moment toward this luminary without sentimentality but simply in acknowledgment, I turned my head forward amid the rustling of the invisible dried corn-stalks which had replaced the brambles and small trees that had hugged the banks of the river. Suddenly the cornstalks gave way, and just visible on the horizon was a thin band of light punctuated by two faintly upward straining points. What could that be, I thought to myself—but at once I understood: there, from where I walked perhaps forty miles distant (having put in a solid ten before nightfall), there were Minneapolis and St. Paul, the two glittering humps of light their distant down-towns. From forty miles away I had seen my destination; and as the sight of the eyes is a form of possession, in a sense I had already arrived. Without hesitation, without even formulating the challenge which had been posed, I accepted it; and with no cessation of my pace I walked all day, closing a thousand-mile trek with a feeling of strength inestimably greater than when I had set out from Pittsburgh's Northside toward the end of August, awaking one bright and humid morning, donning my backpack, and beginning to walk toward the Ohio River and the trains making their serpentine way along its opposite bank.

Now, forty-four days later, eleven of them spent resting in Cleveland, Chicago, Milwaukee, and Madison, I crossed the Mississippi and paused on the edge of downtown St. Paul and looked back. What had I accomplished? Nothing: only another day of walking, even if the day of arrival. I felt no different today than when I left Pittsburgh, I was not a man transformed and I had received no revelation. And yet: the course of the river, the driftless region of southern Wisconsin, Lake Michigan and its windy city, the plains and towns of Indiana and Ohio—all was present at once, gathered up by my glance. I am here like anyone else, I thought, it is no different; and yet the land traversed is also here . . .

"WHY DO YOU WALK?" This is the most difficult question I am asked; it is also the most common. My inquisitor this time around was a young student of philosophy at Middlebury College in Vermont, in whose library up the street I was hoping to wait out an impending storm. I was four and a half years out from that morning above Welch, Minnesota, and six and a half years into traveling, whether to the Mississippi or the corner store, solely by foot. By the time this essay is published, more than ten years will have passed since the mid-December morning when I descended from my apartment in deep South Philadelphia and began to walk to New York to spend Christmas with my family. To be sure, I have gotten better at fielding the question over the years, yet really only in relation to the one who asks—what they themselves might under-stand, have experienced, or be inspired by. For as I've grown more able to read my questioner, the possible answers I might give have also mul-tiplied. "Shouldn't you have figured it out by now? Didn't you know from the start? What's the *reason*?" Such sentiments inform many a parry and thrust with those I meet. But there is no reason: reasons are based upon something understood, something settled and firm in the world—and I understand neither walking nor the world.

The young man before me—energetic and youthful, his medium-length hair falling down over his face only to be brushed aside, his eyes darting from me to the street and back again—deserved and would receive his own reply. We were sitting on the sidewalk outside of a café (it was not yet raining), and had started chatting when I'd noticed he was reading Walter Benjamin. He loved it, he told me, and was trying to understand it. He was determined and intense, and his comments were intelligent: a much more focused young man than I had been as a senior in college—or so I liked to believe.

Benjamin, I thought: perhaps I should speak of the *flâneur*? He will have read, perhaps he's reading now, that "Paris created the type of the *flâneur*." But this is not Paris, and I am no *flâneur*, and honesty should not be sacrificed for comprehensibility. Should I discourse on reasons, then? He'll know Leibniz and Schopenhauer on the principle of sufficient reason, surely. And what about Heidegger on the worldhood of the world? That is pertinent too, and no student of philosophy will be ignorant of *Being and Time*.

The air was moist and heavy with the coming rain as I pondered my reply and speculated on his education. I was on a long walk from southeastern Pennsylvania up into New England to stretch my legs and acquaint myself with the territory, learning continually how to do what I was doing while yet spending rainy afternoons in libraries reading, reading, reading. A conversation about the construction of a world: what a pleasure that would be! And how appropriate! Yet as I looked at his at first interested, then eager, and then admiring face—my secret had been revealed again—I remembered what Nietzsche tells us about reading: that we only understand what we have already understood. Experience had vindicated the statement: I myself had reread *Being and Time* in Midwestern libraries as I returned from St. Paul the spring after my athletic arrival. What a reading that was, to understand the text in the midst of trying to understand what makes a world a world. Surely there was no better way to read such a book? I looked at my young friend. "I've done nothing like that," he had said when my current journey was finally revealed. Of course not! These things take time; and philosophy must remain conceptual until you flesh it out of your own accord, from out of your own experience. Isn't that the privilege of life? "Higher learning begins at thirty"—thus Nietzsche again, but he had it from Schopenhauer, in which borrowing there is no shame. As Voltaire says, it is the privilege of genius to be influenced. I'd been foolish and struck out on my own, but perhaps this young man would prove the adage.

"Why do I walk," I mused, leaning back in my chair and taking a sip of my coffee. He was watching me, completely attentive to whatever I might say. Proudly he had told me of having grown up near Walden Pond, which left me believing he might accidentally take me for some kind of modern-day Thoreau. But I am no Thoreau, no Whitman or Emerson either. How helpful that would be!

I smiled at how difficult this question always is, and also at how seriously he was taking it. That was the proper approach, I thought to myself, for these things are indeed serious. Life is not a game. I mustn't remain abstract or wax poetic—he's a dedicated kid, he wants answers and he wants to believe in them. I meet with this from time to time, not as often as I'd like to, but more than one might expect. Yet how does one encapsulate in a few words what it means to awake to the rising moon and the challenge of a city on the horizon? How does one tell of the experience of sitting in Hyde Park in south Chicago in the languid heat of September and having all of Hammond and Gary crowding in upon you, not as a memory but as the substance of what it means to sit there in Chicago? The attendant in the convenience store in north Hammond had said to me, silencing her friend's warnings about the upcoming neighborhoods, "But think of what he's seen! Think of what he has seen *today*!" How does one speak of that, not the objective event but the way such an arrival forces a change upon the world, which responds and demands a corresponding conformity to its new expectations?

Across from us there was construction where the little Otter Creek cut through Middlebury: a sign had told me that traffic was being diverted here and there because of improvements on the rail line running below the streets and adjacent to the river, improvements undertaken in expectation of Amtrak's new "Vermonter" service through Middlebury. Perhaps I might inspire him with a story of Illinois thunderstorms, but all that would be poetry for this young man. Let me rather come down to earth.

"You've been to New York, right?"

He laughed at me. "Of course."

"Of course. And when Amtrak service gets up and running, you'll be able to take the train down to the City, right?"

"Sure, why not?"

I took a breath and another sip of coffee and then looked up at the low clouds. "Okay, let's say that you take the train to New York. What does New York mean in that case?"

"What does it *mean*?"

"For you it's a choice: you finish classes on Friday and figure out if you have the time and the money to go. If you do, then you walk down to the station and buy the ticket, hop on the train, and head to New York. What matters in this is the *choice* you make; and New York— the actual city of New York—is simply something you can choose. You make the choice, and suffer through however long it takes to get there, and then it's yours. New York in all this is predicated upon your choosing it. The *world* is for you something you can choose, and is founded on your desire, your will to choose it."

"Okay," he said, nodding.

"Now, imagine you walk to New York from here: you still must tabulate your finances, count the days, figure out if you have the time and desire to do it—"

"Right, that's the same."

"—but then the choice is only setting out, beginning. After that, everything between Middlebury and the City is what matters: the weather, the towns, the roads, the people; whether you're tired or hungry, whether you meet with friendliness or distrust. Between here and there *everything is more important than you*, everything must be faced, no mile, no mosquito, no neighborhood can be avoided. It is still you that makes the choice, of course, and still you that arrives; it is still New York into which you finally walk; but what such a New York is predicated upon is the *world* you have had to pass through to get to it; whereas the other New York, the one you take the train to, is predicated only upon yourself, your desire for it, and the choice you make in order to realize that desire. In the first instance the self is founded upon the world, in the second the world is founded upon the self."

My young friend was very silent at this, and for the time being I was not inclined to go on, adding only—recalling that pause above the Mississippi in downtown St. Paul—that by walking to New York he would place the city into the world he had traversed. "And believe me," I added suddenly, hoping he took my words at face value and not as mysterious tokens of some other reality, which they were not, "when you arrive after a walk like that you'll sit in Madison or Union Square or wherever you stop and all of Connecticut, Massachusetts, the whole thing will be there with you. I would say *as you*, but that sounds esoteric, and believe it or not I'm not an esoteric guy." He smirked. "But I mean it, if you walk there—maybe not the first time you try (that will be suffering), but eventually—if you walk there the whole journey will be present."

I was trying to entice him against my better judgment—had I gone too far? He was enlivened, to be sure; he already had half a mind to drop out of school and set out, I knew that, though my direct advice would have been to continue studying. Look! Even his bookmark was back in *The Arcades Project*, dutifully closed, and his coffee was by now quite cold. I had sensed a sincerity in his questions, an almost uncanny understanding that he was missing out on something that might be much closer than he realized, and so I had opened up to him—but wasn't it always going too far? When we parted I quietly avoided his obvious desire to have some sort of contact information: no, he'd be better off with only the inspiration. That way he'll be able to succeed and fail on his own time, claim his discoveries for himself, and build up his own vocabulary in his own conversations. Let him be the strange, suddenly arriving one who sits with the student of philosophy burning to *experience* the efficaciousness of the concepts and the truth of their inception: I knew where to get such things, and was not jealous of the discovery.

Breaking the silence, he asked me another question, one I field less frequently though still from time to time. In a way it's the same question when posed by the subtler intellects I come across. "But why did you *start* to walk?"

That I had handled this question unsatisfactorily before didn't make it any easier this time around. I looked down at the pavement, and he added unexpectedly and most revealingly: "Because I can imagine myself walking, but I can't imagine getting to the point where I start to walk."

I was very pleased at this: I had been right, this young man was much sharper than I had been at his age. What an honest assessment of oneself! What a sensitive differentiation! How was I to respond to this? A wave of elation surged through me at the pass he had forced me into: attempting to formulate what it means to be in a way which has hitherto eluded me.

The first light drizzle was beginning to fall, but we were both anchored there awaiting my reply. I turned my head and fixed my eyes on the red and white sign of the bookshop down the street where I had, to my delight, found and purchased Hermann Fränkel's *Early Greek Poetry and Philosophy* an hour before, which the proprietor would mail on ahead of me. Something about the confluence of the unexpected literary find and the youth's marvelous question stamped Middlebury with a sense that has never left me, though what it is I cannot say.

I began to speak. "A decision takes place in a world where everything, in a certain sense, is understood. I don't mean completely understood, but understood well enough that where you are and where you want to be are apparent, and the path there capable of being decided upon. If one *decides* to walk, make no mistake, such an act will only ever take place in the same world one began from: it will be a walk with a 'reason,' and you'll find exactly what you are looking for, if you know what I mean.

"The point, however, is to *desire* the world, this one right here, just as it is. Maybe one starts walking; and if one is paying attention, maybe one notices that when you walk to the next town over, let's say, it's a little different, this experience of arriving in town. Do you follow this difference, this experience? Not everybody has the time or inclination to follow such things—that's fine: who would want to say how people should be? After all, there are a million reasons *not* to walk.

"This seems to me to be how one might arrive at walking as a *necessity* rather than a choice: slowly, from out of a desire to be present, you strip away one crutch after another and tear yourself down to just being there. Who knows why anyone ever starts such a process! But it does happen, sometimes someone simply can't go on; and then, from out of a desire to remain in the world *like that*—remaining as present as possible—one might begin to *need* to walk everywhere. As a choice one reaches out and grabs life: This is why we should walk! This is what walking means! All that is a kind of tyranny, implementing ideas on reality, even if one means to save the world. One gets no further than where one started, although there is always a great fuss along the way. Such people are frightful; as Thackeray put it, 'Always to be right, always to trample forward, and never to doubt, are not these the great qualities with which dullness takes the lead in the world?'"

I paused for a moment to let the quote settle in, and then continued. "But the other way, by clearing things out and paying attention: if one does this then perhaps one might arrive at the necessity of walking without ever making a choice. And not just the necessity of *walking* . . .

"So it was for me. Sometimes I turn back to those years before I began walking, I 'summon up remembrance of things past,' as the bard says, and find myself in a state of perpetual wonder: Why did I start to walk? What made me set out? I do not know: don't trust someone who always has an answer! I remember thundering across New Jersey in bitter cold yet in the highest of spirits, clearly aware that I was going to try to only walk from that point on, but not at all sure why this had to be. I simply understood that if I was going to be honest with myself I could not go back in good faith."

The budding philosopher interrupted me enthusiastically. "But that's the key moment! Why couldn't you go back? What made you not *able* to go back to taking the train or driving or whatever?"

Deeper and deeper he pressed me toward a statement that I wasn't sure could be made. There is always something humbling about speaking to young people. Why had I gone forward and not back? There was no reason: reasons erupt from out of the world one inhabits. My reasons now are tied up with *walking*, and not vice versa. I had *had* to go forward.

I looked at him and could not suppress a smile. "Aren't the greatest thinkers those who are continually starting over again, admitting they know nothing, never resting in the conceit of knowledge?"

"Those are my favorite. When they're old they write books that begin, 'And so it seems that I have to consider the matter more carefully.'"

"Plato began learning a new language at eighty," I reminded him.

He laughed gleefully. "It's fantastic! What a way to live!"

He was truly a young man after my own heart. I recalled another such youth whom I had sat with in Rochester, New York, several years before, a poem by Keats tattooed on his arm; and a young woman, just a few days before my Middlebury adventure, who had burst into tears while we talked. "Why are you crying?" I had asked, amazed and not a little surprised. "I don't know," she'd replied, shaking her head and trying to smile through the tears, "it's just so beautiful." Yes, it is beautiful; but the credit lies with her for understanding that. There is nothing particularly heroic about walking; but surely for a young woman to allow herself a moment so intimate and vulnerable standing before a grown man and a complete stranger—surely that is real heroism if any such thing still exists, the recognition of beauty and the courage to let that recognition overwhelm you. How rarely one comes across such forthrightness!

"Well," I went on before my philosophical inquisitor, "why do you think that the great ones are like that? Is it because they keep on asking questions?"

His teachers also must have been good because he sensed a trap. "No. Wait. They do keep on asking questions . . ."

"I mean *why* does one have to ask questions?" He knew his limits, too—and I'm back in St. Louis for a moment being led around the city by the daughter of the restaurant owner who'd befriended me the day before when I had stopped in his Northside café to fill my water bottle, just over the bridge from Illinois. It was dusk and I had been describing the days and nights that had brought me to her city. Reaching out to grasp a low-hanging branch she had halted; and very quietly, almost as if she were speaking to herself, the silhouetted trees of Lafayette Square looming above us, she had murmured, "Perhaps I'll travel someday. My place is here now."

Back in the present my young friend was speaking again. "Why does one have to ask questions . . ." He shook his head. "I don't know."

I didn't know either; but long experience can lead one to the point of being able to formulate the problem precisely, and I had learned this is often more valuable to a young listener than a blunt statement, no matter how well-founded. One must tell them the truth, but not how to get there.

"It's a matter of how you are related to the world. The *world* is what solicits the questioning, not the questioner. So one comes to the point where, in order to be honest with oneself, one has to ask the question, one has to try to walk: one has to ask one's questions with one's life."

This was a line he liked, and he told me so, eliciting more memories which I let fall away.

"One goes and goes," I continued, "clearing everything away and being honest with oneself, paying attention, seeking no sanctuary. Certain things might become necessary from out of this, maybe walking becomes necessary—and why is that? Because you've actually created a world that you can't be in *unless* you walk. Then to take the train to New York doesn't mean the same New York anymore, but a different one, and you want the one that's in that world where everything matters more than the self, and your task is to confront the world and question it, and not to keep on choosing and choosing, no matter how helpful the choices are which you make. Now you know such a world is there; and having walked for a while—a few years at least—you no longer feel like yourself *unless* you walk. That is when it becomes a matter of necessity to go about things in such a way—"

"In order to be in the world."

I shrugged. "You know the philosophers as well as I do. Isn't this what they're talking about?"

We both paused, and I decided that he would have to answer this question for himself. The drizzle hadn't abated at all, and I was beginning to want a little solitude.

For a while he said nothing, and I was just about to rise and disappear into the world, never to see him again, when he answered me, or perhaps continued a dialogue with himself begun long ago—yet how long ago could it have been? He was eighteen, no more—I might have been witnessing the *beginning* of a dialogue which would define a life.

"Do we construct our own world, then? Does each one of us possess our own?" He shook his head. "It can't be, there has to be a common world. But then how could you have *walked* here and met me? It's impossible! For you, New York is *two weeks away*, maybe more: I can't fathom it!" Again he shook his head, brushing his hair out of his face. "It isn't the same, but the difference isn't in you or me, how could it be?"

I remained silent, watching him out of the corner of my eye, already having lost almost all my desire to speak.

"No, like you said, it's the world that elicits the question, not us. So it isn't in you or me that the difference lies, and it is the same space, the same New England that you're walking through and I'm not. Do you know when Heidegger talks about the artifact in the museum?"

I nodded my head.

"Of course you know it. He says that the *world* of the artifact is no longer there, it's in our world now, and that is what is different, that is why it is an artifact and not an image of the god or whatever." His eyes were fixed on an invisible point in the distance, and his voice was firm. "But that is easier to grasp than this, because time has passed. In this case, here, we're not talking about a thing, and we're not talking about the past: we're two human beings, right now, sitting next to each other, yet also in different worlds." He rubbed his forehead and laughed abruptly. "I don't know. What does it mean? But it's possible; it's possible that you can come to that point."

There, however, the gulf opened up; for to me it was no longer a possibility but a necessity, not a hope but a real world that I inhabited. For him it was intangible and unreal: so be it! A glimpse ought to be good enough. I did not want to push the conversation to the point where his words might reveal whether he wanted *reality* or only to speak of it. Is that not, in the end, each man's own affair?

(while walking)

Adrienne Mackey

I'M SITTING IN the back of the trolley as we travel from 61st and Baltimore to Center City, and the reporter from the *Philadelphia Inquirer* is asking me whether the 100-plus-mile walk we just completed around the city's border is art.

"Well," I say, falling back into my default artistic-director-of-genre-defying-arts-company mode, "this walk came from a program, 'Cross Pollination,' designed to explore interdisciplinary artistic collaboration. My goal in creating it was to give space to artists to explore and research. I didn't want the aim to be making a product. I wanted us to better understand the processes that gets us there."

He considers this before following up with, "So what were you researching by walking 100 miles around the edge of the city?"

I take a moment in silence to think about a response. I have a physical sense of the answer to his question. The problem is it's difficult to form it using words.

IT IS THE END of lunch on Day Two. The group decides to play a game with the fortune cookies that have come with the check. Instead of the more familiar "in bed," we add the phrase "while walking" to our tiny paper prophecies. The words in front of me read:

> *You find what you're looking for; just open your eyes!*
> (while walking)

THE CONCRETE DETAILS of the thing are easy to talk about.

There are four of us, technically six if you count the reporter and archival photographer who crossed the finish line alongside us, who have completed a journey today. Over five and a half days we've walked around Philadelphia. Not in the casual "Oh I went for a walk around the city" way that one might mention in passing. No, Ann de Forest (a writer), Jacques-Jean (a visual artist and photographer better known as JJ) Tiziou, myself (a theater director), and Sam Wend (my company's resident scribe) have quite literally walked the perimeter of the city we live in.

As we bounce along the trolley tracks, I'm quietly trying to unpack the trickier question of purpose in what we've done. In my silence Ann pipes up to the journalist about her long-standing fascination with maps and her writing on the architecture of urban spaces. JJ follows up with an explanation about how perspective shifts when we move from the center to the edges of a place.

"Were you taking pictures?" asks the reporter.

"Well . . . ," JJ answers, understanding that this is his expected role to play. He says that, yes, he has taken pictures, but not in the way he would have if he were at an event he'd been professionally commissioned to shoot. He's brought none of his fancy gear on this trip, just the camera on his phone. The last day, he explains, he even refused to take any photos at all so that he could really just "be" in the surroundings.

THERE ARE TWO main reactions we get when we tell people about what we are doing. The first is along the lines of:

"Really? Like . . . ALL the way around? That's a long walk!"

The other, the type the intrepid reporter seems inclined toward, is:

"So then, are you doing this FOR something?"

Our answer is something akin to "sort of."

Ann, JJ, and I are artistic creators in the different genres of writing, photography, and theater. We are doing a residency in which we are allowed to spend a week doing whatever feels like a useful exploration of our combined talents and interests, with Sam alongside to document and ensure correct navigation through our travels.

But also, not really. It's not *for* anything in particular. Which, I'm starting to realize in the quiet trolley moment, is kind of the point.

Members of team "for something" always want to know if we are tourists and seem confused to learn that we all reside in the city we are circumnavigating.

The "that's a long walk" group always want to confirm that the northeast section of Philadelphia is really, really big.

THE EXPERIENCE lives in my mind in snapshots.

On the first day JJ offers a Scandinavian saying that becomes a motto for our trip:

> *There is no bad weather,*
> *Only bad clothing.*

GENERALLY THE WALKING begins between 7 and 7:30 in the morning and ends around 6, just after the sun has set.

Yes, there has been bad weather. The first day it rained. The fifth day it rained a lot.

We take the train to the starting point and make sure to hit a station by the end of each day's journey. The first time it was an accident and afterward it always just worked out.

We eat lunch along the route. The first day was pizza in Overbrook. The second day, a Hibachi buffet on Cheltenham. Andy's Diner, just across the far northeast border in Bucks County, fed us on the third day, and on the fourth, Port Richmond's adorable Syrenka, a Polish cafeteria with amazing stuffed cabbage. On Day Five we found a sports bar called Players in the DoubleTree Hotel near the airport, and on the fifth and a half day we tried to eat Jamaican near the ending point but it was going to take too long and so instead we decided to find ramen once we got to Center City.

No, we didn't really find any neighborhoods that made us feel unsafe.

Yes. It *is* tiring. My feet hurt. Still, it feels worth it.

"Okay," says the *Inquirer* man. "But why are a bunch of *artists* taking this trip?"

THERE'S A GAME that emerges somewhere around the golf course at the end of Cobbs Creek on our first day. The game goes like this:

> *Walk the line of the city limit clockwise.*
> *Point to your right and say, "Philly."*

Point to your left and say, "Not Philly."
Notice whatever you notice.

MEMORY. TAKING A TOUR. Regret. Urban identity. Maps. Engaging with one's surroundings. In early planning meetings, as best I am able to remember, this is the mix of words and ideas expressing our desires for our collaboration. There are suggestions about trying each other's mediums in a mini workshop format. There's a question about whether it's possible for a writer to see the way a photographer would, for a director to compose a scene like a story. We talk about the places each of us go in Philly. We talk about the wish to have space to process our creative work. We talk about the magical moment of artistic genesis, what it looks like at the very start of making a thing.

At some point we start coming up with more concrete ideas: meeting people on the street and learning their stories, or trying to find the places of unique and authentic food. We think about whether we are capable of finding a "representative" sample of the city. We talk about walking toward City Hall, this central marker of our landscape, the way I feel it when I jog the Broad Street Run in the spring with its ten-mile line from north to south. We talk about what's ambitious but accomplishable in a week. Margins excite us. At some point there's a thought about "seeing from a new perspective" and how this figurative sense might be made literal. I think Ann is the one who actually says it:

"What if we walked a big circle around the entire city?"

It's so big but so simple. A perfect container for all our questions.

CHILD OF AMERICAN SUBURBIA that I am, I remember moving into the city with a hope that I would finally *be* somewhere, that I might truly experience myself mattering within the place I'd decided to exist. Arriving in Philadelphia in my early twenties, fresh from a collegiate education aimed at honing an emerging creative sensibility, I was excited to learn, experience, and see everything I could. Unlike the spacious sameness surrounding me on the walks to and from the large and well-funded public grade school of my youth, Philadelphia felt like a place where things uniquely mattered: a complex maze of mysterious specificity, a space in which one might finally get down to the work of *doing* innovative and boundary-breaking art, rather than merely thinking about it. Alas, nearly immediately I found myself missing the focus of the educational space. I was so busy juggling half a dozen part-time jobs that I could only squeeze bits of play rehearsals into dirty base-ments during the scant hours remaining between necessary efforts to survive. I distinctly recall one morning several months into that first year out of Swarthmore when I found myself walking to my least favor-ite day job—a predawn barista shift at a too-expensive Rittenhouse cof-fee shop—and noting a sense of ennui uncomfortably familiar to my middle-school self. While the 4 a.m. sunrise over the Philly skyline was certainly more beautiful than the endless rows of Midwest ranch hous-ing, the sense of yearning to have definitely landed still remained.

"Is this being an artist?" I mused as my feet carried me away from home and toward ten hours of nonfat lattes. "Am I doing it? Is it hap-pening now?"

Ten years later, on a 102.7-mile trek, starting in West Philly and tracing a line through Manayunk to Chestnut Hill to West Oak Lane to Tacony Creek to Fox Chase to the Greater Northeast, past Torresdale, Holmesburg, Bridesburg, Penns Landing, the Navy Yard, over the Platt Bridge to Hog Island, around the airport to Eastwick and West Philly again, the word "interstitial" keeps popping into my mind.

"BUT IS IT ART?" the reporter wants to know.

So, too, do many people I talk about this project with. They want to know why, what for, and what will come of all this. They want to know if Ann will write a story, if I will make a play, if JJ will create a photo essay of our adventures, and how Sam will document this for the com-pany website. My first pause in the back of the trolley will continue to be the instinctive response whenever the question arises. It is the moment I try to explain something I've been sensing for some time.

I COULD NOT have done a project like *Walk Around Philadelphia* ear-lier in my career. It would have made me too nervous. I don't mean nervous in the way it felt when we were cutting across a branch of Poquessing Creek into the backyard of the *non*-Philadelphian hom-eowner (his property falling distinctly on the left of our Philly/Not-Philly line) with the giant dog, a man who avidly did *not* want us to move any of the rocks in "his" water. I mean in the sense that five years I ago I could not conceive of a creative project without a discernible ending *thing*. So much of my artistic life was devoted to endings, to beautifully crafted and labored-over products, each successively more expensive and well marketed. It was a tricky moment several years ago when I looked down at the audience from the stage manager's booth during my most successful artistic thing to date and realized that the thing-ness of what was happening felt entirely alienating and weird.

What I love about theater is the connection to others. There's something about the vector of collective artistic process that transmutes *every* moment of exploration into potential significance. I love being in rehearsals and receiving their surprising discoveries, witnessing an actor try an unexpected take on a line that suddenly opens up a new aspect of the story. I like building the sequence of narrative, juggling and re-juggling the order of what's been created to squeeze out the most cohesive journey. I love the sensation of being in progress, in transit, in flight, of knowing together that we are headed somewhere. I love that there are no "in between" spaces we just have to get through, that every moment is filled with ritual and presence in the present tense.

The arrival of the performance is an afterthought and often, frankly, a letdown.

So, for a long time, I'd been in this weird bargain with my art. I pretended that what I cared about were these *things*, these end points, these performances of plays, and I worked really hard to make them impressive and well made. This was the means, as I saw it, to get enough funding and recognition to buy time with people, working together in the moment on solving complex problems in ways that were exciting and new and entirely unanticipated.

Alas, a system set up to focus on endings is a wildly inefficient way to go about enjoying a journey, and I sense that the secret truth at the heart of my work is that I don't want to *have created* amazing works of art, I want to *be in the midst of creating* them. I want to live in the arc motion. I want to suspend as long as possible between a beginning and its inevitable end.

AROUND CHESTNUT HILL, Ann and I get to talking about our backgrounds. Ann is sixty. I ask her what her road to becoming an author has been, if she has always known that writing was her passion.

It turns out that Ann has done a lot of things. She danced as an undergraduate, and we chat about Meredith Monk (whom I've studied from a musical perspective) and the site-specific piece Ann created in college in response to Monk's body of work. She talks about a graduate degree in art history and the eventual recognition of a growing interest in the process of setting thoughts into words on paper. She talks about writing about architecture, then as a journalist, and eventually moving to fiction. She talks about how her own experiences do and don't influence her creation of a character. She talks about getting to a working methodology after a long and meandering set of experiments and circumstances.

Her college dance teacher, she tells me, used the Laban system for recording gesture.

"Do you know about Laban?"

It sounds familiar but I ask her to remind me. She says that it categorizes types of movements one makes so that they can be written down and remembered.

"Slow and indirect," she says, is the way her movement was always described. She says this is a metaphor for her life and her artistic process. Slow and indirect.

ONE DAY I get freaked out as we are walking into the Police Academy Bomb Disposal Unit, and the jangly feeling of fear follows me all the way through the trail past the bald eagles' nests that the cigar-smelling Gus from Point Pleasant tells us we have to see. It's okay, I decide. Not every part of the journey has to feel "nice."

Trash is the only unifying feature of all the landscapes we encounter. While punchy on the morning of Day Two, we come up with a song that sounds like a Bach canon.

> *Beer!*   *Beer!*
>   *Beer!*
>   *Waterbottlewaterbottle*
>   *Beeeeeeeeer!*

One of the heels of my shoes is uneven, and over time the imbalance pulls a muscle deep in the center of my right foot. It hurts. Bad. At home in my apartment later that night I find I can hardly walk. It still hurts as we set out on the morning of Day Three. With each step I feel a hot and dull ache in my sole. I breathe in, I breathe out. I note each tiny shift in the ball. I practice rolling all the way through my toes. I make contact with every part of the heel. Is it possible that any human has had a more intimate understanding of their feet than I do? Surely this must be impossible.

EVERY TIME we find ourselves in a place that one of has been before we shout, "I know this place!" and gather for a story. It is a tradition that has emerged over the course of our pilgrimage, along with "Bridge Self-ies," a flask of brandy shared at the end of the day, and taking our socks off under the table at lunch.

Weeks before the expedition a mentor offered me the advice to take walks over the next few months. He suggested it might open up space for contemplation in my creative practice. "Does it count if it's done all at once?" I wonder, and make a mental note to ask.

On the cold and wet Day Five, a Navy Yard worker spontaneously quotes our "no bad weather, only bad clothing" maxim and we all cheer.

"This is fun," says JJ. It is raining and I am soaked and I am walking on a high bridge that brings out a small fear of heights that makes me a bit woozy. I look out over the oil refinery wasteland and try to see it as beautiful. This *is* fun, I think. Anything can be fun if you simply shift your perspective.

"BUT IS IT ART? What is the value of *artists* taking this very long walk?"
    The question lingers long after the end of the trolley ride and the departure of the inquiring *Inquirer* man. Maybe the reporter with the tape recorder really did ask this question as insistently as I remember. But maybe it is also possible that this is the question nagging *me*. For a bit, at the start of the trip, I tried forcing myself to takes notes on the usefulness of things, like "Take a picture of an object along the way and create a scene based on it" or "Idea: a pageant play on the edges of the city." Quickly, though, the falseness of making the experience fit a particular form and discipline felt like a mantle that needed to be taken off. (*There is no bad weather. Only bad clothing . . .*) I remark how I have taken so much care in the way I dress my body for this trip. I am careful to think about what clothes will be useful for a particular piece of the passage, shedding any sense of how well they might serve in other contexts. I wonder how well I have outfitted my mind. Is it possible to similarly let go of skills and mindsets that may not serve an emerging way of being? How should I outfit my perspective best for the coming tasks at hand?

I still do not have the perfect words to explain the truth that lives in the physical embodiment of this experience. But I desire to write this thought, one that would pop into my head, unexpected, throughout our journey:

There are no interstitial spaces.
(while walking)

Beneath Our Feet

The Three-Century Walk

Kalela Williams

My NEW FAVORITE shoes are cowboy booties—textile uppers, soles etched to give them traction, real-feeling faux brown leather with brass-colored studs, and a bunion-forgiving bevel ending in a tapered toe. They were marked down at a South Carolina Boot Barn, and I bought them on a whim for a honky-tonk-themed party back in my home city, Philadelphia, thinking that learning line dances might be more fun with the right footwear. Sure enough, unlike my only faint grasp of right from left, these ankle-high shoes served me just fine as I awkwardly kicked around on the dance floor.

But it turns out these boots are really made for walking. I can spend a long time in these size-eight shoes, can walk for blocks or several miles. I most often wear them to work in Center City, strolling across the flat slates of Love Park as I trek from the subway station to work on weekdays, then back again. On weekends they take me over the uneven cobblestone of Old City, or the neat gray Belgian block that paves the narrow alleys knitting together the broader streets in Society Hill, which was once a thriving historically Black community called the Seventh Ward.

During warm-weather months I lead Black history tours in these neighborhoods. Or I used to, before the COVID-19 pandemic ushered us all indoors and quieted the thrum of out-of-towners. But I like to think of resuming tours once travel steps up again, because I always greeted my group with something to talk about, and left them with more to think about. My tours are small, at the most eight people, and conversational. In Old City, my little group will shuttle right by hundreds of others crammed in a queue to gawk around inside Independence Hall, or the throngs more who suffer a long wait for a quick glimpse of the Liberty Bell. And you know what? I don't knock it. I moved to Philadelphia as an adult, so I was once one of those people when I first visited. And sure, I even jogged up the Rocky Steps and pranced around the summit, bobbing my fists in the air, just as I ate underwhelming cheese steaks (wiz wit) at both Geno's and Pat's, and struggled to understand the hype.

But I never rode a double-decker tour bus—they seem cheesier than Pat's or Geno's. Sometimes when I'm guiding a tour, one will cruise by, as red as an emergency and emblazoned with advertisements. The megaphoned guide drowns out the sound of my voice. It's fine—those busses pass by quickly. They'll cover miles more ground, but those tourists are missing what mine see. When you're languishing in line or sitting on a bus, stories can't be told, can't be learned. Walking is the only pace to know them—otherwise, there's too much time, or not enough.

This weekend's group meets me at the Visitor's Center, and I give them a minute to go inside and grab a coffee or water, use the restroom or stuff their tote bags with glossy buckslips advertising big museums and landmark sites and those double-decker-bus tours. Then I check everyone in. Cheryl and Angela are retired teachers, one visiting from Tennessee and the other, Los Angeles. I have a soft spot for them—my mother was a teacher. Alejandro, in his twenties, is traveling alone—he's Colombian, moved to Boston three years ago, and works for a labor union. Denae and Brian are a couple in their mid-thirties. Denae works retail, while Brian does mortgage loans and, like me, is a writer. When I hear they're from Macon, I grin, telling them, "I'm from Georgia!" Macon is nothing like Atlanta, where I grew up, but it's always fun to compare notes. Doug, an economy professor, is the only white person and the only Philadelphian in our group. He'd developed an interest in Black history, he says, as most of his research focuses on the impact of trade, goods, and services.

"That works out, because we can start with all three of those concepts," I tell him. "Look down."

Everyone in my group does. For most of the block, the slate sidewalk is demarcated with carved lines about twenty feet apart, like inches marked on a ruler. Etched beneath each line is a name and occupation: James Lang, Ropemaker; William Bell, Merchant; John Pemberton, Gentleman. They show what was once the location of row houses during the eighteenth century, the names pulled from directories from the time period, almost certainly the homes of white men. Doug tells me that he's lived in Old City for fifteen years and never noticed this sidewalk. It's not the first time I've heard this from Philadelphians on my tour. But these names are details only walkers can notice, because you have to be standing right over them.

They say as much about whose stories we know as those we don't, I tell my group, as long as we know how to look. Enslavement was part of the fabric of Pennsylvania's beginnings. While the Lenni Lenape were being pushed from their land, or decimated by disease, enslavement took root with the Swedes, the Dutch, and later the English who sailed up the Delaware in white-masted ships, some of which groaned with the weight and sound of chained Africans who suffered in their dark holds. In Africa, these men, women, and children may have walked for weeks, yoked together and goaded by whips, to reach the continent's coast and confront a brutal future. The Gradual Abolition Act of 1780 was the first meaningful legal act to end slavery in Pennsylvania, I explain.

And so the names of white men beneath our shoes, and the homes they once lived within, obscure but don't eclipse the legacies of Black women and men, I say. Enslaved people would have walked the very thoroughfare we stand upon, from the seventeenth century until the nineteenth century. Black women cooked, cleaned, cared for others' children. They walked to collect laundry, carrying it in large baskets balanced atop cloth-wrapped hair, or they bustled to and from the market on the east end of High Street. Black men labored and stevedored, loading products from incoming ships onto wagons bound into the city, also driven by Black men. The goods and services that William Bell, John Pemberton, and indeed the entire city depended upon, thrived upon, were underpinned by unpaid labor. We, I tell my group, as we walk to our next destination, are following the footsteps of these who supplied it.

"This is the kind of conversation we have at my office about labor," Alejandro offers. "It's a rigged system." He and Doug slip into conversation, with Denae, who works at Lowe's, joining in.

As we cross Market Street, one of the city's busiest thoroughfares, and cut across the grassy sprawl of Independence Mall, I describe how it wasn't just enslaved people whose work fueled the city. Black men made an income as porters, pushing wheelbarrows or dollies stacked with kegs and crates and barrels from the docks or from shops, using thick leather straps to carry lighter bundles. Or they trekked to other day-work sites before the light of dawn struck the sky. Early mornings would have seen free Black women walking miles from their homes and setting up the food trucks of their day, sometimes on the steps leading up to that very building. They stirred kettles of a soup that was chunky with vegetables and beef tripe, calling out, "Pepper pot, spicy hot!" This "toothsome concoction," as described in the *Philadelphia Tribune* by an 1890s Black historian and journalist, William Carl Bolivar, hailed from Caribbean kitchens but became known as a beloved Philadelphia dish.

Other free men and women vended hot corn, sold peanut candy, or roamed through the throng of foot traffic with trays of sweet cakes balanced atop their heads, hawking their goods throughout the cacophonous air. Chimney sweeps, "whose cries might be heard a long distance off," advertised their services, then sauntered to their customers' homes, long-handled brushes leaned over soot-dusted shoulders. With these itinerant workers, one could argue that it wasn't just the products or services they sold that earned their living—it was mobility, the willingness to travel far throughout the city, and for that they could only depend on their own two feet.

Like the white men whose names are inscribed on the sidewalk, there are some Black men and women whose identities we know. James Forten, a Black freeman, would have ambled down the waterfront after checking in with his staff along the docks, before jogging up the narrow stairway of the sail-making loft he owned. A veteran of the Revolutionary War, he was one of the city's wealthiest men. On Cherry Street, Helena Harris, described in a 1794 directory as "a black woman of considerable parts," would have made her way to greet a roomful of schoolchildren. Helena had lived in England, teaching white school children, the article on "colored schools" elaborated. I even look down at my own feet and instead of blue jean cuffs and those cognac-brown cowboy boots, I imagine what she might have worn: black leather pumps, their brass buckles gleaming under a hand-sewn worsted wool gown and linen petticoat.

As my group leaves the heart of Old City, we also move from the eighteenth century. Our pace is leisurely, so it's along this walk down Fifth Street that I give the group members real cotton for them to touch and hold. As we pass the dried plants around, each person feels the tiny, hard seeds hidden inside soft fluff. What's sharp about a cotton blossom—sharp enough to draw blood if one doesn't take care—are the brown bracts surrounding the pillowy puff. I caution my group to watch their fingers.

We've reached what was once the Second Bank of the United States, a thick-columned marble building, as white as a gravestone. Inside, I tell my group, men in fancy silk cravats and frock coats would have pored over documents and papers, playing their part in the domestic slave trade. When cotton became king in the early nineteenth century, it was the Second Bank that was a major credit lender to wealthy human trafficking firms like Virginia-based Franklin & Armfield.

Doug takes especial interest. Of course he'd known about the economic shift from tobacco to cotton, but he had never thought about the human cost. This new economy kicked off the exodus of a million people who, over a half-century, were forced to march from the Upper South—Virginia, Maryland, and Kentucky—into Deep South cotton-growing states. In fact, three sisters of Harriet Tubman, Mariah, Linah, and Soph, were part of this long, sorrowful walk over rough dirt roads, disappearing from their family's cabin and from historical records alike. Plodding hundreds of miles in poor shoes or on bare feet, shackled together in coffles of sometimes hundreds, all of these enslaved people must have grieved their kin left behind as they relived the terrifying march of their ancestors from inland Africa to the coast. As ever, families rarely left together, and almost all were separated in the end.

As we continue walking, I notice Angela is still holding her boll of cotton, rubbing the fuzz between her fingers, her brows furrowed. I ask her what she's thinking about. "It's like a cloud grown from the soil," she says. "My parents talked about picking cotton. In Georgia." She nods at me, at Brian and Denae. "They were sharecroppers. They planted and picked, day in and day out, but I've never so much as held a boll in my hands. I had no idea what it felt like."

As we turn right onto Walnut Street, I describe my own family's relationship to cotton. Both of my parents were raised on South Carolina farms. My mother and father were the children and grandchildren of farmers, who themselves were the children and grandchildren of free and enslaved laborers who plucked cotton row by row; as well as white men who made their livings from the picking; and Catawba Indian women whose ancestral homelands were eroded with each new field tilled. All of these ancestors spent a good deal of time under the sun.

Maybe some inherited memory of so much time spent outdoors is in my blood, but there's nurture, too. Cascade Road, my childhood street, was a far cry from an urban neighborhood. Our little house was on the outskirts of Atlanta's outskirts, fringed by dozens of acres of pine trees and poplars, far from any neighbors but close to history. More than a century before I was born, the Battle of Utoy Creek had blazed through that wilderness, bullets ripping through bark and bodies.

But for my siblings and me, the outdoors was a place of safety and recreation. We took long walks down a foot trail leading through the woods, the air sweet with the scent of honeysuckle, pine, and wild muscadines. During the summers, we were shipped off to the family homesteads in South Carolina, where we spent hours wandering the sprawling properties of both sets of grandparents, tromping the same land my parents once did. My maternal grandparents' land has been in the family since Reconstruction, so generations of feet trod across the same gardens and grassy fields that my own ashy-brown legs tromped over as a child.

Hearing this, Cheryl tells me it's no wonder I give tours, all the on-foot mileage I logged growing up, and my childhood playgrounds practically being historic sites. It makes sense. So does walking and history, Brian adds. History isn't just what happens, it's what we make of it, he says. "It's almost like walking lets me shake loose of all these thoughts I have lodged in my brain, and gives me ground to explore them."

We cut across the diagonal path of Washington Square and head south for six blocks. The length of the walk gives us time to ask each other questions, to share more about our workplaces, our families, and our passions. We talk about politics, about what's happening in the news. And then, as if by mutual agreement that we need space, more than being tired of talking to one another, we fall into silence. Walking gives us time to think, time to reflect, time to notice passersby and consider how each and every one of us is living an individual life with our own particular joys and worries, just as people before once did. My own thoughts jostle from the recesses of my mind into the fore of it, as I think of how it's because those who lived before me walked as enslaved workers or free workers in low-wage jobs, I am able to follow their footsteps in freedom and opportunity. Not all of my Black sisters, brothers, and cousins can say the same, I know, remembering an article pointing out that the Black-white wealth gap in the United States has not changed since 1968. But though we walk an unfinished road, it's been paved and paid for by the work of our predecessors.

The corner of Seventh and Pine Streets, in a stately old neighborhood aptly named Society Hill, feels miles away from the tourists crowding Old City. It's a quiet, tree-lined street of tall three-story homes and mothers pushing strollers to the noisy playground, of joggers with dogs, and couples strolling to Whole Foods. There are scattered businesses tailored to the well-heeled, like a bridal studio and an antique store open by appointment only, and a coffee shop that hosts poetry readings and sells high-priced coffee. I don't knock it—I love their chai lattes. But I, along with most members of my group, stand out. Most everyone else around us is white. However, a century ago, we would have fit in just fine.

This neighborhood, once part of Philadelphia's Seventh Ward, was a thriving Black community of abolitionists and activists. In the decades leading up to the Civil War, one might have leaned out from their second-story window to see the leonine mane of Frederick Douglass bobbing below, for he would have walked these streets to meet fellow activists when he visited Philadelphia. Harriet Tubman, whose swift feet took her from the Eastern Shore of Maryland to Philadelphia, led her freedom seekers here before the 1850 Fugitive Slave Act forced her to guide them more northerly to Canada. Before that year, Black residents of the Seventh Ward had greeted weary freedom-seeking walkers for decades. Organizations like the Vigilance Committee raised funds to help provide for former enslaved folks, to get them on their feet after being on their feet so long. And churches threw open their doors to offer community, to provide a sense of family for those who had left theirs in cotton fields and ramshackle cabins.

My group turns on Sixth Street, where Mother Bethel A.M.E. Church looms into view. "Oh, wow," Denae takes in a breath and pauses to snap a photograph. It's a tall, beautiful stone building with proud-looking, arched stained-glass windows. Beneath the towered façade stretch long-throated gargoyles, quintessential Queen Anne style. Even though the building only dates from the 1890s, the site has been the meeting place of a congregation for more than two centuries. As early as 1794, parishioners gathered into a log blacksmith's shop. By the early nineteenth century, they occupied a simple but commanding building with a steeply gabled roof and a round, ox-eye window. Toward the end of the nineteenth century, the church expanded its physical space and dressed up its architecture into what it is today. As I walk toward the stone stairs leading up to the heavy wooden doors, I reimagine my boots as calf-leather pumps, the flounce of a gauzy dress floating above them. Atop my head would be a broad-brimmed hat trailing with wide, silk ribbons, like those in surviving early-1800s lithographs showing folks in Sunday finery promenading to worship at Bethel A.M.E. and neighboring St. Thomas African Episcopal Church.

After lingering at the church, we turn from Sixth Street onto South Street. "Whoa," Alejandro raises his eyebrows. "It's like a totally different city." He's right. The character of the neighborhood has suddenly changed, as we shift out of Society Hill. We're greeted by eclectic body-art shops and colorful kink stores, bars with funky names like Tattooed Mom's and Wooly Mammoth. It's a diverse stretch of Philadelphia, with folks having every skin hue and hair color of the Pantone chart. Kids on bikes whiz by, popping wheelies and exasperating drivers who jostle for street parking that seems more mythical than available. On the sidewalk, my group is out of that fray, and we're following the footsteps of a Philadelphia hero, Octavius Catto, I tell them, as this young, nineteenth-century activist lived in a boarding house near Eighth and South.

Perhaps it was along South Street that his peer Emilie Davis witnessed him and his compatriots marching in uniform to board a train. "I saw a company of colerd recruits they looked quite war like," she recorded in her diary in June of 1863. She worried for her friends, as the men, led by Catto, were meeting a call to arms issued by the governor, who had requested emergency troops as Robert E. Lee's Confederate army lurched toward Pennsylvania. But as soon as Catto's emergency regiment arrived at the state's capital city, they were sent back, their valor refused due to the color of their skin. In her tiny pocket-sized diary, Davis admitted, "I feel glad and sorry."

But many of Emilie Davis's friends and neighbors would later have their turn to serve in the Civil War when the U.S. Colored Troops were authorized. Nearly 11,000 Black men, trained at Philadelphia's Camp William Penn, would march and camp, march and camp, then fight beneath the shadow of the Blue Ridge Mountains at New Market Heights, among the sprawling cotton warehouses of the Confederate capital city of Richmond, and in the pine-fringed meadows of Olustee. My own grandfather's grandfather, having fled enslavement, once bled on that Florida battlefield. He was lucky to be merely wounded, his loved ones undoubtedly grateful when they saw him lumbering home.

The war preluded a new and terrifying wave of violence against African Americans, including lynchings in the South. Philadelphia was not spared. Less than a decade after the last battlefield shot was fired, on the very street Octavius Catto strolled each day, he would scramble desperately for his life. In 1838, the year before his birth, Black men had lost the right to vote in Pennsylvania. In 1871, he and fellow advocates fought to take it back. For his efforts, Octavius was named a target by white supremacists. On Election Day that year, as he "quietly preceded homeward," according to a *Harpers Weekly* piece, a white man, Frank Kelly, "leveled a pistol at his head." Catto ducked for cover behind a passing streetcar but three shots rang out, one ball striking his shoulder and another perforating his heart. "He fell immediately," the account recorded.

Alejandro shakes his head, saying that MLK Jr. was like the second coming of Octavius Catto.

"In some ways, absolutely," I respond. "Except that Catto bought a pistol that same day. He knew he was marked."

"Both men knew," says Cheryl. We grow quiet, perhaps thinking of Memphis, where Dr. King met his last day.

In silence, we walk a block south. At Ninth and Bainbridge Streets stands the Institute for Colored Youth, an elegant Italianate red-brick building framed by tall wind-rustled trees. It's now a condominium, but beyond its asphalt driveway, it looks much the same as it did in a black-and-white photograph from another era. Octavius Catto was a student at ICY before he taught there, and Emilie Davis attended night school as an adult. Educators and students alike at this school were advocates for abolition.

During the Civil War, Black Philadelphia women led organized protests against the discrimination practiced by trolley car lines that gave them no choice but to walk miles to school or work, and made them all but unable to deliver supplies to Union troops. Women like Catto's fiancée, a teacher named Caroline LeCount, and the Black poet Frances Ellen Watkins Harper stepped onto trolley cars, adjusted their bustled skirts, and took a seat, refusing to budge.

They were manhandled and physically thrown from cars, and they protested despite the admonishment of Black men in their communities. But these women were had-it-up-to-here furious that their lack of mobility pinioned their economic freedom. What had done well enough for their grandmothers—roaming the streets, hawking hand-made products—wasn't enough for these women who had the privilege of education, owed to those very ancestors' fortitude. And more vitally, walking could not serve their desperate need to contribute to the war effort, and to serve other causes. I look down at my cowboy boots and imagine instead brown and tan Victorian boots, with cunning French heels and black buttons marching up the sides, the toes poking beneath ruffles of a voile gown, sewn with a Singer machine. Such is what these women might have worn when they decided upon the very last day they would walk, and the first day they would act.

Mobility and political enfranchisement were what the Black community needed, because it was growing, stepping into a new arena of challenges. Neither Caroline LeCount nor Frances Ellen Watkins Harper, nor Emilie Davis or Octavius Catto, saw the day when the Seventh Ward's Black population boomed at the advent of the Great War, and the new heart of Philadelphia's Black Seventh Ward beat west of Broad Street. But during the Great Migration as folks boarded trains and later, packed their whole lives into automobiles, their descendants welcomed Southern newcomers.

But my tour doesn't travel this far, ending instead a few blocks from Broad Street. And strangely, no one complains of hurt feet, even though we've walked an exceedingly long way—three centuries. We hug and exchange email addresses, and after the last wave goodbye, I turn south, homeward. I could take the subway, but it's a mild and pretty day, so I'll walk. And my thoughts shapeshift my boots one more time into a pair of sturdy brown penny loafers. And I imagine these shoes, soggy with rain, taking me to work down miles of sidewalk in Birmingham, while a mustard-yellow city bus glides by, empty. I see them among thousands in the glorious crowd on the Washington Mall, where a quarter million dreams sail on the promise of Dr. King's words during one of the most inspiring marches history has gifted us. I see these shoes striding resolutely over the asphalt of the Edmund Pettus Bridge, though my knees quaver.

A breeze cools my face as the sun warms my shoulders. I feel buoyant, lifted. And just because I want to—and because of these who walked before me, I can—I do a little grapevine and kick-ball-change like I'd learned in that line dance workshop, and keep going. Snug in my cowboy boots, my feet feel good. I had made a sound 30-percent-off investment.

SO MUCH HAS happened since I wrote the first draft of this piece, and at the pace the world's events are taking us, so much more will undoubtedly occur before it's published. Congressman John Lewis, who stood at the helm of those who crossed that Alabama bridge, is gone. Before his death, the feet of thousands struck the streets once more, compelled to march anew, beginning where a Black man begged to breathe beneath a blue-clad knee in Minneapolis. These marches quickened, they gathered strength and purpose with every tragedy, every outrage—of which there has, equally tragically and outrageously, been no shortage. People of every race walked in cities across the world, millions of masked mouths shouted for equality. All told, the Black Lives Matter movement may be the largest collective demonstration this world has ever witnessed.

So I see my forays through the city as merging me with a greater story, one that cannot end, just as it never fails to change. The act of walking is one of revolution, and one of continuity. My brass-studded boots have all but lost their tread, and the threads of their seams are fraying. They'll wear out soon, I know, but they are not what move me.

Tunnels

Rahul Mehta

1.

The women sitting behind me on the commuter train cycle through conversation topics: the stable where they both keep horses, their children who attend the same Waldorf school, the Paris vacation one of them took last fall, the rain that fell and all but ruined it. The women are white and boarded the train in one of Philadelphia's wealthiest neighborhoods. I note both of these facts, even as I chide myself for doing so. Irritated by their privilege—irritated by my own irritation—I am already directing unkind thoughts their way when their conversation turns to—their voices dropping to a whisper—the tunnels.

"Colorful" is how one of them describes them, the underground pedestrian corridors that connect the subway stations in Center City and run for several blocks beneath Broad Street, tunnels the women resort to walking through—as do I—when the weather is too harsh to walk above ground, tunnels I am guessing we will walk through this morning given the whipping winds, the freezing rain. I have seen what they have seen: the extensive homeless population that seeks shelter down there—folks, with their belongings in bags or carts, sitting or lying on cardboard; bodies wrapped in dirty blankets or buried in

"Tunnels" originally appeared in the November/December 2019 issue of the *Kenyon Review Online*.

sleeping bags; mostly men, mostly people of color, sometimes women, on rare occasions children; folks dealing drugs; folks buying drugs; folks doing drugs; once, a circle of six or seven people passing a needle. I have also seen a woman combing her daughter's hair, humming; a man reading a beat-up Tom Clancy paperback; a man listening to the news on a portable radio and cuddling with a pit bull; a man unfolding, shaking out, and refolding his clothes, and placing them carefully into a soiled duffle bag.

It's awful, one woman says. *Sometimes you don't want to see that. It's been a long day. You just want to go home.*

I don't know whether to feel sad or angry, the other woman says. *They could change their lives if they wanted to. It's not easy, but they could change. Not all of them, but most of them.*

It's awful.

It's sad.

They sigh, and then, their voices returning to normal volume, they move on to the next topic: the online clothing concierge website they both subscribe to.

My stylist is terrible. She keeps sending me loud prints. Do I look like a loud person?

That's not you at all.

2.

There is a moment, a moment that I have perhaps misinterpreted, a moment that maybe means something different than I think it means, a moment when we have gotten off the train and we are walking through the station, into the tunnels, and I am walking through a doorway and the women are just behind me and my tote bag gets caught on the door and I am stuck and I have to turn around to get my bag unhooked and there they are, we are face to face, and the women look—and maybe this is the part I am misinterpreting, assigning meaning that isn't there—the women look, what? surprised? irritated? scared? to be face-to-face with a brown, male-presenting person they do not know and who has stopped and turned around in a doorway for reasons that maybe aren't readily apparent to them? I don't know if they are thinking any of these things. What I do know is that they do not smile, even when they realize—if they hadn't already realized—why I have stopped in the first place.

3.

Maybe I'm wrong. In spite of my gender presentation, my skin color, it's hard for me to imagine anyone feeling threatened by me. After all, the tote bag that got caught on the door is one that I sewed myself and has shimmering gold peacocks on the outside and, for the lining, hot pink fabric dotted with cartoon skulls.

Do I look like a loud person?

That's not you at all.

But it is impossible to know what people might feel threatened by. It is impossible to know what people wish they didn't have to see.

4.

Later that day—despite the whipping winds, the freezing rain—I shuttle above ground between department stores, in search of a new winter coat. I find one I love. It fits perfectly. Is $250 too much to pay for a parka if it's replacing a jacket I bought eighteen years earlier?

I look again in the fitting-room mirror. I see a person who is stylish, self-assured. The faux-fur trim on the hood frames their face, makes their eyes look brighter, makes their skin glow. It's me, but better.

For much of the past six years, working as an adjunct college creative writing teacher, I have been hovering not far above the federal poverty level. This is based on income, although I know that income is only part of the story when it comes to true poverty. I have resources many in my income bracket do not, including generous, financially comfortable family members whom I can ask for money should I need it, who routinely offer me money even when I don't ask.

Recently, my fortunes have changed, and I feel flush for the first time in years. I have a full-time teaching job and, at the moment, my salary is perhaps 30 percent higher than it's ever been in my twenty-plus years of adulthood, although it is still probably less than a tenth of the household income of the women on the train. Still, I am more like them than I am like the folks in the tunnels. For now.

On the way to the register, caressing the luxurious trim on the hood, I think to check the label and realize that the faux fur is real fur, fox fur. I return it to the rack.

5.

I am embarrassed by how much I enjoy wandering through the cavernous department store, sliding across the shiny, tiled floors, gazing up at the gold chandeliers. I stop to contemplate a cashmere throw. I am ashamed by how much I enjoy the deferential way the sales clerk asks me how he may help.

6.

As a small child, I was terrified of tunnels of any sort. When my family took road trips and we had to pass through one, my parents would go to great lengths to distract me so I wouldn't scream and cry. I don't know what frightened me so much, but I'm guessing it was the darkness, how everything that had been there—the sky, the trees, the great world around me—was suddenly gone.

Now I marvel at the structures as feats of engineering, the way they burrow through hard earth, through mountains, underneath rivers, the way they bridge distances, connect people and places that are close but far away.

7.

The next day, I will be walking through the woods—woods in which I twice have had what I would describe as a spiritual experience with a fox, woods I have driven the short distance to in a car my parents bought for me the year before. The weather will still be gray, even if the whipping winds and freezing rain are gone. I will be tapping out this essay on my phone while walking, and there will be a break in the clouds, and the flecks of mica sparkling in the stone and in the dirt will dazzle my attention away from my screen, and for a moment, for better or for worse, the women on the train and the folks in the tunnels and the department store with its shiny, tiled floors and the parka that was me but better will all vanish, and this moment will be the only moment: the sparkling mica, the silvery creek below, the birds I cannot see but can hear, though I haven't learned their calls. I will finish this essay weeks later, one afternoon after teaching, sitting in a café in

Center City; in front of me, beside my computer, a four-dollar cappuccino and a honey-gold canelé on a black porcelain dish; waiting to order at the register, a man in Gucci loafers holding a chihuahua in a Louis Vuitton dog carrier, two more Chihuahuas at his feet on narrow leather leashes and in houndstooth sweaters; on a wooden bench next to the door, a disheveled, seemingly homeless man I have seen here before, trying to get warm. Below us: tunnels.

Finding Purchase

WALKS OF WITNESS ON STOLEN LAND

Nathaniel Popkin

1.

The day had begun before sunrise with a bumpy ride in a camper van. Then a bus from Curacautín to Temuco, about two hours. In Temuco, on a noisy street a few blocks from the market, I managed to get us an Uber. The driver's wife was in the hospital delivering their fourth child. The baby was to be named Rosa Isabella, if memory serves, or perhaps Isabella Rosa. The road to the airport was slippery on account of fog, but the driver didn't see the need to slow down and in minutes Xandra and I were sitting at a café next to the security line and a waiter in uniform was serving us cake and coffee.

At the airport, we rented a car, which we drove from Temuco to Los Ángeles, a city Roberto Bolaño described as "full of one-story buildings and dirt roads, . . . city of nighttime raids"—orchestrated by Pinochet during the military coup. We headed southeast to Santa Barbara and for the first time I saw the Bío-Bío. It trickled under the bridge from Quilaco. For centuries until the military invasion of the early 1860s, the once-ferocious river had marked the frontier between Chile and the indigenous Mapuche people. We ate a three-course lunch in a cozy spot on a side street owned by a gregarious chef and afterwards I photographed a monument to those detained, disappeared, and executed during the coup, in September 1973.

Three hours later, following the road along the river, we turned off in sudden darkness and faced a wall of barking dogs. A man came and opened the gate. He said he was the brother of Melisa, the woman who had advertised the cabana on Airbnb that I had reserved. Inside, he turned on the lights and fetched some wood for the stove. In late autumn, the temperature falls in the Andes as swiftly as the darkness. Another brother came to help. His name was Fernando and he was a journalist. Seeing that we were in search of the story of the damming of the Bío-Bío, he told us to find him in the morning.

Fernando Acuña was broadcasting on Radio Bío-Bío when we were let into the studio, inside a compound dedicated to Mapuche autonomy and social services, a couple of blocks from the center of the town of Alto Bío-Bío. During a break he served us espresso. My traveling companion, Xandra van der Eijk, asked if Fernando could introduce us to anyone in the village whose land had been taken when the Bío-Bío was dammed and Mapuche territory flooded. A materials artist, Xandra documents chemical adaptation to man-made climate change and ecosystem degradation. Her work catalogs change but also loss, in order to convey the dimensions of ecological grief. We had driven to Bío-Bío from the artist colony where we were both in residency to make a preliminary investigation into social and material aspects of the river's ecological ruin. Fernando brought us to the town's library to meet a man whose community cemetery was flooded when Endesa, the Spanish-Chilean energy company now known as Enel Chile, constructed the Ralco dam in 2004, about 16 miles upstream. "They came in the early morning, without warning, and flooded the cemetery," he said. Miniature Mapuche flags decorated the library tables.

After a private tour of the Museo Pewenche de Alto Bío-Bío by the museum's director (Pewenche are a subset of the Mapuche people) and further conversation with Fernando on the legal battle to retain water and mineral rights under threat by the Chilean government and multinational corporations, we bought some snacks and headed out of town.

By the time we set out, it was already midday, only six hours of light left, and we had several dams to visit. Xandra hoped to take water and soil samples at the various sites. We both wanted to observe first-hand the ways in which the imposition of dams had displaced the Mapuche from their ancestral land—physically and spiritually. About fifteen minutes from the museum in Alto Bío-Bío we reached Pangue, the first of six dams Endesa constructed on the Bío-Bío to generate hydroelectric power. We drove past the crown of the dam to get a view of the massive lake it had formed, the placid water navy blue or turquoise depending on the angle. Illuminated, the hillsides were golden and dry, as if, somehow, we had landed in Sicily. The tranquility was a mirage. A photograph I took from that vantage reveals the trick—the solid concrete wall of the dam holding back the epic river like a monstrous human hand, all of it protected by barbed wire.

I turned the car around and we drove back to the entrance of the dam complex. A rusted sign in front of a leaf-strewn path declared that this was the private property of Empresa Electrica Pangue, PROHI-BIDO EL PASO. We read the sign as an invitation, or a challenge: It was finally time to walk.

We climbed over the unintimidating wooden gate and went toward the powerhouse behind the dam wall. Under our feet the smuggled river spun the turbine, generating electricity transmitted along the lines above our head. The turbine made no sound, or perhaps in that moment it was idle. The absence of sound pronounced itself clearly, though, if not without menace: a dam steals the voice of a mighty river. In the still air, a brown horse grazed a few feet from the electrical transformers. Past the machinery we came upon a white horse whose legs were so short it appeared to be standing deep in a puddle; the horse gazed at us impassively and we walked on.

At the artist colony a few weeks earlier, a Mapuche ecologist, leading us on a hike through Conguillío National Park, taught us to follow indigenous tradition and ask permission to enter the forest. But now we were in fact trespassing, and half afraid. A nervous fear electrifies any good walk. With it comes adrenaline and adrenaline awakens consciousness, the feet themselves unzipping the landscape and the mind, revealing worlds.

The landscape was illuminated by the rays of autumn sun, which cuts low but also tenderly, as if by touch. The forest was thick, and despite the subtropical Andean foliage, the path reminded me of dozens of trails near the upper Delaware River, in the northeastern United States, land taken by fraud from the Lenape people, land that I consider my own. Perhaps it was the gravel underfoot or the angle of the earth rising from the path, the fragrance of sun warming bark and branches, that made me sense the merging of histories. I thought of that other river, alongside which I've existed for most of my life, as we came to the end of the trail and as we turned back and then, as if by some external force, or possibly gravity, followed a steep paved road down into the river valley. The trees rising above us filled with birdsong that broke the languid silence. The river, sequestered, existed here only in memory.

It was later, when I read Nathaniel Nash's 1992 account of the river in the *New York Times*, that I realized the beauty and power we had missed, arriving nearly three decades too late. "The Bio-Bio's natural beauty is nothing less than breathtaking," Nash wrote, "with churning rapids, towering waterfalls and soaring river embankments. Four species of large wildcat hunt along the river banks. Andean condors soar overhead and virgin forest stand untouched, bordering much of the 120 miles of river. International kayaking and rafting organizations consider the Bio-Bio one of the world's greatest challenges."

A half mile down we came to another road. A directional sign pointed to the top of the dam and to the below-ground machinery: "CORONAMIENTO" up; "MAQUINAS" down. There was a third destination—up, down, or straight ahead—covered over by green tape. The sign dated from the era of the dam's construction, that much was clear. But we didn't understand, not until later, researching the history of the dam, that these roads signified something more. Certainly installed ahead of the dam's construction, the roads and sign marked the first intrusion into the breathtaking landscape, a new phase in the long war of colonization. Every war begins with a map of intrusion.

Before the dam's construction, and nearly thirty years before our exploratory trek, the *New York Times* had sent Nash to Chile to document the conflict of "Economy vs. Ecology," as the newspaper termed it. In 1992, the economic argument seemed clear. One-third of the Chilean population was deeply impoverished. Rural development depended on access to electricity. The reporter took notice of the ecological dimension as well. The dam threatened the cultural life of the Mapuche-Pewenche, a life closely tied to the dynamic ecosystem of the river and surrounding forest. One Mapuche woman, Lucia Renado Huenchucan, told the reporter: "The dams will be the end of Pehuenche [*sic*] life. We don't trust these people. Yes, we are poor, but we want to live as we have always lived, with the old customs of our ancestors. We want our children to speak our language. The dam will ruin that."

We walked, with each step making witness: of the ruin indeed brought about by the dam, this one and five others. A ruin recorded in the passive construction of Wikipedia as if no other outcome was possible: "With the loss of the whitewater rafting venue, displacement of indigenous Pehuenche people, who had lived in the area for centuries, also occurred."

We'd just passed the old road sign when we heard a vehicle in the distance. Our joint instinct, in the moment, was to hide in the trees. We crouched down as a truck came up the road, laughing at our own stupid fear of being caught in a faraway land by some imagined authority for jumping a fence, for violating private property. For walking on an earth replete with fences, which demand trespass (never walking have I encountered as many fences as I did during a month in Chile). PROHIBIDO EL PASO: the feet answer, no. But more than contrarian, the feet are here, in this spot, indignant and righteous.

Crouching still, we breathed in the scent of shaded forest. We commented on its deceptive beauty. Xandra had begun to notice the ways the utility company Endesa hid the monster's hand. The dense forest was a double disguise: the hydroelectric installations that have neutered the river—a living element to the Mapuche no different from a mother or a baby brother—are one element in the ongoing ecological domination, which includes deforestation for cattle grazing and the removal of water and mineral rights. Long before this road was installed, trespass came to mean precisely displacement, conquest, and "pacification." Mapuche language, customs, political agency, and land have been under continuous attack by colonization, beginning in earnest in the 1860s, when the frontier of the Bío-Bío gave way. Soon after, the Chilean government decided not to concern itself with a treaty with the Mapuche that prohibited the sale of land to settlers unless the land was clear of Mapuche claims. Until then the fierce river had meant protection, a line on a map that signaled the native people could go on practicing the old customs of their ancestors. Ignoring the agreement, the government was free to defraud the Mapuche through counterfeit titles, wills, and proofs of sale, inviting Swiss, German, and French immigrants, along with Poles, Italians, Austrians, Belgians, and Spanish, to forge past the frontier, south beyond the Bío-Bío to the Malleco River and from the Malleco still further south to the Cautín.

Hidden in the trees, we watched the truck creep along. When it passed, we tried not to make eye contact with the driver. He didn't seem to notice us. Or he decided not to stop. We were hungry and now it was almost two in the afternoon. Xandra had water samples to take. Back in the car we continued east toward the Ralco dam. The road became gravel and dirt. Along the side down into the valley were the bone-white trunks of drowned trees, exposed when the water level of the dam is low, as if it were a graveyard that had never been dug.

We tried to reach the Mapuche cemetery that Endesa had flooded, but light was slipping away. Was it there? We got out to try to see; we attempted to climb down into the valley to bear witness but couldn't locate the path.

Between dusk and dark is the hour of enchantment. The sky had become the color of a deep-sea aquarium, the dirt road a sand bar. Once more, the landscape had disguised its true self. Perhaps for the Mapuche this was still its magic power. But then, no more than a few miles back toward Alto Bío-Bío, on our left we spotted a fire. Or rather, the fire seemed to erupt from inside the earth, white hot at the ground then gold then orange, the color of spirits. It burned, I thought, with vengeance. But whose?

2.

A year later, I'm driving for the first time since on a gravel road. My son, Isaak, 17, is in the passenger seat. This is Randt's Mill Road; in this section, it runs parallel to the Tohickon Creek. The stone building at the end is Randt's Mill, built by German settlers in the 1780s, about four decades after the Pennsylvania government decided not to concern itself with a treaty with the Lenape people that prohibited the sale of land to settlers unless it was clear of Lenape claims. The decision was made during a swindle known since 1735 as the Walking Purchase. This is also stolen land.

Like the Mapuche, the Lenape lived in dynamic, interpersonal, and cosmic relationship to a river that bordered their territory. English colonizers called it the Delaware, and it has never been dammed (though that nearly changed in the 1970s). The Delaware was so integral to Lenape life that colonizers began to call them Delawares and still, to this day, though most Lenape live in Oklahoma, 1,300 miles from Randt's Mill Road, they identify by this name. The earliest Lenape negotiations with Pennsylvania officials, in the early 1680s, fixed the Delaware River as the eastern boundary of Lenape territory. Those negotiations resulted in ceding the land from what is now northern Delaware to the Neshaminy Creek and allowed the founder of the colony, William Penn, to build his capital city, Philadelphia. In 1735, the sons of William Penn, who were now the proprietors of Pennsylvania, were badly in debt. They needed cash; the quickest way to get it was by selling land to Irish, German, Scottish, English, Dutch, and French immigrants—in precisely the same manner that Chile dispossessed the Mapuche of their ancestral lands by opening the territory to Europeans. For Pennsylvania the sale of land would have a second benefit. The colony could rid itself of Lenape people—only this meant betraying the original intent of William Penn to treat the native people as "brothers."

Penn's original agreement, mythologized in a painting by Benjamin West, established the rule that Pennsylvania officials couldn't sell land to settlers without first purchasing it from Lenape sachems. The parcels had to be clean of Lenape claims, but the land Penn's sons wanted to sell to immigrants was not. The Pennsylvania governor, James Logan, came up with a solution. He discovered a never-ratified and only partially written treaty elaborating the sale of land from the Lenape to William Penn as far north from the border of the Neshaminy Creek as a man could walk in two days. The distance was estimated to reach near to the spot I'm driving, on Randt's Mill Road, on the south side of the Tohickon Creek—not over or beyond it. Logan announced the discovered document, which itself may have been completely forged, as fact. To substantiate the fraud, Logan produced a fake 1680s map, showing the expanse covered by the supposed treaty. Where the Tohickon Creek runs, however, the name "West Bank, River Delaware" was inserted instead. The map, wrote historian Steven Harper, "seems to have been carefully prepared to convey the impression to the sachems that all they were relinquishing was land below Tohickon Creek, as the Delawares had been willing to do since 1686." For what Logan wanted was the land at the forks of the Delaware and the real West Bank, River Delaware, known now as the Lehigh River, 67 miles north of the Tohickon. He exploited Lenape sachems' poor grasp of English and leveraged the bad will of Lenape enemies willing to vouch for the authenticity of the treaty and the map. All that was left was to hire men to walk two days.

Randt's Mill Road delivered us to a collection of farmhouses, the miller's old house, and the mill, with its attractive outlet arch and rustic stone construction. Then the bridge over the fast-running creek. I drove over the bridge and parked on the other side. We were here to walk, with our footsteps to perform and therefore somehow make witness to the fraud of the Walking Purchase, the event that more than anything else has shaped the geographic contours of my life. A walk that should never have taken place.

Logan's walkers, Edward Marshall and James Yeates, aided by a team of advance men and supply horses, passed this spot, the Tohickon Creek, before lunch on the first day of the walk. Logan had promised both men 500-acre land grants in the territory they were taking with their feet along with a payment of an English half-crown, about nineteen dollars in today's currency. They were mercenaries in a war that might well have felt right and just.

They walked at race speed. By dinner they'd crossed the Lehigh River into the desired territory known as the Forks. The Penn sons coveted the Forks for an imperial town, which soon became Easton. From there, early the next morning the hired walkers kept going until Yeates collapsed from over-exertion. Dying a few weeks later, he became another casualty in the war. Marshall continued race-walking the 65 miles to Minisink, dispossessing the Lenape people of their entire ancestral territory on the west side of the Delaware River (it's that spot, far north toward the river's source, where I indulge in the privilege of swimming every summer).

A few years later, a Lenape man named Teedyuscung began to speak out. He had been effectively dispossessed of himself. "This very Ground that is under me was my Land and Inheritance, and is taken from me by Fraud," he told the governor of Pennsylvania. There is no way, he said, that I can "tell you what the Damage is." It was unnamable; it was everything.

The lackluster steel and concrete bridge over the Tohickon Creek at Randt's Mill had been installed by the state of Pennsylvania in 1927 to replace a rustic wooden covered bridge, a style the European settlers preferred that is pervasive throughout Bucks County. Such bridges, originally designed so the covering would protect the wooden trusses from the elements, now convey an air of charm that serves as a disguise for ethnic cleansing. Perhaps it's better that the current bridge is merely utilitarian. The point for me is to walk across it, with each step unzipping the doors to my own conscious mind.

Isaak and I share a snack of potato chips and granola bars. I remark that we're missing our afternoon coffee and we step out of the car. A filmmaker, he has his camera to record the place, to seek through imagery its meaning. But how hard it is to see! At the crest of the short bridge we stop to admire the classic northern woodland scene, the creek bustling through rocks and tree limbs, and the bright early spring foliage that, like miniature bulbs, twinkles in the shade. Immediately, I want to walk back and start over, zip it back up, unzip again. Perhaps zipping and unzipping I'll disturb myself to recognition, or penance: by crossing this creek, mercenaries severed an entire people from their homeland and gave it, eventually, to the likes of me. I don't want to cross too fast! Isaak, ahead already, is filming the mill on the other side. I turn again and walk back to start over. As he trains the camera on me, I come to understand that symbols have no power to reverse time.

The short, strangely ungratifying walk emits, however, a bitter prayer—or a question: How is it that I, great-grandchild of European immigrants, consider this Lenape river valley—the dulcet river itself from which I have drunk for over half a century—my own?

3.

I have been reading about you this past year, between the walk at Pangue and the walk at Randt's Mill. After leaving Alto Bío-Bío, confronted with the fact of colonial violence against the Mapuche, I returned home to face the theft of the Lenape homeland. Months later, I collaborated on an interview for a documentary film I had written, *American Experiment: The Struggle for Philadelphia*, with a former assistant chief of the Oklahoma-based Delaware Tribe of Indians, Michael Pace. On a hazy autumn day, I stood at the edge of the Delaware River with him. Michael was wearing a single feather in his band. He spoke of you. "A very well-known chief," he said. "A lot of the bones of our people still lie here. Their spirit is still right here." This is how I came to know you, Teedyuscung, and learn the story of your life.

We were both born in Trenton, on the Delaware. The Pennsylvania authorities tried to use your place of birth against you. They tried to argue that your only real inheritance, which anyway had been taken from you and your people, could be in New Jersey. But the river to you was never a border. It was a matter of life, and always moving. To dam a river is to dispossess it.

Two hundred sixty-nine years separate us, Teedyuscung, but in fact the history of time records our footsteps in the same place. Up and down the river, in its dark gorges, meadows of bergamot, its creeks filled with turtles, the banks cascading with dragonflies, chaotic city streets, too. My favorite image of you, Delaware King, is standing before the Pennsylvania State House, on Chestnut Street, with your checkered breeches, English coat, hoop earrings, and single feather. I would only wish this land were still your inheritance and I, in the Mapuche tradition, could ask permission first to enter it.

The history of time records the footsteps of Edward Marshall and James Yeates, the men who walked from the edge of Philadelphia at the Neshaminy Creek all the way to Minisink. They proved, though speciously, that a walk can be a powerful act. On the Randt's Mill bridge I walk, as faint symbolic gesture, to reverse that power. But you had other, more direct, means of recourse. You complained to high officials and your complaints were supposed to be taken all the way to the king of England. You drank away your pain, only intensifying it. Wearing an English coat, learning the religion of the German Moravian Nikolaus Ludwig, Count von Zinzendorf, you tried to assimilate, at times capitulate. When that didn't satisfy, you sent vigilantes for Edward Marshall, killing his wife and children. You set colonizers' houses and barns on fire. You tried to burn away their grazing grounds and fences.

None of these acts reversed fortune. "I sit there as a Bird on a Bow," you said. "I look about, and do not know where to go."

In the end, as you slept, colonizers set your house on fire.

I think often of the fires you set and the fire that killed you. I recall the delusory scene Xandra and I witnessed at the edge of the Ralco dam. The photographs I took from the car show a fence in the foreground and behind that a fire pit, raging, and some distance away a stand of eucalyptus trees fully engulfed by flames. Like the dams, eucalyptus is a tool of dispossession. Mineral-depleting and practically disposable, the trees are planted by forestry companies to supply the paper industry. They replace native forest of coihue, raulí, and araucaria, the latter tree the mother of the Mapuche people, itself now endangered.

Who set the fire, and why? Was this the property of a Pewenche-Mapuche family who, capitulating to the economics enforced by colonization, grew eucalyptus? Was it time to burn the old trees and start over? Or was this an act of resistance, like the fires you set, Teedyuscung, an act of insurrection? An act of erasure, like my walk across the bridge, meant itself to unerase.

4.

But what follows when time itself erases memory and history, as it's told, is written by the victor? There is no ambiguity to the State of Pennsylvania's sign, from 1949, marking the start of the Walking Purchase:

"The historic Indian Walk began here, Sept. 19, 1737. Expert walkers, hired by the Penn family, covered 66½ miles in a day and a half, adding 1,200 square miles to the area open for sale and settlement." The marker, like the directional sign at Pangue, claims for itself a precise and unconditional narrative. I walk for penance, and as witness, to complicate that narrative. To imagine that a narrative doesn't contain a precise beginning, middle, or end.

In his interview, Michael Pace said it was important to acknowledge the genocide of his people. "We never want to talk about that but that's exactly what really happened," he said. But, at the same time, Lenape refuse to live in the past. "Today, we try to take a different tack. Because today, we try to remember that that wasn't us. That was our forefathers. And so, today, we can do something about it."

What Michael does is teach the Lenape language, in which he spoke when he said for the camera, "I am happy that I am standing up well today in our old homeland." He is alive today, a lifelong Oklahoman, and that, he implies, is enough. He need make no claim on the original Lenape homeland. Michael walked with the camera and crew along the edge of the Delaware River. He said it should be called, in Lenape, the White River, for it reflected back so much light.

That moment returns to me as Isaak and I cross another bridge, a short distance from where the Tohickon Creek flows into the Delaware River. The pedestrian bridge at Lumberville (so named by colonizers who turned the trees of the Lenape forest into commodities) takes the walker out above the broad river, sylvan in all directions along the banks. It is the luxuriant image, to me, of home, and I can't take my eyes from the soft contour of the banks, the lissome forest cresting the hills that rise gently from the free-flowing water. Witness thus becomes a matter of love. The ineffable love exists to reconcile the ownership of a stolen thing. Only nature can't be owned.

For many years, Walt Whitman lived along the Delaware in Camden, New Jersey, directly across from the spot where we interviewed Michael Pace. Whitman was restless. His walks were epic in scale and, often, he traveled on long journeys to Canada, New England, into the heartland, and across the United States. These travels went in multiple stages. Much as Xandra and I got ourselves to Alto Bío-Bío, by camper, bus, Uber, and car, Whitman went by steam ferry from Camden to Philadelphia and then by streetcar to a train depot. And from that train depot to another and another until, having drunk of the beauty of the machines as well as the stars, the poet would arrive at his destination. But time would always freeze for Whitman when he was on the Delaware, often crossing back and forth for no reason but love. On the banks or on the steamship, in the morning or the dark of night, he conjugated with the river and the sky above: "the splendor indescribable," wrote the great poet of description in 1879. The splendor indescribable is the gift of nature. It can never be owned, but it can be stolen. That is the agony of my witness and the source of sublime hope. Some day, the dams removed, the Bío-Bío might awaken again.

100 Miles in Chicagoland

JeeYeun Lee

Walk One: Vincennes Trail,
October 2, 2019

I'm standing at Michigan and Wacker at the southwest corner of DuSable Bridge in downtown Chicago. I'm chilled and awkward, trying to act like it's normal to wear this Korean dress and pose for pictures early in the morning. Commuters around me rush to work, heads down, coffee in hand. I'm in front of a tall relief sculpture that depicts a white man wielding a sword to protect white women and children from Native men with tomahawks and arrows. It memorializes an event in 1812 that the carved inscription describes as a brutal massacre, whose white victims "will be cherished as martyrs in our early history."

This place is the heart of settler Chicago's story. The footprint of Fort Dearborn, created to protect American trade, marks the sidewalk on the south side of the Chicago River. The bust of Jean Baptiste Point DuSable, recognized as the first non-Native settler of this region, graces the sidewalk on the other side. And the location itself, where the river meets Lake Michigan, is what made this region irresistible to European settlers—the magical link between the Great Lakes and the Mississippi River. Now the center of Chicago tourism, this spot is where visitors crowd onto boats for river tours of Chicago's famed architecture.

This essay is based on edited versions of Instagram posts that the author made during her walks.

Standing in front of *The Defense* by Henry Hering (1928) depicting the Battle of Fort Dearborn in 1812.

It's the perfect starting point for my project to track settler colonialism in today's environment. For five Wednesdays in October 2019, I begin here and walk for twenty miles. Each week, I head in a different direction, on diagonal roads originally forged by Native people. The board game Settlers of Catan has colonization right—you have to build a road before you can build a settlement. The irony is that early settlers used roads forged by Native people. In *An Indigenous Peoples' History of the United States*, Roxanne Dunbar-Ortiz quotes David Wade Chambers: "early Native American trails and roads . . . were not just paths in the woods following along animal tracks used mainly for hunting. Neither [were they] routes that nomadic peoples followed during seasonal migrations. Rather they constituted an extensive system of roadways

My routes during the 2019 project, following roads originally established by Native people.

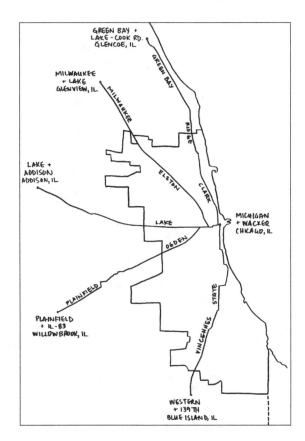

that spanned the Americas." Settlers took those roads and paved them; now they are our highways. Indigenous civilization undergirds today's infrastructure.

It's still dark outside when I start my first walk. The streetlights are on, shining orange through the damp and drizzly mist. I head south on Michigan Avenue, starting down the Native route renamed by settlers as the Vincennes Trail. The path used to hug the shore of Lake Michigan, which now lies a few blocks east due to generations of landfill. In 1914, the Pokagon Band of Potawatomi Indians sued the city of Chicago for that landfill. They had been among the signers of the Treaty of 1833, which designated the eastern boundary of land cessions as Lake Michigan. But the city had since created land beyond the shore, acres of landfill that we know today as Streeterville, Grant Park, Soldier Field, and other valuable lakefront property. The Potawatomi argued for return of this unceded territory, or payment for its purchase. The

Supreme Court ruled against the tribe, saying that they had abandoned their right of occupancy: "for more than half a century no pretense of such occupancy has been made by the tribe." An odd and impossible argument, since that land had been underwater in 1833, and the treaty had required the Potawatomi to leave.

Native peoples were forced to cede their lands around what is now Chicago in a series of six treaties from 1795 to 1833. Villages of Potawatomi people had dotted the region, where they lived with Ojibwe and Odawa kin. Menominee, Ho-Chunk, Sauk, and Meskwaki peoples had also lived in the area, and before that the Miami and Illinois confederations.

I don't like occupying other peoples' lands. Coming from a place that was colonized in the last century, I am acutely aware of the injustice. The least I can do is witness the present-day occupation of the land where I now live. I walk to witness how the logic of taking has wreaked elimination, containment, and dispossession upon peoples seen as less than human. I wear a traditional Korean dress made in denim, an embodiment of slavery and settler colonialism in its cotton and indigo materiality. I walk through the landscape as an immigrant, settler, "American" and Korean female.

ON MARTIN LUTHER KING DRIVE at 24th Place, a sign announces the entrance to the historic Bronzeville neighborhood. Just beyond is the *Monument to the Great Northern Migration* by Alison Saar, one of the few public art works in Chicago made by a Black woman. From 1915 to 1970, the number of African Americans in Chicago grew from 15,000 to one million, less than 2 percent to one-third of the whole city. Drawn by networks of family and friends, recruited by factories that needed labor, descendants of kidnapped and enslaved Africans thronged to the big city, only to be confined to the "Black Belt." But the numbers of newcomers quickly stretched the limits of their containment. As St. Clair Drake and Horace R. Cayton asked in their iconic *Black Metropolis*: "Where would the black masses, still bearing the mark of the plantation upon them, find a place to live?"

Where indeed? Vicious policies forced African Americans into patterns of hyper-segregation and impoverishment that still exist today. Restrictive covenants, redlining, urban renewal, public housing, redevelopment, and organized violence and harassment by white people—all the mechanisms possible have been and are still being used here in

Alison Saar's *Monument to the Great Northern Migration* (1994).

Chicago to confine movement and deny dignity. It's evident all around me as I walk through the South Side.

THE GHOSTS OF WAR are everywhere. I'm on Martin Luther King Drive and 32nd Street, looking east at a high-rise apartment complex built during a period of contested urban renewal in the 1960s. One hundred years before that, this was the location of Camp Douglas, a Civil War Union Army camp that held over 26,000 Confederate prisoners of war during its four years of operation. One out of seven died from smallpox and other diseases, and many are buried in a mass grave marked by a thirty-foot monument at Oak Woods Cemetery just a few miles south. Surrounded by the graves of prominent Black Chicagoans like Harold Washington and Ida B. Wells, this memorial to Confederate soldiers has become an affront to racial justice activists who are now demanding its removal.

IT'S DRIZZLING AGAIN as I cross State and 51st. The mist blurs the air above the empty fields where the Robert Taylor Homes once stretched for blocks. Completed in 1962, the infamous public housing project housed 27,000 people at its height, 20,000 of them children. The development was demolished in 2007, its existence and its ending both evidence of what Saidiya Hartman calls the "brutal disposability and precarity of black life" ("On Working with Archives," interview in *The Creative Independent*). Ironically, the project was named after Robert Taylor, the first African American chair of the Chicago Housing Authority board, who had quit his position when City Council opposed scattered-site public housing in order to preserve racial segregation in the city. Today, only a fraction of the housing rebuilt on the demolition site is affordable for low-income families, despite the promises of the Chicago Housing Authority. In a capitalist logic where land only has value in its use, the emptiness of these lots proclaims the disposable value of the people who used to live here.

I'VE WALKED for hours now, past storefront churches, empty lots, vibrant murals, and a street sign designating an honorary Emmett Till Road. Late in the afternoon, I cross the edge of the city into suburban Blue Island. This spot was once an actual island when Lake Michigan was enlarged by melting glacier water, and it is still the highest point in Chicagoland, 100 feet above lake level. It also used to be the site of a Potawatomi village located along the Vincennes Trail. Appropriately, I immediately see a sign on a field advertising "Land Available." Land, which had been Indigenous peoples' collective inheritance, was turned into property through treaties. The U.S. government promptly turned around and sold it to American settlers, financing its fledgling national budget.

I came across a quotation in William Cronon's *Nature's Metropolis* by Émile Boutmy, a nineteenth-century French political scientist: "The striking and peculiar characteristic of American society is that it is not so much a democracy as a huge commercial company for the discovery, cultivation, and capitalization of its enormous territory. . . . The United States are primarily a commercial society . . . and only secondarily a nation." As I finish my first twenty-mile journey, I wonder: How would we relate to land (to each other, to anything else around us) without this structure of settler colonialism?

Walk Two: Barry Point Trail, October 9, 2019

The 1816 Treaty of St. Louis, a "treaty of Peace, Friendship, and Limits," was Chicago's second formative treaty. It relinquished a strip of land ten miles wide on both sides of the Chicago River, creating Indian Boundary Lines at the north and south borders. The lines were meant to keep Native people out. Today, I'm walking southwest right along the middle of this strip on Ogden Avenue, the first road paved by settlers as the Southwestern Plank Road, now a section of the famed U.S. Route 66.

It's warm today, the sky intensely blue and clear. I've left downtown's skyscrapers far behind when I reach North Lawndale. Decades of systemic disinvestment show in the boarded-up buildings and cracked sidewalks around me. This neighborhood is featured by Ta-Nehisi Coates in his seminal 2014 article "The Case for Reparations," where he talks about the plunder of Black bodies, Black labor, and Black families as the foundation for white democracy. He features stories of Black North Lawndale residents about their experiences of segregation and redlining, and how they organized the Contract Buyers League to fight discriminatory real estate practices. In the essay he goes on to compare slave ownership to home ownership: equally aspirational in its time, equally unthinkable then to envision ending it. "Imagine what would happen if a president today came out in favor of taking all American homes from their owners," he writes; "the reaction might well be violent." As I leave this neighborhood, I wonder: how did we start thinking that ownership of anything was a right? How do we dispossess the American dream, predicated on land as property instead of something we are part of, connected to, related to? How do we unhitch our aspirations from their origins in violence?

TRANSPORTATION is a big theme today. I'm in the suburb of Cicero now, and for blocks and blocks I walk past the Cicero Intermodal Terminal for BNSF, the largest freight railroad company in North America. Containers get moved between trains, ships, and trucks here, conveniently located near the railroad tracks, the I-55 highway, and the Chicago Sanitary and Ship Canal. A quick internet search brings up a 2014 EPA report on this terminal's high levels of diesel pollution, which waft

A dramatic shift on Walk Two, from the Cicero Intermodal train terminal to the lazy Des Plaines River.

over its surrounding residential areas, right where I'm walking. Exposure to diesel exhaust has been linked to asthma, cancer, heart attacks, brain damage, and premature death. Of the 340,000 people who live within a half mile of an intermodal terminal in the Chicago region, more than 80 percent are Latinx or African American. Environmental justice activists call these areas "sacrifice zones."

DRASTICALLY YET CASUALLY, the environment changes from polluted industry to small-town main street. There is no transition. I'm in the suburb of Lyons now, and I'm taking a moment on the bridge to watch the slow-moving Des Plaines River. Just a little south of here is the Chicago Portage National Historic Site. It marks the place where Native people carried canoes between the Chicago and Des Plaines Rivers, thus traversing from Lake Michigan and the Great Lakes waterways to the Mississippi River and the Gulf of Mexico. From the moment settlers first learned of this strategic portage, they dreamed of a canal to open up transportation for trade and settlement. The canal was finally completed in 1848, financed by selling the land along its shores. This transportation hub is why the settlers created a city here, why *Chicago Tribune* columnist John Husar once called this spot "Our sacred ground . . . Chicago's 'Plymouth Rock.'" The 1493 Doctrine of Discovery, a Catholic decree that gave land to anyone who "discovered" it in the name of a Christian monarch, reaches its tentacles into this time and place still, disguising the act of taking with the language of finding.

I'VE SWITCHED OVER to Plainfield Road now, and the sun is still beating down when I pass by the entrance to a subdivision in suburban Western Springs. A plaque on a boulder sitting among landscaped flowers reads:

> Last Camp Site of the POTAWATOMIE INDIANS in Cook County 1835; Erected by LaGrange Illinois Chapter Daughters of the American Revolution MAY 15th 1930.

According to the Western Springs Historical Society, the last Potawatomi people to leave Chicago by the terms of the 1833 treaty departed in fall 1835. The group of about 70 people slept that first night of travel here. It was a farm then, belonging to Joseph Vial, a settler who came from New York and bought 170 acres right after the land was taken through the treaty. Vial paid the U.S. government $1.25 per acre, the equivalent of $33 today. A sign above the subdivision walls advertises that "Timber Trails" is still building and selling new homes. They are priced in the $600,000s. Land was taken, people displaced, and resources extracted in order to make this placid suburban scene possible. All through these walks this question persists in my mind: How do we see what has deliberately and violently been made unseen?

STILL FOLLOWING the Potawatomis' trail of exile, I pass through some of Chicago's toniest suburbs—Burr Ridge, Willowbrook. The houses here are huge and intimidating. They display what I have read: that these suburbs are falling short on a state mandate to have at least 10 percent affordable housing in their communities. No surprise. Keeping working-class and poor people out is precisely what they were designed to do. The Ambiance subdivision in Burr Ridge, a gated community of multimillion-dollar homes, was built after residents shot down a 1969 proposal for low-income housing. Willowbrook was incorporated in 1960 by its 167 residents to prevent the development of low-cost two-bedroom homes. One of the stated purposes of its current zoning code is to conserve the taxable value of land and buildings. I finish my second walk a short while later in a supermarket parking lot, wondering if zoning could be used to conserve the land itself.

A home in Willowbrook.

Walk Three: Lake Street Trail, October 16, 2019

I'm walking west today, an important direction for settlers in the new United States. Lake Street parallels the first railroad track built in Illinois, the Galena and Chicago Union, the genesis of Chicago's comprehensive rail network that tied western settler farmland and grazing fields to eastern markets. Railroads drastically shortened the amount of time in which people expected goods and information, and changed our relationship to time by instituting standardized time zones, essential for preventing accidents, thirty-five years before the U.S. government would adopt them. Just another way this project reveals to me the extent that capitalism and settler colonialism shape our daily lives.

Lake Street itself runs under the tracks of the "L" train. First built in 1892, the system of elevated tracks was mostly retained by Chicago even after other cities replaced them with subways. So now the trains clatter above me for the first few miles of my walk. The periodic passing of trains punctuates the feeling of desolation around me. On either side of the elevated tracks are empty lots and vacant industrial build-

Both sides of the elevated tracks on Lake Street feature empty lots and vacant industrial buildings.

ings. Research confirms what I see: Industry has been leaving the West Side of Chicago for decades, going to the suburbs where land is still plentiful and cheap, and municipal governments desperate for jobs offer taxpayer-funded incentives. The result? Less than 15 percent of manufacturing jobs remain in the city from fifty years ago. The unemployment rate for African Americans in the city, many of whom used to work in the manufacturing sector, is now twice the regional average, which might explain why they're leaving. Since 2010, one out of four African Americans in Chicago, once the largest racial group in the city, have left for the suburbs or gone out of the state altogether in a reverse migration to places like Atlanta and Houston. Who will we become without our Black neighbors? What happens when it's our turn to get eaten up by capitalism?

RUNNING PARALLEL a few blocks south of my route is I-290, known as the Eisenhower Expressway. I hate this perpetually congested highway, and so I feel superior today, as if my walking is faster than driving on that damned road. Built in stages during the 1950s, it was part of a new superhighway system intended to relieve traffic but conveniently deployed to eliminate "blight," code word for working-class neighborhoods and communities of color. Highways take up enormous parcels of land: construction of the Eisenhower displaced about 13,000 people and 400 businesses. Early in the day I walked through the Near West Side; almost 40 percent African American in the 1950s, the neighborhood was decimated by the highway. I cross the border now into the suburb of Oak Park, whose more affluent residents were able to stop the highway's proposed clover-leaf ramps and got center-lane ramps instead, which take less land.

Part of the highway system: a view from Lake Street.

Past Oak Park are working-class suburbs like Maywood and Melrose Park, with their strip malls, cemeteries, and an intermodal terminal. I end in the suburb of Addison, at a veterans' memorial outside of a Walgreens store. Sometimes everything on these walks seems like a mirage. It all looks so real—the buildings and streets and cars—but from another angle, they become transparent and lift from the ground, floating above the land. Which is more real, I wonder, and which will last longer: what has been built on settler colonialism, or the land itself?

Walk Four: Elston Road Trail, October 23, 2019

My walk today goes along Elston and Milwaukee Avenues. This was another early plank road laid down by settlers on a well-defined Native path. In 1889, white men protested the tollgate along this road by burning down the gate, killing the owner, and taking the planks for firewood. They were dressed as "Indians." Back then, "redface" was a popular mechanism allowing white men to act the "savage" in order to protest the social order. It still is. We live in a country that glorifies armed rebellion against government dictates, but only if it's by white men.

I HEAD NORTHWEST from downtown, through a part of Chicago where white people live. Construction is clearly the day's theme: the neighborhood is booming with new office buildings, condos, and street improvements. I pass the outer edge of Lincoln Yards, a new $6 billion project subsidized in part by $1.3 billion from the city. In exchange for what? Protestors question whether the development will create affordable housing or simply perpetuate racial segregation. A 2019 Urban Institute report says majority-white neighborhoods in Chicago receive 4.6 times more in home mortgages, small business loans, and commercial real estate investment than majority-Black neighborhoods, and 2.6 times more than majority-Latino neighborhoods. I can see that money today, in these improved streets and brand-new buildings, just as I witnessed the lack of it on my previous walks, in neighborhoods deteriorating from lack of investment.

A LITTLE FARTHER, and now I'm near where I live. The entire route today is intimately familiar territory. My brother lives off this street. My car mechanic is on this street. My sister had her wedding at a banquet hall on this street. My mom gets acupuncture at a storefront on this street. The nursing home where my grandmother lived is off this street. I'm about to pass not one, not two, but three Korean supermarkets on this route, where people will actually know what I am wearing. Except they will still be confused because my traditional dress is made out of nontraditional denim, and no one wears this costume in their daily life. I thought the strangest part of this project would be to walk through neighborhoods I didn't know, but it turns out the ones I know are stranger, encountered through the lens of settler colonialism.

IT'S SUNNY AGAIN today, with the light reflecting green off the trees by this stretch of sidewalk. I've reached the edge of the city, where the forest preserve, a golf course, a nearby road, and the entire neighborhood are named after Sauganash, also known as Billy Caldwell. Born to a Mohawk mother and English father, he came to Chicago in the late 1700s and married into the Potawatomi tribe. For his role in negotiating the Treaty of Prairie du Chien in 1829, Caldwell received 1,600 acres of land. He started selling it off a few years later, and then was forced west with other Potawatomi after the 1833 Treaty. Almost forty years later, a man came forward as Caldwell's son to ask about the land. The Bureau of Indian Affairs told him that a portion of the plot, 160 acres,

Walking through my own neighborhood.

had been sold without permission of the U.S. president, a condition regularly built into treaties ostensibly to protect Native people. The land remained unrecovered, and it was sold to the Cook County Forest Preserve in 1917 and 1922. Technically, Caldwell's descendants might still be able to make a claim to this piece of land.

Stories like this lay bare for me the colonized status of this land, pulling the fact of occupation into the present day. I grew up in Illinois, a state that lacks a single federally recognized tribe. Like so many non-Natives here, I'm not used to the idea of Native people actually living on their ancestral land. I end the day at the corner of Milwaukee and Lake in suburban Glenview, in a shopping mall that has several Korean stores and restaurants. My people make a living here, on other peoples' land.

Walk Five: Green Bay Trail, October 30, 2019

It's my final walk. It's drizzling again, a freezing rain. I head north across the DuSable Bridge, past the bust of Jean Baptiste Point DuSable. Every Chicago schoolchild knows him: the founder of modern Chicago, its first immigrant, a visionary and entrepreneur. Of African descent, he was born in Haiti or Canada, and came to the Chicago area as a fur trader. He married a Potawatomi woman named Kitihawa, established an extensive farm and trading post here on the north bank of the Chicago River, then sold it all and moved away in 1800. The farm was later bought by John Kinzie, a leading figure in early settler Chicago. For many years, African Americans protested the city's lack of official recognition of DuSable, while Kinzie, a white man, is commemorated in many Chicago sites. Even the bust was a private donation by a Haitian American. In 2010, ninety years after this bridge was built, it was renamed after DuSable as a result of these protests, and in June 2021, Chicago's City Council voted to rename Lake Shore Drive after him too. Even that necessitated a compromise: instead of replacing the previous name, more words got added, creating the unwieldy moniker "Jean Baptiste Point DuSable Lake Shore Drive."

As uncertain as the facts are about DuSable, almost nothing is known about Kitihawa, his wife, even though it's likely that her family networks enabled his success as a trader. Searching in the archives while preparing for this walk, I looked in vain for information about Kitihawa. How did she grow up, what kind of person was she, what did

The bust of Jean Baptiste Point DuSable, with *Discoverers* (1928) by James Earle Fraser in the background.

she think about or like to do? If the archives don't tell us, will a monument or renaming do the trick? When we add a bust of DuSable on the Magnificent Mile, or perhaps erect a statue of Kitihawa, what are we celebrating? What do we proclaim when we celebrate the founding of anything on this continent, and does it mean something different if those people are Black and Native?

Those are the questions that swirl in my mind as I walk north along the Magnificent Mile, home to upscale shopping and the world's largest Starbucks. This stretch of Michigan Avenue, its iconic status boosted by city financing and a strategic marketing campaign, didn't become a shopping mecca until the 1950s. As restrictive covenants were outlawed, African Americans started to move out of the Black Belt into other parts of the South and West side. Rather than serve their new Black customers, retailers abandoned those neighborhoods, and African Americans, with few neighborhood options, began shopping on State Street, which was then downtown's main retail strip. In a domino chain of retail white flight, State Street's higher-priced retailers pulled up their stakes and moved to Michigan Avenue. Thus, the Magnificent Mile was born. Racism's distaste of proximity to Black bodies extends even to shopping.

NOT FAR PAST the Magnificent Mile, I turn onto Clark Street and come to a high-rise housing complex, the result of 1960s urban renewal. My cousin used to live here, and I once dated someone who lived here. The neighborhood was home to Chicago's first large Puerto Rican community, who called it "La Clark." As working-class people of color started moving closer to the tony Gold Coast district, the city decided that this land was blighted. It demolished the entire neighborhood and financed a $6.4 million housing complex for middle- and upper-income professionals. From 1950 to 1966, Chicago displaced over 80,000 people through urban renewal projects, the most per capita in the nation. Forced to move out to Lincoln Park and Humboldt Park, Puerto Rican youth fought back, forming the Young Lords Party and a national movement for self-determination. No marker, no monument alerts pedestrians to this history. It requires organized resistance to even document stories of resistance.

THE SLEET KEEPS coming down. I'm looking for a place to get dry when I reach Wrigley Field. Looking at the country's second-oldest ballpark, I don't think about baseball history or the Cubs, but about Carol Warrington. In 1970, this Menominee mother of six lived behind Wrigley Field in an apartment with steadily worsening conditions. After two months of withholding rent in protest, she was evicted. Native organizers rallied around her eviction and camped outside the apartment building for three months to protest substandard housing for Native Americans. Led by Mike Chosa (Ojibway), this group became the Chicago Indian Village and went on to stage encampments around the Chicago region for the next two years, occupying buildings and federal properties to bring attention to housing needs for Native Americans.

Most Native people living in Chicago at the time had come as a result of the federal Bureau of Indian Affairs relocation program in the

Iconic Wrigley Field, near a housing site that sparked Native American protests in the 1970s.

1950s, part of its termination policy designed to assimilate Native people as well as end federal recognition for tribes. When I delved deeper, I discovered the BIA commissioner championing this effort had previously headed the War Relocation Authority, the agency in charge of imprisoning Japanese Americans in internment camps. Incarceration, assimilation, removal: sometimes the connections are right there, you don't even have to stretch to make them.

THE OVERCAST SKY follows me north past the border of the city, through Evanston and into Wilmette. This is where my family moved after my first year of high school. We were on the immigrant upward-mobility track, and my mother wanted us to go to "better" schools. Only recently did I learn that this suburb is named after a French Canadian settler, Antoine Ouilmette, and is located on the reserve deeded to his Potawatomi wife, Archange Chevalier. Antoine helped to negotiate the 1829 treaty; in return Archange got 1,280 acres in what is now Wilmette and Evanston. The Ouilmettes lived there until 1840, when they moved to Iowa to join their Potawatomi kin following the tribe's removal. Archange died right afterwards, at the age of seventy-six, and her husband died the next year. Their children sold this land in the following decade, and a land syndicate was formed by white settlers to promote residential development. In the 1920s, the town annexed neighboring Gross Point, and built a 170-acre development named Indian Hill Estates. Wilmette is now one of the ten wealthiest towns in Illinois. Somehow, all of this seems connected to my misery after moving from the city to the suburbs, surrounded by rich white kids. Would things have gone differently for me, for those kids, if we had felt our connection to the land we were on and the people who had come before us?

I'M DONE, AT THE END of my final walk. I just walked through Winnetka, the second-richest town in the state. Now I'm at the corner of Green Bay and County Line Road in Glencoe, the richest place in Illinois, tenth richest in the U.S., with an average household income of $340,000. These suburbs are 90 percent white. In 2013, white families had thirteen times the amount of wealth as Black families, a wealth gap, often attributed to the ongoing legacy of slavery, that Ta-Nehisi Coates defines as theft. For most families, of any color, wealth is acquired through owning property, specifically a home. It is the American Dream. Walking through these neighborhoods where the median value of homes is over $1 million, I am in someone's dream come true. Whose dream? Whose wealth?

IN *AS WE HAVE ALWAYS DONE: Indigenous Freedom through Radical Resistance*, Leanne Betasamosake Simpson (Michi Saagiig Nishnaabeg) says: "within Nishnaabeg thought, the opposite of dispossession is not possession, it is deep, reciprocal, consensual *attachment*." We who are not Native, what is our right relationship to this place, this land? If settler colonialism is a structure and not an event, as the late scholar Patrick Wolfe put it, how do we dismantle the structure? How do we move from the logic of taking and separation to the logic of care and reciprocity?

Life is always like this series of walks, I think. On one hand, there's the plodding mundanity of strip malls and broken sidewalks and dank underpasses. The tedium of drizzle or the discomfort of heat, negotiating uncomfortable clothing and sore feet, achy knees. It's punctuated by an occasional burst of color in an unexpected mural, or whimsy in a storefront display.

On the other hand, there are the stories that have shaped this place, visible on street names, railroad tracks, city boundaries, and really everything that you can see. The ghosts, usually flattened by the hustle of everyday survival, take shape and crowd around, clamor, demanding to be known. If we walk long enough, will we notice them and listen?

What are we to do with the stories—the stories of desperate clawing for survival, of homes lost and made, of grief and terror and humiliation? The stories feel so exquisitely personal, even as the structures that create them are driven by rationale from centuries ago. How do we live together, who gets to call this place home, how do we navigate our untenable inheritance of violence in this landscape of heartbreak? I keep walking, gathering questions, open to signs and whispers rising from the land.

.

Pilgrimages, Routes, and Rituals

The Complacency of Place

WALKING THE VIA JACOBI THROUGH GENEVA, SWITZERLAND

Paula Read

To LIVE ON the border between two countries is live with a certain level of porosity at all times. Or at least it was, back when I wrote the original version of this piece in 2019. We border dwellers are accustomed to the constant presence of the Other, either because border dwellers from the Other Side come to our side to sleep or shop or visit, or because we go there and are the Other. The ancient pilgrim's path I walked is also, by its nature, a walk of traversing borders—the marked and unmarked borders between countries, the invisible borders of the self. One undertakes these walks precisely to find oneself elsewhere, to discover the Otherness, both within and without.

When the COVID-19 virus undertook its own rapid journey across the world, we border dwellers suddenly found ourselves cut off from our other Others. Like most places, we went into a prolonged lockdown. In France, we were only permitted to go outside for an hour of activity each day, which could only take place within a fifteen-minute walking radius of our home. In any case, people scrambled to get themselves on their preferred side of the dividing line, and borders between France and Switzerland were closed.

"The Complacency of Place" originally appeared in the 2019 issue of *Panorama: The Journal of Intelligent Travel.*

All crossings, from the large multi-lane border stations down to the walking paths I used on this pilgrimage, were either severely narrowed and tightly controlled, or completely cut off by concrete blocks. Some walking paths in villages that spanned both sides of the border were blocked by concrete planters filled with flowers in an attempt to soften the impression of fearful exclusion, but the result was the same.

The first time I was able to cross into Switzerland after almost three months, I found myself unexpectedly crying. I hadn't realized just how much of my life is lived in transit on a regular basis, moving between places of being. With the virus ebbing and flowing in a toxic moon tide, we face similar closures on an unpredictable schedule for the foreseeable future.

Of course, I've been very privileged to be able to cross most borders at will all my life, even crossing into a new nationality as a naturalized French citizen. Perhaps that's one reason I've taken it so very much for granted.

It was one of the plague's unanticipated gifts, this appreciation of simple foot-led mobility, the mingling among Others, the chance to walk unhindered in pursuit of oneself.

Day 1

Versoix to Genthod

The path is marked at regular intervals by plaques bearing the symbol of the journey, a scallop half-shell, set into walls and street signposts.

My own half-shell swung against my backpack, keeping my pace in a rhythmic whisper. The grooved lines of the shell represent countless paths that lead in scattered rays towards a single point of convergence. The image denotes the many individual interior pathways that lead to a shared center of spirit. It's an old nonverbal sign that the bearer is a Camino pilgrim, and an invitation for other pilgrims to talk.

The Camino, a pilgrim's path that dates back to the ninth century, was once mainly a Christian journey of faith. It has long been a secular journey of self-discovery, a walk for peace, and a personal physical challenge. Walking the Camino is supposed to bring strangers together, literally from all walks of life, in a harmony of movement. Geneva, as a city, promises to do the same.

I've lived in the Geneva area for over twenty years. Although I wasn't a proper pilgrim coming from afar, I wanted to be a pilgrim in spirit.

I STARTED EARLY on a Friday morning in Versoix, at the border of the Geneva canton. Snugged between the worn roll of the ancient Jura mountain range to the west, the punky new peaks of the Alps to the east, trees rustled the heat in a welcome August breeze. The sun rose over the Alps, benign.

The late summer sun shone down on the town in the middle of Europe known as Peace City. The air carried the sweet scent of grapes ripening in nearby vineyards. Lake Geneva was a carpet of dazzling diamonds set against the backdrop of Alpine peaks, white-capped even in summer. These shores are home to the world's highest density of humanitarian organizations; half of the inhabitants are foreign born. Geneva is one of the most diverse and wealthy small cities in the world, managing to assimilate a large transient population with what looks like little fanfare or strife. Wars come and go, Geneva floats serenely above the fray.

On my previous Camino walk, in the north of Spain, I'd gotten lost. I'd had wonderful encounters with walkers and locals alike; I'd also gotten viciously hit in the head by a drunken Spaniard in Pamplona. Not that I was looking to repeat that particular experience, but I was looking forward to some unexpected moments. And maybe a little less heat.

There wasn't a soul in sight, even on the main road where the Geneva path begins. After the first thirty minutes, I sensed a flaw in my plan: I expected to encounter people who would complicate my walk, but there were no people. I'd downloaded maps as if I might lose my way. But if I'd hoped for getting lost and having an adventure, the path was clearly marked by dust-free signs at every turn. And it was getting hotter by the minute.

HERE WAS the first fountain, clearly marked as a welcoming sign to Via pilgrims. A waterfall of fresh, clean spring water, splashing against a new sculptural fountain carved from a large boulder. Clean fountain water is one of the only free things you'll find in Geneva, but it's a luxury you'll find almost everywhere.

Welcome, lonely stranger.

I embarked on the exquisitely laid-out path through a tree-lined residential area, accompanied only by a babbling brook that shadowed the path. Gravel crunched quietly beneath my walking shoes, birds sang their morning song, and I might have been in a remote forest instead of in the middle of a town.

I've lived here for most of my adult life, raised a child here, and yet I have very few Swiss friends. It's a phenomenon one hears often among long-term foreign residents. That's one of the things I would have to think about on my own: *how can a city be so welcoming and so aloof at the same time?*

Among the top twenty world cities with high foreign-born populations, Geneva is the smallest. In addition, tens of thousands of foreign-born workers flood over the Franco-Swiss border every day to work in the congested urban area. When Switzerland held a 2014 national referendum to limit immigration and foreign workers in favor of Swiss citizens, Geneva and the neighboring French-speaking cantons all voted against it. The national referendum passed on the slimmest of margins based on the German-speaking cantons, none of which have the high levels of foreigners living and working in their regions.

The mere fact of an economy's dependence on foreign workers has never meant that local residents like or accept them. Any language of tolerance usually has discord oozing out the sides like chocolate melting on a hot day.

Two women were walking on the gravel path. Finally! Some chance encounters!

I said the obligatory *"Bonjour!"* that any polite person says in French-speaking areas when there aren't too many people to say it to.

"Bonjour!"

"Oh, *bonjour, bonjour!*" I fell into step with them. They looked like grandmotherly extras from a 1960s movie, all polka-dotted dresses and stockings, hair meticulously coiffed at eight in the morning.

"Are you from around here?"

They both shook their heads and protested. One was tall, the other barely came up to my chest; neither was younger than seventy-five.

"No! We're not from here! We're from Geneva. We only moved here to be closer to our children and grandchildren. But this town is so unfriendly. Not like Geneva."

Geneva, they said, had opened its arms to them in a real communion for half a century. But Versoix! Versoix turned its back, overcharged senior citizens for bus fares, and waited impatiently for them to die.

It was time for them to turn off the path, and I carried on alone.

THE VIA MORPHED into an asphalt road and then guided pilgrims onto suburban sidewalks. It jig-jagged down through the village proper of Versoix, skirted the national railway, then climbed back up into some of the most exclusive parts of the Geneva canton. Lush gated mansions, regal diplomatic missions, startlingly tidy and intact village centers with homes from the fifteenth century onwards. Flowers overflowed and cascaded from window boxes and lampposts. Street cleaners were sweeping already immaculate sidewalks. They said hello as I passed, but the only other people on the streets were well-dressed dog walkers who pointedly ignored me. Maybe it was my backpack and hiking shoes.

The Via traversed a small vineyard heavy with purple grapes that lay in front of a large chateau like an edible tablecloth. The city revealed itself, carnelian rooftops between lapis sky and lake. I had more time for silent meditation than I had anticipated.

I thought, as I often have, of how Geneva hasn't had armed conflict on its territory for generations. Even before it joined the Swiss federation, Geneva's leaders had learned to successfully avoid conflict by negotiating, by expelling hotheads, by compromising between religious factions. It's long provided a haven to incendiary intellectuals like Voltaire, but has been equally happy to turf them out if they didn't conform. The city has an annual event that includes flaming torches and a battalion of costumed volunteers to commemorate a 1602 victory over the French. Filling the cobbled streets of the Old Town with suits of armor, ragged peasants, ramrod soldiers, and original cannons as if the battle had been won just yesterday, the Escalade has always struck me as a curious way to celebrate centuries of nonviolence.

Maybe the militaristic posturing is to remind people that peace is the choice of the strong, those who could fight but choose instead to discuss.

Genthod to Pregny

I missed a turnoff on the Via, one of the only corners that wasn't exceedingly well marked. Admittedly, I was excited to have gotten even a little bit lost. Maybe this would get the ball rolling, encounter-wise.

By this time I was in the area of the city that is almost wholly occupied by the United Nations and other humanitarian organizations, as well as several of the larger missions. I approached an imposing twenty-foot-tall fence of spiked metal, and beyond that, the old World Health Organization buildings. I took a picture, from the street, then noticed the United States flag flying high above the fence. I moved slightly to take a photo of it against the sky, only to have an armed guard get very agitated.

"*No photos!*" He was waving his hand at me.

After the two women in Versoix, this guy, a fellow American, was the first person who had said anything to me on my walk. I was fifty feet away on a public street, and he was getting angrier by the second. He motioned for me to come over and talk to the other guards of what turned out to be the U.S. Mission to the United Nations. The installation has become increasingly fortified over the past couple of years and now looks more threatening than Geneva's local prison. This was not the kind of meeting I'd hoped for.

I backtracked to the correct path.

By now I was worried that I wouldn't be any closer to understanding this city or my place in it than I was at the outset.

Pregny to Geneva

The day was getting oven-hot, the sun was no longer benign, and my back was sweaty against my day backpack. I'd decided to dress the part, and was wearing the same kind of lightweight hiking clothes I would wear if I were walking all the way to Santiago rather than to the Swiss border just ten miles away.

I thudded along one of the main lakeside roads, all traffic noise and wide sidewalks, dodging the sun and trying to stay in the shade of any trees. Now that I was out of the rarified diplomatic quarter and down by the lake, there were tourists everywhere. From having too few possible people to talk to, I had too many.

My half-shell brushed against my backpack, swish-swish, and I kept walking.

I WALKED ALONG the lakeside promenade, pockets of cool air rising up from Lake Geneva. Small flocks of birds bobbed in the shallow water—grebes, swans, ducks, many of them with comet tails of young-lings trailing behind. The Via took me right past the Palais Wilson, the former headquarters of the League of Nations during the 1920s and most of the 1930s.

Geneva, like the rest of Switzerland, was neutral for both of the twentieth century's global conflicts. When the United Nations replaced the defunct League of Nations after the Second World War, Geneva was once again chosen as the European headquarters.

It's easy to take the weight of all this diplomacy for granted. Live in the city for long enough, and it becomes a matter of routine to get stuck in traffic as the world's dignitaries come to discuss treaties and negotiate conflicts. There's a blasé acceptance of these grand comings and goings. Of seeing, as I have, Hillary Clinton or John Kerry stroll through the hotel bar where my book club meets.

Geneva is like one of those old market towns from Western movies, the ones where anyone visiting had to leave their weapons at the town limits if they wanted to come in and trade. Most international residents will work for a time in Geneva, and then leave. New foreign residents will take their place.

I'd expected the Via to be an easy stroll with lots of conversation. But as I made my way further into the city, I was getting no conversation and having to weave through knots of tourists. The crisp mountain views were highlighted by the Jet d'Eau in the middle of the lake, which shoots a fountain of water 460 feet (140 meters) into the air.

FROM THE LAKESIDE promenade up to the main train station, and then back down, I thought this part of the Via Jacobi might have been altered at some point to accommodate travelers arriving by rail. But no—it's the train station that was built near the tenth-century Temple de Saint-Gervais. This stolid Romanesque temple now stands stranded, an island between bus and tram lines. Not a pilgrim in sight, but so many travelers.

Crossing over the river to the Old Town, I headed for my first destination, the Cathedral de St. Pierre. I passed the many (*many!*) private banks, jewelry shops, watch shops, and more banks. Private wealth management is what Geneva does when it's not doing humanitarian work. This has historically included legitimate banking, as well as an array of documented money-laundering. Banking is a cornerstone of Geneva's wealth and its neutral status.

Neutrality doesn't necessarily mean an absence of conflict or conflicting interests, but it can mean an absence of armed conflict on one's own territory. In this city of humanitarian work, it's not widely known that Switzerland ranks among the world's major arms suppliers, or that it long kept an army of soldiers that could be rented out to other conflicts while the federation held itself apart. Neutrality means that energies can be focused on providing the services and places for creating peace both within, and for others, even if the city and country profit from distant conflict.

It's worked well here in Geneva, which is why I can walk across the city and marvel, again and again, at how pleasant, clean, and well-appointed it is. That takes a lot of bureaucratic and organizational attention; it takes a commitment to following rules. And there are so many rules in Geneva, spoken and unspoken, an entire labyrinth of do's and don'ts. I've gotten so accustomed to walking between them that I don't even see the walls anymore.

I finished the first day climbing the steep hill of the Old Town and then, knees cracking and legs aching, the steps of the cathedral's towers for a panoramic view of the area. The cathedral guide that day told me we were in the high season for Via Jacobi pilgrims—July and August—and he usually saw between five and ten people a day.

No wonder I wasn't running into anyone with a shell hanging from their backpack. We were too thin on the ground. The day had grown long with backtracking and musing. I had looked into getting a bed for the night at a hostel, or better yet, at the Camino hostel across from the cathedral. But this was under renovation and, in any case, only had six beds. I would have felt like I was stealing an inexpensive bed from someone who actually needed it. So I left the cathedral, followed the Via signs down the back hill of the Old Town. I hopped on a tram that would take me home for the night, to sleep in my own bed.

Day 2

Geneva to Carouge

On the morning of the second day, legs surprisingly tired from the previous day's walk, I started the Via where I had left off. I was determined to talk to at least one other walker. Stopping off for a cup of coffee, I heard a loud altercation in accented French. A woman was screaming, hurling vile insults and telling people not to look at her even as her voice drew everyone's gaze. It took me a while to locate her on the large tram-stop square at Plainpalais, the university quarter. She turned out to be a Roma woman around my age, black hair escaping a headscarf, cart-wheeling arms, railing against the world. A man told her she needed to calm down. Someone, not him, but someone, would call the police if she insisted on screaming. Other voices concurred. Calm down, or you'll be removed.

"Someone will come and take care of things!" is the reaction of people who trust the authorities to clear away any unpleasantness. But what else could happen in a place where the spotless streets are cleaned again before they are anything less than spotless? In a rich country like Switzerland, peace doesn't come free. Until we figure out how to extend lack of conflict, that is to say, peace, to everyone, someone is paying the price for peace in places like Geneva.

DESCENDING THE HILLS that lead away from the austere stone Via path of the Old Town, the back streets are lined with shops and res-taurants representing and servicing all the various communities in Geneva. If you want to have an accurate inventory of what foreigners miss most from their home countries, walk into the American or Brit-ish or Spanish or Japanese specialty food shops in Geneva.

What is lacking is the assertion of these individual cultures on the Swiss or Genevois culture and identity. Is this a kind of peace? Not the opposite of war, but a kind of tolerance that could be acceptance, or maybe blanketing indifference, as long as you abide.

Geneva doesn't have the pointy liveliness of cities where groups set-tle in, put down roots, and grow their gardens of culture over time. People leave and take their unique cultures with them, or tend to them quietly within their own communities. Refugees are domiciled away from the city center. Likewise, the local *Gens du Voyage* population, a once-nomadic group of travelers, has been relegated to a large parking lot at the cantonal border, where their caravans are out of sight from everyone else. I had passed them on my first day in Versoix, a marginal-ized group made marginal in the most literal sense.

Local Genevois know that outsiders may come, but they will almost always go. Only around one-third of the population in Geneva was actually born there and can be considered native Genevois. The rest are either foreign nationals or Swiss from other cantons in an ever-changing mix. Like the changing colors and currents of the River Rhône and Lake Geneva, it's a constant flow of strangers washing through, border to border.

I realize that I am no different when it comes to making friends with locals and foreigners who are here for the short term. My peaceful life is bought, at least in part, by holding myself at a comfortable distance and walking alone.

Carouge to Saconnex d'Arve

The second Via day was getting just as hot as the first, and with just as little to show for it. The Via took me down quiet back streets, even downtown. Walking across the Pont de Carouge and crossing the soft green waters of the Arve, streaked white with Alpine silt, I left the city of Geneva proper and entered Carouge. Carouge was once a separate township built by Victor Amadeus III, King of Sardinia and Duke of Savoy, in the eighteenth century. Just across the river, it looks and feels different from Geneva.

Low Mediterranean-style buildings, artisanal workshops, no chain stores or restaurants, tree-lined market squares. It's arty, it's alternative, it's the opposite of patrician. It was the place Jews were allowed to live before they were allowed to live in Geneva; it was the place where bars and dancing were allowed back when Geneva allowed neither. It was a refuge from the refuge of Geneva.

Carouge's lively color and movement contrast sharply with the Old Town's somber reticence. I helped a shopkeeper rescue a young cat that had gotten itself into a precarious rooftop situation, and which was howling in despair. A café worker paused to direct the action from across the street, and a man passing by stopped to comment and observe. We problem-solved together, but as soon as the cat was safely inside, the three dispersed as if we'd never spoken in the first place. And since the Via through Carouge isn't very long, I was out of the quarter almost as soon as I'd entered.

Saconnex d'Arve to Charrot

As I followed the Via signs out of Carouge, the urban part of the city ended abruptly at the top of a small hill, and the wide sidewalk narrowed into a dirt footpath through a small park before entering agricultural land. Suddenly, the roofs of Geneva and Carouge presented themselves as a mere backdrop to wide fields of sunflowers and corn, a million yellow suns.

I was on a pastoral path again, weaving through meadows and small breaks of forest. Water fountains marked every village center, and I splashed cool water on my arms and face.

I was walking up a dirt path and had so given up any hope of starting a conversation that I almost jumped out of my skin when a Swiss man in his seventies puttered up on an electric bicycle and surprised me by asking about my half-shell. White-haired, tanned, keen to talk, he'd done the entire walk from Geneva to Santiago de Compostela in one epic walk a couple of years earlier.

A genuine native to the city, he indicated that there was, beneath the surface, a local network of people who would put pilgrims up for free, who welcomed travelers into their homes. This kind of sub-surface network is typical of Geneva—the true locals know all about it, but it's not readily available to anyone else.

"I always look for people walking this part of the Via. For the shell." He glanced down at my half-shell and smiled. "Of course, it's a little hard for me, because I only speak French. And most of the pilgrims here, they speak German, or something else. Still." He shrugged. "One tries."

He was visibly disappointed that I was doing such a short leg of the Via, and that I actually lived in the area. With a wave, he kicked his bike into action and disappeared.

Alone again, I walked for some time through fields that were tinder dry at the end of a long heat wave, past old stone houses and churches that rose out of the earth like they'd always been there. My shell swished against my backpack like a retreating tide and I wanted to be done.

Charrot

I approached the last few hundred yards from the picaresque nineteenth-century village of Charrot. It was noon on a sultry Saturday in August, and locals had put out chairs and tables near the fountain. People were chatting and took no notice of the stranger among them. But then, I made no effort to approach them.

A minute down the road was a metal box posted like a mailbox, or maybe a municipal gas meter. Hand-painted words on the front beckoned: *Information Tampon. Tampon* in this case meaning a pilgrim's stamp, not a feminine hygiene product. Inside was a collection of pilgrimage paraphernalia: an ink pad with a stamp for the local Via station of Bardonnex, a larger village five minutes back; a map and contact information for a local home in case of questions or emergency; a folder of simple maps for the next major leg of the Camino through France, free for the taking. A Post-It pad and several pens to leave notes for fellow walkers.

One of the notes was posted on a message board in French, telling *"Julie"* to *"Have a wonderful quest and I'll miss you,"* signed with a heart. After two days of little interaction, here was a public wisp of sweet emotion. I stamped a piece of paper to take with me, a personal token that I'd done the walk. The ink pad was almost dry, but it's not like anyone would be checking my stamp. The Camino is not a test for anyone but the walker doing the walk.

A vineyard bursting with purple grapes, covering the low hillocks in a cresting wave of future wine. The path led through a few trees, and there was a sign post: *Switzerland wishes you a good trip.* A simple roadblock, open on either side—and that was the border to France. The final steps of the day's walk.

I stood for a moment, and then headed back home.

Walking on Shabbes

Kathryn Hellerstein

WALKING ON SHABBES is different than taking a walk midweek and midday for exercise and errands. On Shabbes morning, I usually bang out the front door, late for shul. Even so, I don't hurry too much. I take my time, walking either all the way down Lincoln Drive, through the traffic light at Mt. Pleasant, or crossing at the corner with Mt. Airy Avenue, where we now, after years of neighbors petitioning the city for a four-way stop sign, have at least a zebra crosswalk to slow down the cars. When the kids were in elementary school, I used to hold their hands and run across that wide street, in the rare moment I saw no car approaching, to wait for the 7:05 a.m. school bus. On Shabbes in those days, when I would cross that corner on the way to the synagogue, sometimes with the kids, sometimes without, I still had to wait to make sure there was no Saturday speeder taking that corner like a racecar. But now, with a zebra crosswalk and Yield to Pedestrians signs installed, when I cross the street, without the children, who have long since graduated from college, I cross without a pounding heart.

Like everyone else in Philadelphia and around the globe, I took for granted the way things were in the old normal. What I had planned to write in this essay was a reflection on how I experienced walking on the Sabbath, the twenty-five hours, beginning when I light the candles just before sundown on Friday evening and ending an hour after sundown on Saturday, during which observant Jews do not ignite fires, in accordance with the biblical injunction not to work on the Sabbath. "Not

95

lighting fires," in contemporary terms, means that we don't, as a rule, turn lights on or off, or the stove, use our phones or computers, or drive or ride in vehicles. I would have explained that I could not dictate or write this essay when I'm actually walking on Shabbes, though on other days I often begin writing poems that way, talking into my phone.

Walking is thus my mode of transportation on Shabbes. But how far should one walk on the Sabbath? The commandment not to travel far on the Sabbath derives from Exodus 16:29, where Moses commands the Children of Israel not to leave their desert abodes to gather manna on the Sabbath, "See that the LORD hath given you the sabbath; therefore He giveth you on the sixth day the bread of two days; abide ye every man in his place, let no man go out of his place on the seventh day." Later rabbinic rulings and customs established distances that may be traversed on foot on the Sabbath. The Hebrew *techum Shabbat* (Sabbath boundary) defines the limited space in which a Jew may walk on the Sabbath and Jewish holidays. According to the Babylonian Talmud, the allowable distance is approximately one kilometer (0.62 mile) from where she or he settled in at the start of the Sabbath; according to the Jerusalem Talmud, twelve times that distance is permitted, or approximately twelve kilometers (7.46 miles).

My husband and I belong to a Conservative synagogue located approximately half a mile from our house, well within the limits set by both the Babylonian and the Jerusalem Talmudic restrictions, neither of which I personally choose to follow. So, over the past twenty-five years, we have walked to Shabbes services. It takes my husband about ten minutes to walk there, and me longer. In the old normal, my husband would leave the house about half an hour after services started at 10 a.m. and walk briskly. I would dawdle over breakfast and reading the newspaper, and much later, find my way out the front door and wend my way to shul, arriving for the last part of the service and in good time for the Kiddush, the light spread of food for the community to enjoy after the end of *davening*, that is, the communal prayer service. After schmoozing with our friends there, we would walk home at a leisurely pace, sit down to lunch kept warm on an electric hotplate in the kitchen, and, after eating and *bentshing*, that is, singing the concluding blessings over the meal, we would read, or lie down for a nap. Later in the afternoon, we would go out for a long walk.

As I reflect on these walks, I can see in retrospect my decades in this neighborhood unspool. I see the children growing up. I see the routes I habitually take change over time without really knowing why. When we first moved to our house here, our walks were adventurous and varied. In recent years, we have trod more or less the same route. In the beginning, we would take one or both of the kids with us, and maybe join our friends across the street and their youngest daughter, to walk half a mile down Mt. Airy Avenue, with its small conjoined twin houses and bright gardens, to McCallum Street, turn right at the institutional brick building that was once an old age home and now houses those with mental illness, and cross Allens Lane. When the kids were really small, we would walk another block down Allens Lane to the playground at the Allens Lane Art Center, where there were swings and a jungle gym, monkey bars, a slide, and a small zip line in the shade of evergreens and maples. When the children were older, we might pause instead at the playing field at the corner of McCallum and Allens Lane, to join a Minyan softball game or to bounce a basketball and shoot hoops. In those days, the long afternoons of Shabbes drew many members of our congregation with young children outside, into the neighborhood, the ball fields and courts, and the woods. Other times, we would descend the path into the woods off Emlen or further up toward the McCallum Street Bridge. We walked through the woods on dirt paths, stepping over roots and around puddles toward Cresheim Creek, which gurgled over rocks. Sometimes we would continue through the woods all the way to Devil's Pool, crossing the creek on stepping stones, often slipping off and getting sneakers wet. Devil's Pool is a place surrounded by boulders where the creek pauses and collects itself, before continuing down to Wissahickon Creek, a wide, deep tributary to the Schuylkill River, with a covered bridge upriver, and some ruins of the mills from the eighteenth century. At Devil's Pool, we sometimes saw teenage boys climbing the cliffs or jumping in to cool off, although the water was not very deep or clean. Once, on the way to Devil's Pool, we saw a place where it seemed that a deer had lain, leaves pressed together, and tufts of fur, and hoof prints in the mud. I wondered then if a doe had given birth, or if a buck had slept there. We would continue on, climbing up the path toward a narrow iron footbridge spanning a ravine, mount a staircase to cross the bridge, our feet ringing on the metal mesh, and end up on Livezey Lane, a winding street of large stone homes that led us back to Allens Lane.

We haven't walked that route for many years, since the kids left for college, and our friends across the street moved away. I read online that

Devil's Pool is now littered with trash, and graffiti scars the cliffs surrounding it, although the Friends of the Wissahickon work constantly to clean up the trails in these woods. Another place I once frequented has vanished into memory. Even though that place still exists, I no longer enter it. I am no longer part of these places we passed through on Shabbes, although they remain part of me.

After the kids grew up and left, we would take our Shabbes walks on the streets of West Mount Airy. Walking home from shul, we would often stop in at Nick Criniti's shop on Emlen, where Tommy the artist, Ronnie the woodworker, and Bill the veteran hung out. On the sidewalk, Nick would put out, next to a dresser and a bookcase, an unusual 1950's lamp and a Pennsylvania Dutch painted kitchen table, with a handmade sign saying, "Hot! Hot! Fire Sale!" This shop had been in Nick's family for at least two generations. His father, or uncle, or father-in-law, and maybe his grandfather, ran a grocery store here, or maybe a deli, that became a pinball arcade, an election polling place, and then a storage unit. When Nick inherited the property, he converted it into the showcase for the furniture and *tshatshkes* he collected and refurbished. David and I would enter the dim shop, a ratty Oriental carpet on wood scuffed soft by decades of shoes, a fan running, and smells of cigarettes and varnish and the hoagies they were eating for lunch. We would examine Nick's hauls of the week from estate sales and auctions, thus shopping on Shabbes—not exactly kosher. We enjoyed the almost-transgression. Talking with Nick and the guys, we would pick out secondhand treasures, bargaining with Nick until we agreed on a price. Nick understood our limits. Later in the afternoon, he would stop by our house with his pickup truck to deliver our selections, for which we mailed him a check an hour after sunset Saturday night. All sorts of things we bought from Nick now surround us, during the house-bound months of the pandemic: Chinese porcelain decorative plates, a custom-made glass cabinet, a corner hutch, a large American machine-made floral Whittall's Anglo-Persian carpet from the 1930s, a Mexican brass coffee set, Chinese vases, two sets of silver-plate flatware, a porcelain Art Nouveau table lamp sculpted as a lanky youth, wooden dressers, end tables, an Eames chair, bookcases, two overstuffed brocade vanity chairs, and a painting of a nude, signed with a semi-famous name, and, on the back, Nazi appropriation stamps and the insignia of a 1940 Paris art dealer, a known collaborator. I still lament the tall mahogany Victrola, complete with a spare steel needle, playing Caruso and ragtime 78s into the Emlen Street traffic, which David wouldn't let me buy.

After lunch, sometimes we walked west down Allens Lane to cross onto Emlen and then turn left into Gate Lane, guarded by a remnant wall that arches to hold a gate no longer there. Gate Lane led us to Elbow Lane, curving past the imitation French country manors built by George Woodward in the 1920s from Wissahickon schist, set back into rolling lawns and gardens, to St. Georges Road. We'd walk all the way, past grand old houses, private roads, and one property of meadows and slat fences that looked like it should have horses. St. Georges Road ends in a cul-de-sac, where ferocious dogs ran loose on the grounds of the last house, a modern split-level, beyond which, thick woods lead down to Wissahickon Creek.

Sometimes, in the old normal, instead, we would walk east on Allens Lane, cross the Regional Rail tracks, and continue to Germantown Avenue. We would often stop at the Mt. Airy Art Garage, a feminist artists' collective, but even after it moved farther south toward Germantown, we'd walk the extra mile to stop in and say hello to Linda and Arleen, the married couple who run MAAG. We would also stop in at the antique store on Germantown Avenue, a more expensive gallery than Nick's grungy treasure house on Emlen. Walking home, west on Mt. Pleasant Avenue, we would visit Maloumian Oriental Rugs to window shop at its years-long "Going Out of Business Sale." If we bargained with Sayyed, he would deliver the Afghani or Persian rug Saturday night, after Shabbes, or on Sunday. How lucky we are that our neighborhood friends have come to understand how our religious practice shapes our Shabbes transactions.

But now our world is different. In mid-February 2020, I walked next to Carpenters Woods, alongside the brittle brown branches, starting to turn supple and red from the sap rising up through them. The crocuses in front of our house, up too early, lifted their heavy buds skyward, their orange stamens and pistils opened like tongues in the throats of purple baby birds waiting to be fed. Daffodils sent up their green spears prematurely, and a few tulips had tentatively unfurled the tips of their flags in a too-warm winter without snow. Now I write from a world utterly changed by the new coronavirus pandemic, which closed all gathering places, stores and theaters, salons and barbershops, schools, universities, churches, and synagogues. The governor of Pennsylvania ordered everyone to shelter in place at home. In Philadelphia, these closures took effect around March 13. But the orders did allow for people to walk outside for exercise in the fresh air. So I continued to walk through my neighborhood, attuned in the confines of this new life to the transformations that spring nonetheless brings. In April, I paused at my own corner and all down Mt. Airy Avenue to sniff the lilacs sending out their intoxicating scent. In late May, I mourned the peonies, on the wane from their blowsy, sensual dance, when they bowed their heavy heads to the derecho storm that blew through Philadelphia. That was just after May 25, when the mayors of major cities throughout the United States imposed evening curfews to try to limit the violence that developed during the otherwise righteous and peaceful demonstrations protesting the police murder in Minneapolis of yet another African American man. The freak winds stripped the peonies of their petals and downed century-old oaks and sycamores. And the yellow-taped-off blocks forced me to change my Shabbes route.

With our synagogue building temporarily closed, services are held on Zoom. But because we don't like to keep our computers on for all of Shabbes, we haven't participated. Instead, since March, I give myself a lazy morning, while David davens in the living room, alone. Then we sit together, each with a heavy Pentateuch on our respective knees, and he chants the Torah portion of the week and then the Haftarah, from the Prophets or the Writings, in Hebrew, while I read along, crossing back and forth from the Hebrew to the English in the adjacent columns. We eat lunch, read the paper, and later in the afternoon, take a walk. Our walks this season of limitations have repeatedly taken us down Mt. Airy Avenue a mile, to Wissahickon Avenue. Sometimes we cross Wissahickon and continue another half mile downhill to the entrance of the Wissahickon Valley Park. We don't enter, though; we don't walk down the rutted trail to Forbidden Drive along the Wissahickon Creek. Instead, we turn around at the fire hydrant and climb back up the street toward home. It's as if the restrictions set on all our lives these months, to shelter at home, to maintain social distance, have set boundaries on our ability and desire to walk wherever our feet lead us.

Now we walk masked. If no one else is in sight, we pull our masks down over our chins to breathe. When we see someone approaching, a neighbor walking his dog, two joggers, a mom and her kids, a couple from our Minyan, another neighbor working in the front garden near the sidewalk, two teens shooting hoops at the curbside basketball net, we pull up our masks to cover our noses and mouths, smiles obscured, and wave. Sometimes we stop to chat for a few minutes, maintaining social distance of six to ten feet, before we all feel that it's enough—the pandemic has trained us not to talk for too long or too close—and continue on our way. This past Shabbes, when the mayor set a curfew to keep the protests from turning violent, we turned back early and hurried to get home by six o'clock.

Maloumian' Oriental Rugs is temporarily closed because of the pandemic. So are Mt. Airy Art Garage and the antique store. Last summer, Nick sold his property to a couple—a ceramicist and an architect—who have gutted and refurbished the space, but have not yet been able to open their upscale studio and gallery because of the pandemic lockdown. Without the synagogue to walk to on Shabbes morning, without these places to visit in the afternoon, it seems that our perambulating imaginations have been curbed. But the checks on where we think to walk now are not the boundaries of Jewish law and custom. It's not that we limit our walks to the one kilometer or the twelve kilometers, depending on the different rabbinic traditions. Rather, in the old normal times, we pushed the limits of the Sabbath laws by stopping in the local shops to talk and look, and those non-shabbesdik connections made our Sabbaths a time to connect with people in our neighborhood beyond our Jewish customs. What have we all lost during this time of closure, when there are few destinations beyond our own homes? What do our Shabbes walks mean, now that we cannot walk to synagogue and cannot make our own rituals for the Day of Rest by almost transgressing? Are our walks now just a time to exercise our legs, to pace down the hours of daylight in the cage of restraint? For the sake of walking, we walk.

Nobody Walks to LAX

Tom Zoellner

I ONCE TRIED TO walk out of Los Angeles International Airport. This wasn't easy.

I'd stepped off a flight from Tucson with no luggage and decided on a whim to walk back to the beach at Venice, where I lived at the time. Though it was seven miles away, it seemed like a good enough idea. A cluster of restaurants near Marina del Rey would be a place to stop for dinner and break the trip up a bit.

So I emerged from the sliding doors at the ground transportation level, the horseshoe-shaped funnel of shade and exhaust fumes that forms a loop between the eight terminals. The goal seemed simple: exit the airport. In front of me was a parking garage and through it was the general direction of Sepulveda Boulevard—the indispensable north-south artery that connects the airport with the west side of Los Angeles.

I had driven into this airport dozens of times and had seen sidewalks threading between the parking garages and administrative buildings that lay inside the horseshoe. But navigating them turned out to be a maze. I had to dart across traffic-choked asphalt and backtrack several times before finding a way that looked like it could eventually hit Sepulveda.

It turns out that L.A.'s grubby gateway to the world is a lot like the city it serves—it makes life rough on the ordinary pedestrian. Leav-

Adapted from "Nobody Walks to LAX," *The Los Angeles Times*, April 8, 2018.

ing or approaching the terminal on foot is considered a highly unusual activity and the structure just isn't built for it. A passenger survey once showed that almost every LAX traveler arrives to get on a plane by using some other kind of vehicle. Cars and shuttle vans deposit 99 percent of them, and 1 percent arrive via public transportation, mainly by the city's light rail.

Those that walk? Too few to be counted. An LAX official told me the only people known to walk into the airport were the pilots and flight attendants staying in one of the corporate hotels that stand at attention less than half a mile away. Indeed, you can sometimes spot them from your car with their dark-blue uniforms and wheelie suitcases, on their drab walk to a drab place.

But this isn't unusual. Airports in every American city have a schizophrenic relationship with foot traffic. Inside, they demand you walk, often long distances, from gate to gate. Some concourses are a modern *flâneur*'s dream with abundant retail shopping and people-watching. Outside, it is the exact opposite: American airports seem to deliberately obstruct pedestrians. It isn't just because of the lack of sidewalks. Our modern airports are ringed with high fences, barbed wire, and stern No Trespassing signs, a literal extension of the legal fortifications erected by the Federal Aviation Administration designed to foil acts of hijacking, vandalism, terrorism, or any number of criminal acts that might result from loose access to the flightline.

Every government in the world knows this: the airport is among the most sensitive patches of real estate in any nation. It is inevitably near the top of the list of targets for any rebel group, perhaps even more of a prize than the presidential palace or the television station. To control those is to control the narrative of who's in charge, but to control the airport is to cut off the best channel of assistance and reinforcements for the regime—and to open a new potential source of your own.

Hence, the fortress model, which stands in marked contrast to the more pastoral imagery that accompanied the first portal of flight in the twentieth century: the blameless word "field." Speedway Field in Minnesota, that later took on the far-less bucolic but more utilitarian name of Minneapolis–St. Paul International. Candler Field, named for one of the South's blue-blooded families, which is today the more awkwardly named Hartsfield-Jackson Atlanta International Airport, the busiest in the country by passenger volume. Pearson Field in Vancouver, Washington that still features a lawn of luxuriant grass between its runways.

The first functioning airport in the U.S. had an even better tag: College Park. Still in operation, this was the meadow in Maryland where Wilbur Wright himself trained army pilots in 1909. A college and a park sounds like a spacious plaza of marble and elm trees rather than a grim stockade of concrete and cyclone fence.

When the barricades hardened around these places after a wave of hijackings in the early 1970s, so too did the sense of a visual connection or continuity with the surrounding landscape. Airports became even more removed and walled-off: bland symbols of the city set apart like a gemstone from its setting: the concentrated and fortified identity of the city itself. In this way, the security perimeter resembles—linguistically, at least—the three-letter codes bestowed on every world airport by the International Air Transport Association, a legal requirement that emerged in the 1930s. Some are more euphonious than others, and have even entered spoken conversation or casual written communication as a jazzy shorthand for the metropolis itself. I have heard locals in Phoenix call their city PHX. *The Albuquerque Journal* routinely abbreviates the name of its city in headlines as ABQ. The Lexington, Kentucky airport adopted the entirely sensible tag of LEX that had already been a municipal nickname; same with the JAX of Jacksonville, Florida.

These X-endings aren't always so visually pleasing, however, especially when they are applied as placeholders for lack of a more logical letter. They sound institutional, a bit like a Supermax prison acronym, which is perhaps appropriate, given the carceral appearance of an airport from a pedestrian's point of view. Portland's PDX comes to mind. The especially unfortunate formulation for the Sioux City, Iowa airport is SUX. And then there is LAX, a standalone word that implies laziness, and yet also possesses a vaguely sinister quality; an unknown factor about Los Angeles, or a dystopian commentary on the vast, ungovernable civic splatter at the edge of the continent. The X sounds like a door slamming shut. "LAX is, in fact, a surprisingly shabby and hollowed-out kind of place," wrote the journalist Pico Iyer, "certainly not adorned with the amenities one might expect of the world's strongest and richest power." One gets the feeling of a truck stop or a bus station more than a mighty gateway to the stratosphere.

Which is a shame, because it occupies a truly spectacular piece of topography at the edge of Santa Monica Bay. The night approach path in from the east that banks in a crescent over the Pacific is one of the most beautiful in the world, a symphony of city lights, mountain hulks, and moonlit water before the dismal reality of the ground takes hold. This former field of lima beans was purchased by the Los Angeles city council in 1928 as a potential rival to the Burbank airport, where most of the mail flights were going in those aviation boom days right after Lindbergh's crossing of the Atlantic. They named the 640-acre parcel "Mines Field" after William Mines, the real estate agent who handled the transaction—an appropriate gesture for a spreading urban entity whose dynamic protoplasm was home and land sales. Not until after World War II did it assume a dominant role in Southern California commercial aviation. Not coincidentally, the marching line of office buildings housing big defense contractors, known euphemistically as "the aerospace industry," sprung up just to its south along Imperial Highway.

But I'm going north, and after wandering through garages, I find a sidewalk that takes me past the arachnoid base of a shuttered restaurant called the Theme Building that looks like an art deco escapee from Tomorrowland. A plaque on the outside proclaims it dedicated in 1961 by then–Vice President Lyndon Johnson. This was the age when jet airplanes seemed like a mere gateway to flying saucers, and when dining at the airport was the height of suavity. That such an aesthetic was described as an undefined "Theme" says a lot about the ubiquity of Space Age assumptions when LAX was at its creative height. From here, you could sip a gin-and-tonic and watch the planes from TWA and Pan Am take off, knowing you would soon be on one of them yourself. What finally killed the Theme Building restaurant, winkingly named Encounters, was the heavy security cordon thrown up around the concourses after 9/11. Gone were the days when arriving early at the airport was a luxury and not a necessity. The establishment lingered, losing money, until 2013. Once at the airport, it seemed, nobody wanted to check their bags and walk back out the doors for mediocre airport food they could more easily get at some corporate outpost near the departure gates. And yet another small link between walking and flying was severed.

LAX isn't even the worst offender against those who want to walk up to it, or around its outsides. I once tried to walk out of Miami International Airport and found it could only be done by chancing a jog down a speedway that didn't even have a sidewalk. Other cities such as Dallas, Charlotte, and Kansas City built their sky palaces far from population clusters, which is respectful in terms of noise and traffic, but makes life tough for those who choose the most basic form of movement. The builders of Denver International Airport were thinking on a century-long scope of growth when they built the replacement to Stapleton Airport far out onto the eastern prairies twenty-five miles away from downtown and ten miles from the last fringes of the suburbs. It is doubtful if more than a dozen people have made the walk; they would need camping equipment to sleep along the way.

The airports I like the best are those that were like the old Stapleton—of the first generation of "fields" close by the population centers that they serve and in some cases, hard by rows of bungalows. They're never in affluent precincts: too much traffic and noise for the cosseted to bear, and city councils bent to their clout and put the early airports next to people without much power. Though born in sin, these working-class airports have a lunch-bucket honesty about them, a sense that catching a flight is a routine matter for all people, those with calloused hands, and not just the elite. I'm thinking here of Love Field in Dallas, Reagan National in Washington, and especially Midway in Chicago. These are the airports of shoe salesmen and factory shift supervisors. Best of all, you can walk up to them from a civilized neighborhood of trees and parks, and catch a flight across the country, or a series of flights that can take you to Jakarta or Paris or Lubumbashi.

As I head away from LAX, I reflect that the airport managers could fix their walking problem simply by adding what architects call "wayfinders," the signs and other visual cues that point pedestrians in the right direction. If the airport encouraged more people to simply walk to and from the Century Boulevard hotels, it would reduce shuttle congestion and perhaps bring a little life to the dowdy corridor that welcomes visitors to Los Angeles before they reach the utter hell of the 405. A few well-placed directional signs might be enough to convince the skeptical that such a foot journey was even possible before dialing up a Lyft. We all have rolling luggage these days, after all.

I crossed one of those internal streets that seem to be used only by airport employees going to and from heavily guarded parking lots, and then found an obscure sidewalk and headed toward a cluster of multicolored cylinders known locally as "the pylons." Besides the Theme Building, they're the closet thing this airport comes to a unique symbol to draw the viewer's eye, a bit like the Hollywood sign—a line of block letters that stands for nothing but an idea.

Immediately in front of the pylons I happened upon a diamond-shaped park immaculately gardened in Key West style and completely hidden from passing traffic. A flagpole bearing the legend "Gateway to the Pacific Rim" stood at the center. Seemingly forgotten by everyone but the landscapers, it is probably L.A.'s best-manicured and least-visited park. I never would have found it without this walk.

Walking to and from the airport is a small private rebellion, a union of high and low tech, a way of asserting one's individuality just before getting into a cattle-chute-like line to meet the TSA agents. The stroll to the airport before ascending into the sky is like a Greek myth, or those lines from Genesis 5:24: "Enoch walked faithfully with God, and then he was no more because God took him away." Enoch stands in biblical lore as the man who didn't suffer a mortal death; he was instead directly "translated" into a different state of existence. The material act of stepping onto a jet vaguely mimics this express train to heaven without the mediation of any other earthly vehicle.

The Via Appia Is Easier Going If Taken Slowly

Liana Brent

Walking: An (Ir)rationale

Anyone who has ever walked along an ancient Roman road knows that you don't get anywhere fast because you're constantly sliding into the spaces between the large basalt stones and tripping over the irregularities. Surely the Romans, who were, after all, masters of engineering and construction, had their reasons for paving roads with *selce*, the giant, grey basalt stones quarried from nearby volcanic sources and cut into irregular shapes. While walking, you have to be constantly alert, always concentrating on the next step immediately in front of you. If you visit the Roman Forum on a hot day, you feel like part of the herd, slipping and tripping along, following the legs of the person in front of you, barely able to look up and appreciate the historical importance of where you are.

As an archaeologist living in Rome for two years on a doctoral fellowship, I was no stranger to the shape and feel of ancient Roman roads. I'd often enjoyed pleasant afternoons exploring the Via Appia Antica on the outskirts of Rome. All the guidebooks highly recommend the experience, an eight- to ten-mile stroll "off-the-beaten-path" (by which they mean outside the city walls and the noise and crowds of Rome's *Centro Storico*), where you can visit Roman tombs, catacombs, and luxury villas. At the same time, whenever I walked on the ancient stones of the Via Appia, I felt paralyzed by my need to look down, unable to take in the landscape around me. This struck me as the ultimate form of tunnel vision, an outlook on ancient roads that was surely no coincidence. After all, I was a graduate student, nearing the end of a seven-year Ph.D. program in classical archaeology. Tunnel vision was an appropriate metaphor for many aspects of my life.

From that bleak view sprang an idea that would shake me out of a tunneled perspective. The idea took shape slowly. I would walk not just eight- or ten-mile stretches of the Via Appia Antica open-air archaeological park familiar to so many Roman tourists, but travel the entire length of the ancient Roman road, from Rome to southern Italy, a distance of some 350 miles.

Construction began on the Via Appia in the fourth century BCE. The road was built in bouts and extensions, radiating outward from Rome, the *caput mundi*, the head of a new power on the rise. From Rome, the road's construction moved incrementally south, first down the coast to Terracina and then to Rome's rival city at Capua.

As Rome subdued a succession of enemies, so the narrative goes, construction on the Via Appia kept pace. The road extended to Benevento, through the Apennine Mountains, over the rolling hills of Basilicata and Puglia, down to the Greek colony at Taranto, and eventually, over the Salento peninsula to its terminal point in Brindisi. By the time it was completed in the early second century BCE, the Via Appia covered a distance of approximately 353 miles, and it remained the principal artery through Italy for centuries. Like all Roman infrastructure, the road would continue to be modified and upgraded in later phases of innovation and renovation. But for the most part, the final form of the Via Appia existed—a continuous line from Rome to Italy's heel—by the time Rome had really started to stretch her legs, so to speak.

My idea of walking the Via Appia wasn't exactly a new one. In 38/37 BCE, the Roman poet Horace traveled on a slightly different route of the Via Appia from Rome to Brindisi, and he later chronicled his adventure in a poem that survives to us as *Satire* 1.5. He noted aptly that "the Via Appia is easier going if taken slowly," a sentiment with which I fully agree. The full route of the Appian Way has been lost and forgotten over time, but over the past six decades, the intrepid and curious have attempted periodically to recreate the ancient route on foot, by bicycle, or in a car. Thanks to recent efforts by the archaeologist Lorenzo

Quilici and hikers like Paolo Rumiz and Marino Curnis, I had a template to follow for the queen of long-distance roads. When Paolo Rumiz and his team walked the Via Appia, they were "foreigners" from northern Italy. My experience, as a Canadian living abroad at the American Academy in Rome at the time, was at an even greater remove. I had no ancestral ties to Italy. My connection to the land was tenuous, despite my field research in the south, and I would feel this keenly along the course of my walk.

Once I made the decision to walk the entire Via Appia, there were a number of logistical details to sort out. Most of the handful of hikers who had attempted this walk before me followed the chronological course of construction, beginning their journey in Rome and ending in Brindisi. But the more I thought about it, the more I realized that my journey needed to be the reverse, from the periphery to the center, from Brindisi to Rome. The trek southward from Rome follows the expansionist narrative, traces the history and development of the road alongside Rome's increasing dominion. By switching directions, I'd be grappling with the legacy of Rome, both ancient and modern. Starting in the south gave me the opportunity to think about what the road, as a metaphor for "Romanization," meant to local peoples and to experience the landscape from their perspective, not just as a history of successive modifications by consuls, emperors, popes, foreign kings, and dictators over the centuries.

Practical considerations also influenced the decision to start in the south and work my way back to Rome. My experiences in Italy have always been heavily mediated by my privileged academic sphere: in archaeological field schools "cloistered" in twelfth-century monasteries, at the gated property of the American Academy protected by security measures nearly as tight as any foreign embassy's. If I had started in Rome, the first sign I had left the carefully curated world that tourists and academics experience might have spooked me, and I'd have been tempted to turn back.

Another reason influenced my decision to start in the south: my archaeological fieldwork in southern Italy. Since 2010, I've worked at an archaeological site in the heart of Puglia: an ancient Roman cemetery within a stone's throw of the Via Appia outside the modern town of Gravina. I'd spent ten summers in the south, always on the eve of the next transition, the next move, the next stage of my life. At the end of every summer, when the excavation equipment was packed up, when all the bones and artifacts were cataloged and deposited in the superintendency, I would make my annual pilgrimage back to Rome, ready for another beginning. On the eve of my most recent rite of passage—that from perpetual student to early career professional—there could, in my mind, be only one direction for my walk along the Via Appia. Besides, the saying is "all roads lead to Rome," not the other way around.

And so, with an abundance of book learning and relatively little practical preparation, I set out in March 2019 to walk the Via Appia Antica, from Brindisi back to Rome, over a period of a little more than three weeks and a distance of 350 miles.

All Roads Lead to Rome

Puglia

Puglia, the famous "heel of the boot," is a land of striking geological and agricultural landscapes. It almost seems like the grey limestone swells upwards, resentfully shaping the rolling hills above. That same stone appears everywhere in the constructed landscape—as dry masonry walls, property boundaries, and debris piled up in roadside ditches. It comforts in its unpretentiousness, simply shaped but meant to endure. Many of the dry stone houses dotting the Salento peninsula have been repurposed, used by squatters, occupied fleetingly by shepherds, sold along with the more valuable land on which they sit, and left to languish. Central Puglia is a land of rolling hills, of wide-open vistas, of agro-commuters who make the daily pilgrimage from their city dwellings into the landscape that, depending on the time of year, feels like a harsh and unforgiving desert or a lush and productive countryside.

On the map, the Via Appia leaves Brindisi and runs across the open plains of the Salento peninsula, Italy's *tacco* or heel, through towns like Oria, Taranto, and Gravina, all potential overnight stops. In the 47-mile span between Brindisi and Taranto, smaller towns pop up every 10–15 miles, so planning the first few days of the trek was relatively easy. From Taranto to Gravina, though, there are few visible traces of the Via Appia and next to no convenient places for someone following the invisible road at a walker's pace to spend the night. My route thus required occasional slight deviations off the Appian Way to places like Castellaneta and a farmstead (*agriturismo*) outside Iesce.

During the first segment of my walk along the Via Appia, I was accompanied by Asa, my partner of several years at the time. Asa is as rugged and outdoorsy as they come: he through-hiked the 2,000+ miles of the Appalachian Trail in a mere four and a half months. Not only is he knowledgeable about practical things like water sources, navigation, and gear, but he never feels the need to fill the silence unnecessarily. When we set out on the first morning, the sky was gray with an ominous drizzle as Asa and I navigated our way out of Brindisi, slipping and sliding along the slick, modern, travertine pavement slabs in the city center. As we approached the industrial outskirts of the city and the rain picked up, I couldn't shake the feeling that I was in over my head. After so many months of planning for this adventure, I was overwhelmed by the reality of leaving the safety of the city and by the responsibility of navigating my way through an unfamiliar countryside. The feeling intensified as I struggled to read the map on my phone from inside an oversized blue poncho, while lumbering along service roads and highway overpasses. My sense of panic rose as cars whipped past us, their drivers undoubtedly puzzled at the unexpected sight of mud-splattered hikers in shapeless raingear.

Despite the rain, my rising panic, and the sinking realization of what I had gotten myself into, the first day gave rise to one of my favorite moments in Puglia. A moment of unexpected calm set in when Asa and I made the turnoff from a real road onto "Strada Comunale 16," a small road that followed the fields from the rapidly disappearing suburbs into the unknown (at least for me). Paradoxically, the terrain I feared the most because I couldn't prepare for its unexpected hurdles was the grounding I needed. This was just after the four-mile mark, and I thought we couldn't possibly be on a road because it seemed like we were trespassing. The dirt beneath our feet wasn't the paved asphalt of modern roads, nor was it the hard-packed dirt of a well-traveled country road. It certainly wasn't the polygonal basalt stones that I knew from the Via Appia in Rome or the travertine paving stones used in many modern Italian cities. Because of the rain, the gravel crunched beneath our feet, and there were bits of broken pottery and tiles everywhere as we followed the tire tracks through the mud.

We trundled on and saw rows of trees with no leaves, abandoned *masserie* (farmsteads) with defunct farm equipment splayed out in the yard like a testament to how slowly things decay in Italy. Over the course of that first day, we saw only one other person: a farmer who was pouring water or some other liquid into the tank of his farm equipment. He didn't seem too interested in us. Chickens and geese ran loose in the yard, and we continued on, apparently as unseen by him as his way of life had been by me during my time in Rome. We covered an ill-advised 24.5 miles, which would come back to hurt me a few days later when shin splints set in, but by the time we arrived in Oria that first night, soggy, drenched, and bedraggled, I felt a real sense of accomplishment, as if this foolhardy plan might be possible.

The rough terrain continued as we made our way to Taranto, past the Ionian Sea, and inland over some of the most challenging terrain of the hike. Five days after setting out from Brindisi, we walked into Gravina, our last stop in Puglia. The seasonal rhythms of archaeology bring me back to southern Italy nearly every summer, when the fields around Gravina are golden in anticipation of the harvest, before they're scorched at the end of the summer to make room for new growth. As we walked through Puglia in March during academic archaeology's "off-season," a palette of new colors filled our horizon with lush grass and the optimism of spring. We strode confidently into the town that has been my summer home for almost a decade, and friends in Gravina marveled at what we had accomplished in an exhausting but rewarding five days. The familiarity provided a brief respite from the strain of continually arming myself to face the unknown challenges that each day brought.

Throughout this first stretch of the Via Appia, we found that the fertile countryside of Puglia was filled with contradictions: rocky ravines that bordered rolling hills; illicit trash dumps, still alight and smoldering next to verdant orange and olive groves; productive farmsteads hampered by the effects of abandonment; bicycle paths commemorating stretches of the Via Appia that no longer survive. By the time we crossed out of Puglia and into the region of Basilicata, we had traversed 101 miles, more than a quarter of the total distance. Our bodies ached as we adjusted to the rhythm of walking, and onward we went, despite the increasing reliance on ibuprofen, a tensor band for shin splints, and ice packs at the end of the day.

Basilicata

If Puglia was characterized by large farmsteads nestled in the fertile, rolling hills, Basilicata was far less cultivated and considerably more wild. Over the course of the Via Appia, this relatively small region of

Italy (population just over half a million, compared to the four to six million inhabiting Puglia, Campania, and Lazio) presented by far the most variable and unpredictable terrain. Our route took us through Palazzo San Gervasio, Venosa, and Melfi, towns known for their Roman and medieval remains. Eclipsed by Matera, Basilicata's famed UNESCO World Heritage Site, these wonderful small towns with rich cultural heritage have not yet become fixtures on the general tourist itinerary.

And it was just outside Venosa, on our eighth day of walking, that Asa and I were rewarded with our first glimpse of what must have been the ancient Roman road. We turned off a state road to follow what appeared to be tire tracks, possibly on private property, and saw the road we'd been seeking for more than a week—not just phantom traces of it, not just archaeological remnants that suggested the Via Appia's former presence, but intentionally placed stones that formed a path. Sure, the stones may have belonged to a later phase or a repaving, but we momentarily forgot our aches, pains, and blisters as we set off in hot pursuit of that unmistakable line of stones.

We clambered through another field, again unsure whether or not we were trespassing. We saw a car parked nearby with someone sitting inside, so we ventured over to ask if it was okay to be on that property. The man's answer was simple: we were free to roam. He even seemed amused that we were out there looking for traces of an ancient Roman road. But he also cautioned us: he'd seen some *cinghiale*, Italian wild boar, nearby. We should stay near the modern roads, he warned. The noise from the occasional passing car would keep them away and prevent a potentially nasty encounter. It seemed counterintuitive that walking alongside a minor highway should offer protection in this intractable part of Basilicata. But it would turn out there would be other times on the journey when I would choose personal safety and expedience over strictly following the ancient road.

As we walked along the long, nearly deserted stretches of modern roads in Puglia and Basilicata, cars often pulled over to ask if we were okay. Drivers weren't accustomed to seeing two hikers with large backpacks, and they were concerned for our well-being. The towns were far apart with few amenities in between. The basic concept of walking, especially in this part of the country where traces of the ancient road were mostly absent, seemed as foreign to them as we did. It was inconceivable to them that foreigners should spend so much time and energy following a mostly invisible path. The Via Appia's fame still endured in the south, but the physical traces had succumbed to the ravages of time.

On our final day in Basilicata, the gently rolling hills of the past week were replaced by the steep ascent into the Apennine Mountains. Climbing up, I had to stop more frequently to stretch my shins. There were many times when, conforming to Newton's first law of motion, I would have remained at rest without an external force—in our case, the race against the setting sun in the days following the spring equinox—to compel me to put one foot in front of the other and repeat until I could take solace in the rhythm of walking as a kind of equilibrium. As we inched closer to Melfi, a tiny city perched on an impossibly high, naturally occurring rock outcropping at the foot of Mt. Volture, we were astounded by the sheer number of windmills—those violent mechanical giants—in an area that seemed like it had otherwise been completely untouched by man's desire to build. By the time we reached Melfi, where an eleventh-century Norman castle and cathedral dominate the town, we were transported into a medieval world of warring Lombard and Byzantine peoples. After a day of wild topographic variation, Melfi felt like a haven, that hill town a civilized refuge from the unsettling pendulum of our 40 miles through Basilicata, moving between the sublime tranquility and the threatening silence of the countryside.

And as our time in that unruly region came to an end, so did Asa's eight-day adventure with me on the Via Appia.

Campania

When Asa left in Melfi, my friend Nate replaced him, and the next leg of the trek began, though not without some difficulty. Nate's train to Melfi was delayed, so we attempted to triangulate and meet somewhere between our two locations in order to avoid losing an entire day of walking. Instead of ameliorating the situation, we found ourselves alone at a train station a few miles off of the Via Appia, with nothing but mountains casting shadows over fields and a rapidly setting sun. There was no cell service and no way of correcting our course, so we were lucky that someone in the train station control room took pity on us and let us use a landline to call for a hired driver. It was an expensive deviation, and the route we had planned to take through the final section of Basilicata wasn't navigable by car. We had no choice but to skip that eight-mile stretch between Melfi and Bisaccia and hand over 100 Euros, a small price to pay considering the alternative was to be stranded overnight at an empty train station or to wait several hours for the last train back to Melfi. After a long and winding detour through the mountains, we were unceremoniously welcomed into Campania, relieved and ready to begin walking in earnest the following day.

The walk between Melfi and Benevento offers few archaeological sites and miles of modern highways. The mountains always dominated the horizon as Nate and I continued our gradual ascent. It often seemed like our adventures mirrored that mountainous terrain; we had more strange encounters between Melfi and Benevento than anywhere else on the journey. One day, a friendly dog followed us for almost eight miles from Rocca San Felice to Frigento. Later that afternoon, we accidentally ended up in the wrong town—or rather, we were in the town where we wanted to be along the Via Appia, but our lodgings were not—and after hitching a ride with a former policeman, we spent the night in a very sketchy B&B above a strip club.

The next day, at the aptly named Ponte Rotto (broken bridge) near Apice, we spent an hour looking for the safest place to cross a swollen, swift-moving stream. We slid around the muddy banks, growing increasingly uneasy about the dog we could hear barking at us, whereabouts unknown. Finally, we decided to change into shorts and carry our packs across the chest-high water like Roman soldiers swimming with their shields above their heads. We took what we thought was the most direct crossing. It was not. We had miscalculated and ended up on the wrong bank, at a fork in the stream. We had to re-cross. After several other minor mishaps that afternoon, we walked triumphantly into Benevento, the conceptual if not the actual halfway point of the walk. Not only was Benevento an important Roman city, but here, in 109 CE, the emperor Trajan created a second branch of the Via Appia, which also ran from Benevento to Brindisi, but along a much gentler coastal route, bypassing the wilderness of Basilicata and Puglia and shaving off at least a day of travel time. Would that I had heeded Trajan's wisdom and skipped over the areas that had created so many challenges for me, but stubbornly I wanted to follow the original route that existed in its final form for 300 years before Trajan thought to refine it.

By that point, I had walked just shy of 215 miles spread over twelve days, inching my way diagonally across the Italian peninsula, with only eight days until my return to Rome. In Benevento, Nate and I parted ways, and he returned, by train, to Rome.

From Benevento, the Via Appia descends out of the Apennine Mountains and wanders through the territory of the ancient Samnites, through Caserta and Capua, and then opens on the first glimpses of the Tyrrhenian Sea at the modern coastal town of Mondragone. I thought the most difficult terrain was behind me. But coming down from the Apennine Mountains also brought the lowest point of my journey, and the hardest part was still on the horizon. After Nate's departure, I walked alone for four of the next six days. I felt vulnerable in ways I never had before. I missed Asa's companionable quiet and Nate's chattier presence, his jokes and insights. Even though the stretches between towns were shorter and I spent more time walking in cities, I was nervous, tensing at every territorial dog I passed, wary of passing people too. Anyone could take anything from me at any point, I kept thinking. More than once I jumped in fright, only to realize that I had been spooked by my own shadow.

For tourists, Italy's Campania region is synonymous with the archaeological sites in the Bay of Naples that were buried by the eruption of Mt. Vesuvius in 79 CE or the natural marvels of the Amalfi Coast. Campania is also the most densely populated region in Italy, but because the Via Appia bypasses Naples, the region's capital and largest city, I never fully experienced that density. The grittiness of this beautiful region, though, was evident at all turns, as was the specter of organized crime, infamous in Campania.

Just outside of Caserta, I found myself hemmed in by a rail line. Once again, I could either backtrack and take a detour or trespass, in this case by hopping a fence and crossing through a scrap metal yard. I chose the latter and ran through as fast as I could, never shaking the sense that I was being watched. Blind to oncoming traffic, I darted through a tunnel beneath the A1 superhighway that connects Naples to Rome. When at last I entered the outskirts of Santa Maria Capua Vetere, I felt a tremendous sense of relief, but too soon. Out of nowhere, a stray dog—the very thing I feared the most—ran at me and bit the back of my leg. Fortunately, the wound was superficial. Still, I sought medical attention at the nearest hospital, where I wrangled with an even more fearsome beast: Italian paperwork. (Though public healthcare in Italy is excellent, the system is weighed down by the number of forms required as well as the number of personnel necessary to figure out those forms.) I was frightened more than hurt, and after figuratively licking my wounds overnight in Capua, I was determined to press on.

The next day, on the way into the coastal city of Mondragone, I wove my way through temporary housing villages and migrant communities that exist outside my accustomed tourist bubble. Yet again, I had to choose the least dangerous option between illegally crossing a busy highway, hitchhiking over it, or going around it through the makeshift housing. I chose to hitchhike. When an old man stopped for me at the side of the road, I took my chances, clutching my pepper spray and concealing it in my sleeve. The man's questions escalated rapidly from innocuous to menacing: Did I want to stop for a pizza with him? Did I have a place to stay? Did I want to go to his place and *fare l'amore*? My embarrassment and impotent anger were matched only by the speed at which I hurled myself from that car as soon as it was safe to do so.

When I limped into Mondragone, I found myself in a seaside town during its depressed off-season. I felt like I was trapped in a carnival after hours, when everyone else had gone home and the lights had been shut off with no warning. I was exhausted from constantly looking over my shoulder and watching out for dangers that seemed to be multiplying at an exponential rate. For the second night in a row, I thought seriously about giving up. I realized I wasn't prepared for the challenges of walking alone, especially when conditions didn't match my expectations. Certainly if I had been walking in the other direction, I would have given up in Campania. But by that point, I had covered nearly 260 miles. I knew I would regret it if I didn't finish what I had started, even if this long-anticipated adventure looked different than what I had originally envisioned.

In Mondragone, I found myself fighting the urge to abandon my trek while wanting sympathy for a situation that was no one's making but my own. After confiding my distress about the dog bite and the unwanted proposition to a friend in Rome, I got the boost I needed to keep going. My friend Vicki agreed to take the train from Rome to Formia, my destination the following evening, and then walk with me for a day. By offering to break up my time alone, if only for a day and two nights, she unknowingly made my decision to keep going for me. With great relief, I left Campania behind and crossed over into Lazio, where unexpected treasures awaited.

Lazio

While Campania's gritty and frankly scary modern overlay had belea-guered me, the abundance of archaeological sites and the visible traces of the Via Appia in Lazio made the final week of my walk much easier and more enjoyable than I anticipated. Home to the ancient Latin pop-ulations and eventually the seat of Rome, Lazio is a mostly flat region with a population hovering around six million, only slightly larger than that of Campania. From Mondragone, the Via Appia meanders along the coast to Formia, inland through the scenic Parco Naturale dei Monti Aurunci to Fondi, then back to the coast at Terracina, followed by a long, unwaveringly straight stretch of nearly 60 miles through the Pontine Marshes and the Alban Hills, before arriving in Rome. So straight is the section near Terracina that it's affectionately known as the Fettuccia (ribbon). I alternated my five days in Lazio between walk-ing alone and with friends. As my distance from Rome decreased, it became easier for Rome-based friends to hop a train and join me for a day. Throughout Lazio, I spent less time in the hinterlands that con-nected towns and more time snaking my way through populous urban centers, often following the course of the Strada Statale 7, the modern Via Appia.

Between Mondragone and Terracina, the Via Appia passed through several Roman colonies that were established on the route of the Roman road. My first day in Lazio took me through Minturno, where the Via Appia served as the *decumanus*, the principal artery through the Roman colony. Even though I was alone there, I enjoyed the hallmarks of a well-preserved ancient Roman city: a forum, temples, theater, and even a latrine. Since I had never been to Minturno—or Terracina or Benevento for that matter—visiting the archaeological sites as part of this longer walk gave me a greater sense of them, not just as strategi-cally placed Roman colonies, but as hubs that organized people and resources in uniquely Roman spatial forms.

From Minturno, I walked to Formia, where my friend Vicki, a fel-low archaeologist, made good on her impromptu decision to join me for a stretch. By chance, she picked the most spectacular day of the walk to accompany me. Setting out from Formia, we stopped at sev-eral Roman remains, including the so-called Tomb of Cicero, a gigantic tomb standing nearly 80 feet tall. Each magical discovery was topped by the next, until we arrived in the archaeological park between Itri and

Fondi, where some of the longest preserved stretches of the ancient Via Appia are visible. There, the layers of history were plain to see: eighteenth-century Bourbon paving stones lay beside the sixteenth-century Renaissance revival of the third century renovation of the road that had already existed for five centuries. Those centuries of infrastructure and intervention were juxtaposed with the gentle swells of the Aurunci Mountains in all directions, and Vicki and I were overwhelmed by the convergence of nature and culture and the ongoing attempts to preserve both. And, after my Campanian ordeal, I too was restored.

As I walked the final 100 miles of the Via Appia, I noticed the presence of the ancient road become stronger. Signs for all manner of businesses—a car dealership here or an event pavilion there—emphasized their connection with the Queen of Roads. Although I'd encountered traces of the Via Appia interspersed throughout my walk—as ancient fragments or as influence on the forms of modern cities—those relics of the road intensified, and my relief did too, as each step brought me closer to Rome. My friend Mark joined me for the last two days, from Cisterna di Latina into the Alban Hills, and on the final day, heading into Rome, our group snowballed to include two other walkers, Talia and Anne. For the last 30 miles, we weren't following mere traces of the Via Appia; it had become the most vocal of guides. When we weren't walking directly on the ancient basalt stones, we could see their outlines under a roughshod attempt at asphalt paving or peeking out in channels for modern plumbing, wires, or drainage, their resilience on full display.

The final day, from Ariccia to Rome, brought me firmly back into familiar territory. I had walked the last 12 miles of the Via Appia Archaeological Park several times in both directions before, but this time, each irregular basalt stone under my feet seemed less like its own unique puzzle piece that never quite fit and more like an old friend. I had seen all these stones before, some covered by overgrowth, others striped in the long shadows of the late afternoon sun. As I walked into Rome, through the suburb that was once crowded with villas, temples, and tombs, past the Aurelian Wall, the Via Appia was suddenly more than the sum of what I could see. It was an accumulation of materials and textures, triumphs and tribulations, big enough to stretch between the Tyrrhenian and Adriatic seas.

A group of friends surprised me, gathered at a makeshift finish line near the Circus Maximus to welcome me back to a Rome that felt smaller and infinitely more familiar after walking nearly half the length of peninsular Italy. Or perhaps it wasn't that Rome had shrunk as much as my perspective and appreciation for the rest of Italy, with all its mountainous ups and downs, had expanded.

The Via Appia Is Easier Going If Taken Slowly

Looking back, two years after walking the Via Appia, I realize that what left the biggest impression were the liminal zones, the invisible transitions where the countryside broke free from the confines of the city, where cultivated areas devolved into wild abandon. Between Rome and southern Italy, between the Tyrrhenian, Ionian, and Adriatic seas, there are many discernible shifts in the landscape that can only be appreciated by going slowly. From years of fieldwork in Puglia, I understood that the borders between the regions of Italy, though fixed on a map, are porous in nature. In some places, they follow defined topographic features like rivers or ravines, but in others, the regions blend into each other so seamlessly that it's only after realizing something essential and definitive about the former region is missing—say, the giant olives trees in Puglia—that you notice you must have crossed a boundary into new territory.

Even though I could boast a passing familiarity with many areas, I learned the contours, rhythms, and harsh nature of the Via Appia by walking it. In the weeks before and after my hike on the Via Appia, people in Rome asked me about what I saw, but I repeatedly failed to articulate the impact of my encounters. Looking back, it seems to me that the sum total of those encounters was resilience—both my own and that of the Via Appia to endure throughout the centuries. While walking, I often had to choose between backtracking and making a detour. Sometimes the detour paid off and I discovered exciting, wonderful new places, but other times, I had to dig deep and find the energy to retrace my steps after taking a gamble on the circuitous route, always conscious of the setting sun or the subtle shifts in the weather.

When I set out to walk the Via Appia, I expected that it would strengthen my connection to the land that's been so important to me for the past decade, and in many ways, it did. I visited archaeological sites that I'd only read about, and I was able to understand my excavation site in its wider regional landscape. Yet what I discovered along the way wasn't so much about the route or even about Italy as much as it was about myself: these days, I'm much better equipped to change directions, shake off the tunnel vision, and embrace unknown challenges on the horizon. I learned that you can't prepare for every scenario, but you can adapt and enjoy the sense of accomplishment after the constant ebb and flow of highs and lows. Walking also allowed me to enjoy carefree moments with friends before our time in Rome ended all too quickly and we entered a strange, new, socially distanced world. Now, whether it's two or twenty miles, I walk in every new place as a way to maintain resilience in the face of unexpected challenges and, in doing so, I always find my way . . . eventually.

The Edge

JJ Tiziou

As I GET READY to walk out of PHL International Airport, I ask myself again why I'm doing this. Leaving the airport on foot, as a pedestrian, is a strange enough thing to do. Yet here I am, accompanied by sixteen companions who've elected to join me on the last leg of my fifth annual pilgrimage walk around the perimeter of Philadelphia. The final stretch involves making an unconventional exit from the airport, edging along highways before diving into the sanctuary of the Heinz National Wildlife Refuge. But much has been unconventional about this adventure.

Walk Around Philadelphia emerged from an artist residency collaboration in 2016 with my fellow walkers Adrienne Mackey, Ann de Forest, and Sam Wend. A year later, in the aftermath of my father's death, I did it again on my own, with some friends joining on the last half-day segment. The following years, I completed some parts solo, some with a friend, and others with a small group. It has become a personal ritual that has also captured the imagination of others. In 2020, I opened the invitation a little bit more broadly, hence that big group striding out of the airport on foot.

Walking around Philadelphia takes me five and a half days, covering roughly 100 miles. Each year I've done it in mid-February, always start-

A version of this essay first appeared in the May/June 2020 issue of *The Pennsylvania Gazette*.

ing at 61st Street & Baltimore Avenue in Southwest Philly and moving clockwise. Each time is different, with new adventures, companions, discoveries, challenges, and ever-changing weather.

Day One begins in the woods, following a trail in Cobbs Creek Park where the western edge of the city is defined by the natural border of a stream. The first of many astonishing contrasts comes when we suddenly emerge onto the back end of a golf course, from there encountering the sudden roar of cars on City Avenue. This long stretch of strip mall is clearly a line drawn by a cartographer—but then we cross a bridge toward Manayunk and find ourselves following another natural border: the Schuylkill River, which leads us toward the city's northwestern edge.

The operating principles of this walk are straightforward. Start somewhere on the city's edge. Decide if you're going to go clockwise or counterclockwise. Stay as close to the perimeter as you can (within reason, prioritizing safety). Don't break in anywhere or blatantly trespass, but explore with a spirit of adventure, open to paths that might not generally be taken. When obstacles arise—and they will—simply go around them. (We call this the "Roomba Rule," bumping our way around obstacles like the little robot vacuum cleaner.) As dusk approaches, find the nearest spot where you can take public transit home. Resume from where you left off. Repeat until you've come right back to the beginning, changed by what you've experienced along the way.

Day Two is a zigzag of straight roads, leading us northeast from the river toward Chestnut Hill, then southeast along Cheltenham Avenue all the way to Tookany Creek Park. From there, the border runs northeast again, alongside a rail track toward Fox Chase. But the first part of our morning takes us up a steep wooded hill behind the Schuylkill Center for Environmental Education and Manatawna Farms. There is wilderness, mixed in with fields and cows, yet somehow this too is Philadelphia. Later in the day it's a strip mall, and then a park. Also Philadelphia.

There's something special about experiencing the city by focusing on its outer edges. One revelation of our first year was how "center-centric" our view of the city had been. We'd catch a glimpse of the skyline in the distance and say "Look, there's Philadelphia!" Then we'd have to correct ourselves: "This, this right here at our feet and to our right, is Philadelphia. And everything to our left, that's Not-Philadelphia."

As someone who's been well established in the city for more than half a lifetime, I thought I "knew" Philly. But the walk provides a humbling perspective on this vast and complex city. Now that I'm intimately familiar with its edge, the whole of Philadelphia feels like so much more of a mystery.

The forecast for Day Three called for cold and constant rain—the kind of prediction that might inspire one to stay at home, but I knew from the first year that the walk truly bears out the proverb that "there is no bad weather, only inappropriate clothing." When you set out in the spirit of pilgrimage, with an attitude of curiosity that's open to discovery, you can bring joy to most any challenge and find beauty around every corner.

There's a spiritual metaphor in this for me: In these turbulent and challenging times, we might wish that the world were other than it is—but I find it more helpful to focus on how we choose to respond to it. What values and virtues do we need to cultivate in order to participate in whatever the world will bring us next?

And so we persevere, with a bushwhacking adventure, as the northeastern border of the city traces the bramble-choked banks of Poquessing Creek. But to get there we first follow roads, stumble into quite an elaborate detour through a new housing development and into some vacant industrial lands. One of the great surprises of the day is a giant crypt in a cemetery whose door swings open to reveal a gorgeous crumbling wreck half overgrown by nature. We see both things along the walk: new things being built up, and old things being reclaimed by nature. The afternoon drizzle intensifies as we wind our way through the paths in the creek bed below Philadelphia Mills mall, and it is properly dark and rainy by the end of this leg, but we are all in great spirits.

This sets us up for a spectacular early morning start to Day Four, with the long Regional Rail ride back to Torresdale timed to catch sunrise at Glen Foerd, a strange palace of a property on the northeastern corner of the city where Poquessing Creek meets the Delaware River. This day is a straight shot down the river's edge, but not without its adventures. Interspersed between newly expanded segments of the Delaware River Trail are a shipyard, a chemical plant, abandoned boats, a scrap metal recycling facility, and of course the prisons.

Questions of privilege hit home for me again here, as I know several people who've made the journey from Southwest Philly to these carceral facilities by the more traditional route of the school-to-prison pipeline. And here I am having accomplished this journey via the more roundabout and far more pleasant experience of a grant-funded artist residency and then by annually continuing a thing that can easily feel like a self-indulgent vanity project.

There's an irony or conflict here. At its core, *Walk Around Philadelphia* is about the most basic human activity: walking in public space. Circumnavigating the city should be accessible to most anyone physically capable of it—but actually doing it requires a significant amount of privilege, and I wonder about how to make this experience one that more diverse participants can partake in.

It's a long trek down the Delaware, and by the time we reach Penn's Landing, suddenly feeling so close to more familiar everyday territory, we're exhausted and our feet hurt. Nevertheless, we push on all the way to Pier 68 by the shopping plaza in South Philly.

Day Five starts off with another glorious sunrise over the Delaware, this time more frigid: it's 16 degrees when we set out. Amid the cast of characters who are joining me on this year's pilgrimage is Ann, one of the original perimeter-walkers from 2016. We were strangers when the project started, but the experience of navigating the city's edge together has made us fast friends, and for the fifth anniversary she's decided to do the whole thing again. This morning we're also joined by Adrienne, one of our other original crew, and it's a joyous reunion.

It's a gift to spend all day walking with friends old and new. Walks open up a special, different kind of space for conversation. They allow for a fluidity, leave room for silences that feel comfortable, create possibility for deeper connection. Ever since the first walk, I've started shaping more of my meetings and social activities into walking-centric ones.

The next stretch is industrial, past shipyards and into the Navy Yard. A highlight of this day is crossing the Platt Bridge. I'm used to driving over it when going to the airport, but it's surreal to cross it on foot. To either side lies a vast realm of oil refinery infrastructure, and visible through the bridge's open grating is a steep drop to the Schuylkill River. We could call it quits at the airport, since technically only a fraction of it is in the city, and we can't quite follow the perimeter directly across the runways, but a spirit of completionism leads us to go the long way around the airport, on what is called Hog Island.

These long stretches can get monotonous. This is where feet really begin to hurt. But there are still sensations to register and discoveries to be made: a jet landing just overhead, a deer carcass just underfoot, the remnants of a campfire in a hidden spot by the river's edge. As we end our day at the airport's international departures terminal, the bright lights and bustling of travelers are a wild contrast to our experience of the city's margins. We are a different kind of tourists, having traversed so many diverse landscapes so close to home.

And once again I find myself in the home stretch, for what we call Day 5.5 because the last segment is shorter than the others. Knowing that such a large group is joining for the last leg, I'm a little bit anxious: how will I keep them all safe, and will the size of the group detract from the experience? Part of me wants to be doing this walk alone as my personal pilgrimage, part of me wants to facilitate small groups going out and doing it on their own, and part of me has a great time leading this motley procession on what might be the most unconventional tour of Philly ever given. And it works out splendidly, with everyone enjoying the adventure as we navigate the edge of a toxic Superfund site, discover where all the old rusting dumpsters end up, wander beautiful creek beds, and have a joyous reunion with two more walkers who intercept us just ahead of Mount Moriah Cemetery.

As our group cheerfully makes it back to Baltimore Avenue, I relish the ways in which this project creates new opportunities for rich connection between participants who spend all day walking, talking, navigating obstacles, and coming to new understandings of the city together.

Ever since completing the first walk around Philadelphia, I have wondered: What would it be like if we matched together a city councilperson, a citizen just returning from incarceration, a historian, and a plumber and sent them off to explore the city's edge together? Could this experience of discovery, and the conversation and connections that come through it, be used as an experience for civic groups?

In September 2020, as the city continued to struggle with the many impacts of COVID-19, I developed an "organize-your-own-group" and "choose-your-own-adventure" version of *Walk Around Philadelphia* in conjunction with the Philadelphia Fringe Festival. This offering provided a pandemic-safe opportunity for about 125 Philadelphians to engage in this unique experience.

Participants were able to pick up a perimeter kit of supplies, including a route map, from my front porch, access additional resources online, and then set off on their own exploration of the fringes of the city, at their own pace. A group of mixed-income homeschooled high school students completed the entire perimeter, as did several groups of retirees. Sliding-scale registration helped support stipends for walkers whose financial circumstances would otherwise have prevented their participation.

I continue to seek ways to make the experience of *Walk Around Philadelphia* more accessible to others for future iterations of the project. I'm not sure where this project will go next, but I do know that it will take me 'round the city a few more times, God willing.

The Walkable City

Walking It Slant

MY CATERCORNERED INCLINATIONS

David Hallock Sanders

DIAGONALS HAVE long attracted me. When I doodle, I doodle in diagonals. Diagonals are prominent in my quilt designs. In sixth-grade square-dancing class I learned to bow (diagonally) to my corner. Around the same time I learned that squaring the diagonal of a rectangle would give me the sum of the squares of the remaining sides of the resulting triangle. Thank you, Pythagoras.

When I was a boy growing up in L.A., I'd play a walking game with my father in which our routes would be decided by the toss of a coin. At each intersection, heads would send us to the left, tails to the right. Sometimes sequential flips of the coin would simply circle us back home, but other days, chance would lead us on stair-step diagonals to distant destinations.

Another travel game of my father's involved a map and a drawing compass. We'd set the legs of the compass for a reasonable distance, I'd close my eyes, and my father would rotate the compass until I called, "Stop!" Wherever the point pointed, that was our walk's destination. Sometimes we used the same device for bicycle rides, and one memorable day the compass point landed on Santa Monica Beach, thirty miles away. That sent us off on a southwest diagonal bike ride across L.A. to the shore, where we swam and ate hot dogs before beginning the long ride back.

Conceptual diagonals also appeal to me. My father used to read poetry aloud at the dinner table, and among his many favorites was an Emily Dickinson poem that included the line, "Tell all the truth but tell it slant." Dickinson was writing about the need for a gradual revelation of dazzling Truth, but I have embraced her line as a guide for slanting my way across the landscape of life.

Years ago, when I first encountered the Microsoft Excel program, I was intrigued by its immense cyber landscape of data cells. I was curious how much terrain the program encompassed, so I ventured diagonally across the grid from its first cell (A1) to its last (XFD1048576)—a vast 17,179,869,184 cells away. When I told my mother what I had done, she said, "Of course you did."

Objects situated at opposite ends of a diagonal are said to be cater-cornered to one another (or sometimes kitty-cornered, although no cats are involved). It's a phrase thought to be derived from the now obsolete word "cater," meaning the four-spot of a die. It's easy to visualize those four dice pips lined up catercornered to one another. Other sources say the phrase comes from "quatre," French for four, which also suggests the catercornered pips.

Long diagonal walks particularly intrigue me. In my teens I read with awe and yearning *The Man Who Walked Through Time*, Colin Fletcher's account of hiking the length of the Grand Canyon on a winding diagonal across Arizona. More recently I read Rory Stewart's *The Places in Between*, and marveled at his fascinating, and often harrowing, story of walking across Afghanistan.

In 2018 my wife, Nancy, and I decided to take our own long walk—this one across Scotland. Far less daunting than those by Fletcher and Stewart, but still with its challenges, our catercornered trek followed the Great Glen Way along a diagonal from the town of Fort William, on Scotland's west coast, to Inverness up on the east coast. The walk took us eight days to complete. Some days we climbed highland hills. Other days we walked along tumbling rivers. Many days took us past stunning lakes, including the famed Loch Ness.

That trek was a marvelous experience, especially the opportunity to walk with Nancy, just the two of us alone. We'd been told to expect a lot of fellow walkers on this popular route, but in fact we encountered very few. That alone-ness gave much of our days a kind of time-out-of-time quality. Sometimes we walked together, chatting side by side in the cool of lush forests. Other times we drifted into our own reveries, climbing single-file up steep mountain switchbacks while our thoughts pursued their own courses.

Harry J. Stead, a writer in West Yorkshire, England, describes walking as a source of personal inspiration. "Usually," he notes, "I walk without a plan. I have nothing to achieve; the beauty is in the walking, in the journey itself." And then, he says, "quite suddenly, ideas arrive. Stories unfold. Meaning and purpose are restored."

That combination of simplicity and inspiration was certainly true for our Scotland walk. Each day held a single, clear focus: just to walk from "here" to "there." Each day unfolded in the open air of a phenomenally beautiful environment. Each footstep provided accompaniment for ruminations and realizations. Even on days when joints ached, or blisters formed, or rain moved in, walking held a profound, peculiar joy. Most evenings we ended up in a pub for some simple food and drink, a great joy in itself. Then we slept deeply, and woke to begin walking again.

Nancy and I began preparing for our Scotland walk a few months in advance. We bought new gear, including, most important, some excellent hiking shoes. To break in the shoes (and ourselves) we undertook several local walks of increasing distance. We were advised that, before we left for Scotland, we should complete at least one full-day walk equal to the longest days of our trek.

So one Saturday we set off for an eighteen-mile, round-trip, cross-city walk from our home at the southeastern edge of Philadelphia, near the Delaware River, up to the Chamounix Equestrian Center, located diagonally across the city in the northwestern corner of Fairmount Park.

Much of Philadelphia is laid out in a grid—a design that reaches back to even before the city formally existed. English Quaker William Penn, for whom Pennsylvania is named, envisioned a "greene country town" here, and sent his surveyor general, Thomas Holme, to create a design for the town based on a grid pattern. Philadelphia has since grown far beyond its original grid, but the city's x and y axes still dominate.

I often cross the city by subway. One subway route follows a straight line along the x axis (under Market Street), and the other runs along the y axis (under Broad Street), with the lines crossing beneath City Hall. Of course, when you're traveling underground, your primary view is of the passing stations and your fellow sardines packed into the train car.

But up on the surface, some city streets manifest as long, satisfying violations of the grid. Yes, the grid still holds dominance—in one direction streets are numbered, in the other they're named after trees. But subverting the grid, here and there, are notable diagonals. Some of these slanted streets—like Passyunk and Moyamensing near my home—developed organically from, I believe, old Native American walking trails. But others are deliberate impositions on the grid, like the grand slash of the Benjamin Franklin Parkway, created in the early twentieth century to reflect the European-inspired City Beautiful Movement and to echo the Champs-Élysées.

Walking these slanted routes offers a catercornered relief from Philly's checkerboard layout. When we began our walk to Chamounix we were solidly on the grid. We headed across Philadelphia on South Street, once the southern border of the city and at one time Philadelphia's prime destination for gambling, prostitution, and illegal liquor. Now the street, considerably tamed, is the home for a wide array of commercial establishments, such as coffee shops, galleries, clothing stores, and a large number of eateries that range from soul-food restaurants to ice-cream parlors, and that feature foods from a world-tour of locales, including Germany, Italy, the Caribbean, Mexico, Morocco, India, and many more.

Tamed perhaps, but the street can still hold surprises, as it did one earlier day when Nancy and I, on another cross-city walk, were passed by an African American cowboy in leather chaps and cowboy hat riding his horse down the middle of the street.

South Street led us across the Schuylkill River, and from there we angled north and west in a diagonal route that followed no particular plan. Would we go left at the next intersection? Right? Straight? Who knew? We decided when we got to each corner, an echo of my childhood walking games.

When I walk the city, I sometimes notice my perspective shifting. One moment I'm immersed in my immediate, ground-level stimuli—the sights, sounds, smells of where I am. The next moment my perspective can take flight and soar into the sky, to where I can imagine my location as though looking down at a map: I am *here*, in relation to *there*, and *this*, and *that*. Each of these perspectives instills in me a different emotional quality.

Walking the city I can feel very much the urban wanderer—a *flâneur*, as the nineteenth-century writer Charles Baudelaire named it. Of course, much of the time I walk with an intent to arrive somewhere specific. But very often I also wander without aim, navigating the urban environment simply to enjoy its spaces and structures. And by walking the city slant, I feel I am doing some of both—taking routes that may be shortcuts to a destination as neighborhoods come and go, yet in other ways are ventures through unfamiliar territory. Going somewhere known by an unknown path.

I think I've always combined this love for both the known and the unknown. For both structure and discovery. For example, I hold two graduate business degrees in planning, but I've also devoted many years to teaching and performing improvisational theater.

These dual influences—to both plan and improvise, to both set and challenge boundaries—have long shaped me. I can recall that even as a very young child, when given a new coloring book, I would first keep my crayon carefully within the lines, then make deliberate excursions outside to color beyond the borders.

I also see these influences in my craft as a quilter. I tend to design carefully controlled quilt patterns, plotting them out on sheets of graph paper. But then I violate those patterns in some subtle way. It wasn't until years into my quilting that I learned this was a long-honored tradition in quilting—to design a "flaw" into a design so as not to compete with God for perfection.

Now I approach my city walking with a similar attitude. While I may plan a specific route, I'm also willing, maybe even eager, to violate those plans as I go.

Of course, this always creates the possibility of getting lost.

Today, when I think of my father's walking and wandering games, I have to add another chapter. When my father was seventy he began to lose himself in a ten-year descent into Alzheimer's disease. One manifestation of the disease was a tendency to wander. Increasingly, my father lost his sense of not only where he was going, but also where he had come from, and even where he was at that particular moment.

In the early stages of his disease my parents lived in Cambridge, and I lived nearby in Boston. I worked at Harvard at the time, and one day after work, walking through Harvard Square, I noticed an apparently homeless man sitting on the sidewalk. I had nearly passed him before I realized that it was my father. When I asked him what he was doing down there, he responded by asking, with an odd, jaunty smile, what I was doing up *there*. I laughed, joined him there on the ground, and we sat together for a while before I accompanied him back to his home.

Soon after that I helped my parents move to an apartment in Philadelphia, where my father continued to decline. The disease eventually devastated his memory. He routinely lost things like keys, dates, and his train of thought. Increasingly he lost names: of objects, of places, even, in time, of his seven children. He forgot how to read, how to write, how to hold a conversation, even how to eat—probably his four favorite activities.

For a while he continued to take walks by himself around his Philadelphia neighborhood. My mom pinned his address and phone number to his clothes in case he forgot where he was. These solo walks came to an end the day that a stranger found him lost and crying on the streets, and drove him home.

Over time my father forgot how to turn his body left. At doorways in his home he would always turn right and right and right again, repeatedly ending up in the bedroom closet, confused and frightened. It felt like a sad version of our coin-toss walking game, now with a loaded coin that only came up tails.

My father finally forgot how to move his body entirely. He became bedridden for the last years of his life, first at home, then in a nursing home where, for years, he appeared perpetually lost. The man in the bed little resembled the man he once was. I began to feel that my father was gone. His nursing-home aides, however, told a different story. They saw what he had retained, not what he'd lost. Amid his incoherent growls and sobs and gibberish, he still preserved enough of his personality to inspire one aide to tell me, shortly before my dad's death, "Your father has such a great sense of humor!"

Years later, memories of my father can still be conjured by the simple act of walking. They were right there with me on my cross-Philly trek, as Nancy and I continued playing our version of my father's walking game—Left? Right? Straight?—on our way to Fairmount Park and Chamounix.

Fairmount Park is one of the largest urban public green spaces in the country. It was created in the nineteenth century as an effort to protect the city's water supply and preserve open space in a fast-growing city. Now it serves as the verdant setting for a wide range of cultural institutions and historic structures, including the elegant Memorial Hall, a Beaux-Arts reminder of the groundbreaking 1876 Centennial Exhibition.

One historic landmark after another greeted us as we walked through the park and up Belmont Hill, our tired legs now registering the climb. Finally we reached our destination, the Chamounix Equestrian Center, tucked into the far corner of the city.

The equestrian center is the home of Philadelphia's Work to Ride program, which offers urban kids a range of horsemanship activities—including riding lessons and an amazing polo team—in exchange for working to care for the center's approximately thirty horses. I imagine the Chamounix Center is where our earlier urban cowboy had started his ride, taking his own catercornered slant across the city on horseback. Not surprisingly, another feature of the center is an impressive, and constantly replenished, stack of manure, which Nancy and I periodically raid for our compost piles at home and at our community garden plot.

On this particular day no one at the stable was riding. Some of the horses were inside in their stalls, others were outside walking the pen, and some were just hanging by the fence to soak in the day. Nancy and I visited them all.

Eventually, however, it was time to head back.

We had chosen a different, less familiar, path for our return, one that took us through the Brewerytown section of the city. I felt that our training for Scotland would be incomplete if we didn't visit a pub. Brewerytown, true to its name, offered several options, including an actual brewery, where we stopped for a bite and a beer.

But once hunger and thirst were quelled, we roused ourselves once more. We took stock of our location, visualized our destination, and plotted a new slant across the city.

Even from just this one day's crosstown walk I was feeling a subtle shift in my relationship with Philadelphia. I felt as though the city and I had begun to know each other a little better. That we'd begun to share some previously unshared secrets.

But then again, that may have just been the beer.

Regardless, I felt newly inspired—to paraphrase Dickinson—to walk the world but walk it slant. So we gathered our packs and set off again, this time on a new, catercornered route home.

Aberrant Angeleno

Ann de Forest

THE TOPOGRAPHY of my youth did not encourage walking. My family lived in a succession of sidewalk-deprived canyons, my first remembered house on a precipitously steep street, the second on a narrow, winding one that a friend's brother, who sometimes drove me home in high school, compared to the rough roads of Greece. In my earliest memory of walking, we are fleeing a fire in our canyon, our panicked babysitter giving me no time to put on shoes. I can still summon the burn of asphalt on my feet.

This was in Los Angeles, infamous as a place where nobody ever walks. My city taught me to view walking as a kind of aberration. To be an adult who had to walk was to be deprived. From the window of our car, I would see other people out walking. Outlandishly costumed men and women we passed on Sunset Strip or Hollywood Boulevard walked, performing for an audience unseen. ("Crazy," my mother said, or once, spotting a man with long hair, beard, and striped caftan—our first hippie!—"He must be in a Biblical movie.") Raggedy men I glimpsed ambling in the weeds alongside railroad tracks walked. (Hobos, my parents called them, more pity in their voices than disdain.) Mrs. Heilweil, who came from New York and didn't even know how to drive, walked. She was not deprived, just eccentric. She also took the bus. I was five years old and I pitied her too.

Thus, my life as a walker began inauspiciously. At summer camp, where walking meant hiking, I was labeled a bad walker. I was scrawny, short, abysmally unathletic, with a wandering mind not conducive to the brisk, steady pace my counselors wanted to enforce. Even now, as I remember those brutal hikes, I can see myself straggling far behind the line of green-clad Girl Scouts as we marched in a unit on a road overlooking pine woods. (We didn't even hike on trails, but on the shoulders of paved mountain highways). We sang in unison too. Perhaps "The Happy Wanderer" (*val de ri, val de ra, val de ri, val de ha ha ha ha ha*). Ha ha ha indeed. Inevitably, as the gap between me and the rest of the line lengthened, the counselor would blow her whistle and call me to the front, where she could keep her eye on me. Behind me now, the other girls whined that I was slowing everyone down. Thirst compounded the torture; I remember my throat parched and my head so light that the air seemed to spin around me in tangible bits. The heavy metal canteens we were all supposed to carry banged against my hip. I could hear its enticing slosh. Hydration wasn't in the vocabulary of the Girl Scouts handbook. We had to keep moving. We marched past splendid vistas, high slopes covered in cool pines, a verdant valley below, a sparkle of lake. While dawdling at the end of the line, I could glance up, down, and all around me, marveling at fallen pine cones, wheeling raptors, the changing shapes of clouds. Up front, though, our relentless pace kept me from focusing on anything but my need to push forward. Conscious only of the glaring eyes on my back, the whispers behind me, I was propelled by the desire to avoid further shame.

Still, I walked. What child doesn't? Though I logged many hours in the pre-seat-belt era bouncing and flopping in the back seats of various family station wagons, my parents weren't always willing or available chauffeurs. To get around my neighborhood I had to depend, like every other kid on our street, on my own two feet. The going could be treacherous. My brother and I, and later our little sister, learned to listen for cars and time their approach, scurrying onto the thin, weedy shoulder as they roared past, tires spitting gravel on our calves. Beyond our own more rustic stretch of road, where houses were perched against a steep hillside or, like ours, sat below the actual street, the canyon widened, and the street along with it. The houses "up the street" were newer and more uniform, all single-story ranch homes, vaguely Japanese in their geometry, with driveways and garages, many sporting basketball hoops. This is where all the neighborhood kids congregated, to wheel around on skateboards and bicycles, shoot baskets, thump handballs against garage doors, or play elaborate games of freeze tag and kick the can. Except for the lack of sidewalks, this extension of our street could pass as the kind of neighborhood families lived in on TV.

But beyond that sun-bleached suburban haven our street narrowed again into a lane, marked "private," which tall, shaggy eucalyptus trees cast in perpetual shade. The first time I walked up there, I felt like I'd entered some secret, magical portal. I was with my friend Jasmine. A Catholic school girl, Jasmine was always game for transgression. I would follow along, motivated more by a mix of curiosity and boredom. The sounds of wheelies and bouncing balls and boys shouting faded. Crows cawed. Somewhere a creek trickled. The houses tucked into the grove of trees spread farther apart. We crunched on the purple leaves, peels of bark, and fallen nuts scattered in the dust. The tang of eucalyptus filled the air. The road ended abruptly, in a steep canyon wall, higher than any house, sand-banked against mudslides. Just beside it, though, was another surprise: a clapboard farmhouse and stable with a white picket fence that seemed to belong to some other era, some other place. Horses grazed behind the fence. Sensing our presence, they lifted their heads and bounded over, nuzzling our palms in search of sugar.

Walking had brought us this moment of magic. For kids in that blissfully unsupervised era, walking was not just a default means of transportation when no other mode was available. It could be transporting, which was different. And, because not many grown-ups I knew did walk, except out of necessity, my own two feet felt like they held a secret power. I could use them to explore. I could use them to escape.

Escape is what my friends and I did every lunch period at the end of eighth grade. My school was building a new campus on the rundown grounds of a country club nestled into another L.A. canyon, in the San Fernando Valley (which we called "the other side of the hill"). For the spring quarter, the seventh and eighth grades, in confirmation of our in-between and out-of-place educational status, were relocated to temporary quarters, in a pre-fab assembly of one-room classrooms that would soon face the wrecking ball. Our displacement to the edge of the school's property, in the crease of the canyon, somehow empowered minor rebellions.

Behind the asphalt playground rose a high slope that leveled into a rough, overgrown plateau, destined to be graded and further flattened to become our new campus's playing field. Until then, though, it was unknown territory, which three friends and I decided to explore every day during lunch. Lunch period was just twenty minutes, and looking back, I don't know how we managed to slip away from the strict supervision on which our school prided itself. We must have made an incongruous picture, four thirteen-year-old girls in the blue blazers, pleated skirts, knee socks, and saddle shoes that were our required uniform, wandering in raspy thickets of scrub sage and dry chaparral. Every day we found a new path, poked in a new direction, discovered puddles and rivulets, and named the places we happened upon after ourselves—Patti Lake, Cydney Creek, Debbie Island. We could look down at our classmates and the patrolling teachers in the schoolyard below, diminished and oblivious. Nobody seemed to know we were missing. We would hear the bell ring to signal the end to that day's wandering, and fly down the hill to take our seats in Geography class, exhilarated. As our teacher, Mr. Ahmed, lectured about the California biomes, I leaned down to pick burrs from the ankles of my knee socks.

Looking back on that liberating spring, I realize my friends and I were not fleeing our reality as much as expanding it. On those lunchtime explorations, we enlarged our sense of the spaces we inhabited. We experienced the disjunction between the tangled wildness of the upper canyon and the orderly built structures and paved surfaces that constituted our school below, but we also forged a connection—physical and conceptual—between the "safe" spaces whose boundaries we pushed against and through, and these unplumbed mysteries that could be found just a few steps away.

Doug Aberley, in a book he edited, *Boundaries of Home*, describes the "cognitive maps" aboriginal peoples created as they migrated through the territories they hunted, foraged, and inhabited: "The ability to map territory into a sustaining familiarity . . . to know a new place quickly and well, and to adapt to its circumstance, may be the most important unique attribute of the human animal." Though we eighth-grade schoolgirls did not rely on the overgrown plateau above our school for material sustenance like food or shelter, this daily act of marking our movements through a space most adults we knew would dismiss as a weedy lot did sustain our spirits. It was our secret place, which kept yielding new discoveries, and the exhilaration we felt there held a measure of the sacred.

Those three months were the most freeing days I can remember in my years as a "lifer" (the irony of that term not lost on me) at a school whose motto, "self-expression through self-discipline," stressed the latter at the expense of the former. Alas, the rugged, unmanicured terrain of our eighth-grade lunchtime explorations was doomed to become purposeful, the golden chapparal mowed down, the uneven ground smoothed and paved over with bright green sod. In high school, I too felt like I was being flattened and tamed. Was it because that brief, daily ramble was no longer accessible? I had always been a kid with a humming, chattering brain and an overactive imagination, but without a physical outlet, a way for my body to move along with my mind, my brain, in overdrive, churned with anxiety and worry and fear.

A summer camp in Arizona high country offered a measure of salvation. Unlike the tyrannical Girl Scout camp, this camp had a staff and an ethos that accepted, even celebrated my slow, meandering tendencies. For five weeks every August, I was happy and alive. Then, the winter I was fifteen, a friend from that camp invited me to visit her over the Christmas holidays. Her family lived just outside New York City, and we went into Manhattan for a day of sightseeing, museum going, and shopping. Before we set out, Mrs. Pearl, my friend Holly's mother, made me memorize the streets of Manhattan, below Central Park, in order. Beginning with 5th Avenue, headed east: Lexington, Park, Madison, 3rd Avenue, 2nd Avenue, 1st Avenue, FDR Drive, the East River. Headed West: 6th Avenue (also known as Avenue of the Americas), 7th Avenue, 8th, 9th, 10th, 11th Avenues, with Broadway cutting through at a diagonal. "The Bronx is up." She had me point, just like those tap-dancing sailors in the movie *On the Town.* "The Battery's down."

I was thrilled. Mrs. Pearl, not unlike the staff at the camp where Holly and I had met, had seen some capacity in me I didn't know I possessed. She saw me as curious, adventurous (she said as much), a latent navigator. Maybe she sensed that growing up in Los Angeles had given me rare insight: compared to the sprawling vastness of my hometown, the neat checkered streets of skinny Manhattan Island would be—conceptually, physically—a piece of cake. Maybe Holly had already shown herself helpless with directions. Whatever the reason, Mrs. Pearl gave me, and not her own daughter, the responsibility of holding the grid of Manhattan whole in my mind. And I happily accepted this charge.

Mrs. Pearl's affirmation undid, at least temporarily, the damage inflicted by those grim Girl Scout counselors. If those sourpusses could only have seen me zipping up and down the streets of Manhattan reinforced by Mrs. Pearl's implicit trust, energized by the tall buildings that drew my gaze up and up, the unfamiliar smells (roasting chestnuts!), and the fast-moving walkers all around me. It was cold. And the unaccustomed chill ignited me too. Or maybe I hadn't yet had a chance to discover the potential of my newly long legs, following my ninth-grade growth spurt. I had bought a long suede coat and thigh-high boots for this trip east, and I strode—brisk steps in brisk air, marveling at how much distance I could cover so quickly. Walking in winter, my own breath billowing around me like the clouds billowing from trains in old movies to meld with the steam from the subway grates, walking straight and fast in a city surrounded by other walkers, was invigorating. And my mind and my imagination felt as alive as my body.

I no longer pitied Mrs. Heilweil—or I pitied her for a different reason. How exiled she must have felt, how lonely, ambling on the sidewalks of West Hollywood, shamed for doing something that seemed natural, normal. Walking. Now I wanted to be Mrs. Heilweil. That New Year began with my realizing that, as much as I loved California, New York—or a city like New York, a city with winter, a city that took shape under your feet as you moved through it, a city where everyone walked—was the place for me.

That New York trip was a watershed moment, and I wish I could say that from that moment on my trajectory was clear or that I realized, with that sharp flash of an epiphany, that all I needed to thrive was to be in a place where I could move and think and dream and invent and discover and absorb the wonders of the world around me all at the same time. A place where I could be among others who also moved, who understood, in my own romantic interpretation, the connection between movement and thought. But I had a long slog ahead of me, two and a half years of high school to get through.

Of course, my life was not as dismal as I paint it here—though I certainly felt it then. I am surprised, as I write this, how readily I can summon that anxious, mopey, alienated teenager I once was. Fortunately, I did have a companion in adolescent misery. My best friend, Debbie, she of the eponymous island, also had nervous energy to burn. Like me, she was fixated on going to college back East, as Californians like to say. Like me, she was sure, every time she took a test, that she'd failed. Like me, she spun out scenarios for the future—some reassuring, others disastrous—to vault over the unhappy present. And somehow, without really thinking much about what we were doing, she and I started to take walks together. We didn't necessarily consider walking an antidote to the anxieties that plagued us. At first, our walking accompanied the socially sanctioned activity of shopping, meandering through the self-styled "villages" of Westside L.A.—Westwood or Beverly Hills or Santa Monica—and in and out of shops like treasure seekers, running our fingers through clothes racks, book stacks, record bins, not necessarily with the desire to acquire anything, just absorbing the plenty on display. Our conversation meandered too. Walking and talking complemented each other, and deepened our bond.

At some point, we must have realized that shopping in Westwood or the outdoor mall of Century City was a pretext for simply ambling in one another's company. So we started walking for walking's sake. Whenever we went to the beach, we took long walks, letting the waves fizz up over our toes. Once, on a whim, we decided to walk the entire length of Ventura Boulevard, one of the main thoroughfares of the San Fernando Valley, which ran, straight and flat, some nineteen miles along the foot of the Santa Monica Mountains. From the perspective of a car window, the storefronts of Ventura Boulevard rolled by unvaried and monotonous. On foot, the storefronts and mini-strip malls and supermarkets and car dealers, punctuated by driveways and parking lots, took on singular identities. That linear sprawl also contained vestiges of small-town amenities. Community gathering places like libraries, rec centers, movie theaters, and pharmacies gave Ventura Boulevard, from our pedestrian perspective, an old-fashioned quaintness, a sense of history that we hadn't expected to find.

We especially enjoyed walking on residential streets in neighborhoods adjacent to, but far tonier than, our own, playing a game in which we would pick a specific house—our Southern California surroundings offered an eclectic array of possibilities—and fill in the details of the lives of the families who lived there. Architectural style, we decided, was destiny. And so we moved from musing about the current residents' lives to projecting our own future lives into those homes. Pick a house—red-roofed Spanish Colonial, miniature Tara with its columned portico, or shingle-clad New England saltbox—and the specifics of what jobs we would have, what types of people we would marry would follow.

Looking back, I appreciate the free-wheeling invention that these walks allowed. We never saw anyone else on those sidewalks, but that absence of real people stimulated our speculations. We had grown past the stage of imaginative play. We wouldn't be caught dead dressing up Barbie dolls and placing them in their Dream House. At the time, Debbie and I might have believed that the stories we were spinning about who we might become by inhabiting these houses reflected our own desires for what adulthood might bring—an admittedly conventional, middle-class vision of marriage, home ownership, and children. But we were really crafting fictions. Walking the empty streets of the foothills of West L.A. and the San Fernando Valley, we listened to the stories the houses whispered to us. We told them to each other. And that storytelling, in retrospect, sparked a deeper empathy for other lives, other possibilities, and became a prelude to our both becoming writers.

I survived high school. On graduation day, I sat with my classmates on a temporary platform placed over the emerald football field that had replaced the scruffy wonderland of our eighth-grade adventures, baking in the unrelenting sun, and received my "walking papers," that is, my high school diploma. I was headed back East for college and, as it turned out, the rest of my life. Philadelphia, the city where I ended up settling, is organized on a rational grid like Manhattan, except the blocks are shorter, the buildings lower, and the streets pleasantly shaded. In Philadelphia, everything—the rows of brick and brownstone houses that lined those shady streets, the ample, inviting, handsomely proportioned urban squares—seemed scaled to human dimensions. When I first moved there, I walked everywhere, from river to river, stitching myself through a warp and weft of streets that composed an appealing urban fabric, becoming part of the life of the city as it became an integral part of me.

UNTIL I WENT back East, I didn't know that anyone hated L.A. "There's no there there," people I met at my New England college would misquote Gertrude Stein to me. "It doesn't have history. Everything's so new." "There's no center." "Nobody ever walks there." Those comments rankled me. I knew they were wrong, though I couldn't always find convincing words to counter their smug certainties.

I wanted to tell them that "there" in Los Angeles was fluid and varied and vast, that just because a place wasn't easy to reduce to synecdoche, like New York or Philadelphia or even San Francisco (the California city my East Coast friends all claimed to love), it wasn't placeless.

So I would gush about Southern California's multiple biomes, which had filled me with wonder and pride when we studied them in Mr. Ahmed's eighth-grade geography class. Couldn't they see that a city that encompasses an ocean, several mountain ranges, dusty deserts, and twisting canyons, as well as the expected urbane pleasures of department stores, bookshops, movie theaters, and museums, was dynamic and fascinating? To me, the appeal and wonder of L.A. was in its contradictions. The quirky canyon I lived in was a case in point. Coyotes howled in our hills, and my street ended in a eucalyptus-shaded lane with an old farm and stable at the end, and yet we were included in the city's broad confines no less than downtown civic icons like the white obelisk of City Hall. "That's not a real city then," my friends said, unpersuaded.

Worse, the writers whose ideas attracted me and inspired me to become a connoisseur and chronicler of urban form, like Ada Louise Huxtable and Jane Jacobs, bashed L.A. too. Sprawl, freeways, and dependence on the automobile severed neighborhood ties, eviscerated communities, and led inevitably to what Huxtable called "urbicide." Perhaps the most damning assessment comes from geographer Yi-Fu Tuan, who invented the field of "humanistic geography." In his 1970s book *Topophilia*, he denounces long auto-centric corridors like Ventura Boulevard:

> The pedestrian is given little consideration in an automobile city like Los Angeles. Even in the 1970s some streets have no sidewalks; many others are long arteries scaled to the speed of the car; and in some sections pedestrians risk being picked up as vagrants. The streets are noisy. . . . Little of the noise is human. Indeed not many humans are to be seen.

Yes and no. There's so much I could argue with in Professor Tuan's pithy dismissal. For one, New York, where horns honk, brakes screech, and sirens wail all hours of the day and night, strikes me as far more cacophonous than L.A. But what I resent most is the implication that a place like L.A. cannot engender sentiments of *topophilia*, defined by Wikipedia as "a strong sense of place, which often becomes mixed with the sense of cultural identity among certain people and a love of certain aspects of such a place."

Granted, walking on a crowded city street surrounded by strangers, where everyone is moving with independent purpose to a separate destination yet shares the same dynamic current of energy, generates a heady sense of social cohesion. But there's something to be said, too, for walking in a place where walking is considered an aberration. Learning to walk in a city where a suburban block could suddenly morph into a dark country lane, where a monotonous commercial strip could reveal its small-town origins, where eclectic houses whispered elaborate stories of their inhabitants' imagined lives, opened my eyes and mind and heart to strangeness and surprise.

And being attuned to strangeness and surprise has proven, in all the cities I've walked in my life, the surest way to fall in love with the particularities of a place.

During the lockdown imposed by the pandemic, when the parameters of where I usually walk in my Philadelphia neighborhood started to feel confining, I decided to vary my route. A glimpse of cherry trees in bloom drew me onto the deserted campus of a pharmacy college. Beyond those trees, vibrant with bees, I ventured onto the vast black asphalt of a parking lot, empty of cars. I strolled past a small power plant, whining loud, generating heat and light for classrooms nobody was using, past a pumping well guarded by a chain-link fence marked with the seal of the city water department, past a warren of dumpsters and recycling bins, and another chain-link fence that bore signs in cheerful primary hues alerting potential passersby to the presence of hazardous waste. The parking lot tapered to an abrupt triangular point where two streets—42nd and 43rd— liberated from the impositions of the city's grid, collided like clandestine lovers. Beyond the street signs was a metal gate, and beyond the gate was a rough gravel-strewn path leading uphill.

The gate was open, and the ascending path was enticing. I turned to see if anyone else was around. Alone, I walked up, struck by the unkempt tangle of woods to one side of me. My heart pounded. My hackles were raised. I was aware of my own vulnerability as a woman walking alone, even if this was a bright mid-morning in late spring and most everyone was indoors working from home.

The path was steep but short, and I soon reached a broad plateau crisscrossed with railroad tracks. An Amtrak train barreled past on its way south, and I considered these tracks with a pang of nostalgia for a time when traveling to the places these tracks led—New York, Boston, Baltimore, D.C.—was not so fraught.

But the more stunning sight lay beyond the tracks, the sparkle and sway of the Schuylkill River. I was transported. I knew the river, in theory, defined the edge of my neighborhood, but the overlay of roads, parking lots, and train tracks had long since rendered the water invisible and inaccessible. Standing high on that railroad embankment and gazing down on the water's sweep and curve in both directions, I felt like I had stumbled upon a discovery. I felt like I was seeing the familiar river for the first time.

"What is that?" I jumped at the voice behind me and turned to see a woman, around my age, walking up beside me on the wide shoulder at the edge of the tracks. We were both wearing masks. I wasn't sure what she meant by her question.

She clarified. "What water?"

"The river," I said. "The Schuylkill."

"I never see it."

This surprised me. "Why did you come up here?"

"I see you," she said. "I follow you."

That made me happy—that I, once maligned straggler, could be someone else's guide to discovering the city in unexpected ways. We talked a bit more as we headed down together. She came from China originally. Like me, she had lived in this neighborhood bordering a heretofore unseen river for more than twenty years.

Newly discovered neighbor. Newly expanded vista. All in the course of a walk.

I didn't tell her that day where I'm from. Though maybe I should have. Because that morning when I walked down an unpromising parking lot and ventured up a deserted path where the road seemed to end, I was walking the way I'd learned how to walk, the way I walked as an aberrant kid in Los Angeles, small steps of rebellion leading to discoveries and new connections.

A Walker's Paradise

Mickey Herr

My MISTAKE was attempting to multitask.

By the time my mother had collected too many doctors—each specializing in a different part of her body—we had grown weary of the constant need for follow-up and lab testing. An upcoming cardiologist appointment required a prior blood test, so my brilliant idea was to stop for a quick blood-draw before her radiology check-up. In between point A and point B lay three city blocks and the place I hoped was the key to my plan, Di Bruno Bros., a popular gourmet food emporium my mother could never resist.

My mother woke up cranky. But I reminded her that she enjoyed visiting with the radiology nurse. And if we stopped by the lab *today*, it was one less trip later. And treats. There would be a flaky croissant and a triple-cream brie.

My husband dropped us off at the corner of Ninth and Chestnut streets. We waded through the busy lobby and stood watching people jostle onto over-packed elevators before we finally were able to squeeze into one and make it to the second floor. My mother had graduated to a rollator, a walker with wheels. But she was still a slow walker.

In a busy medical building, she was one of many using a cane, walker, rollator, or pushing a stroller full of children. Everyone was in the same boat. We had the system down. My mother knew which seating area to roll to, as I entered her name at the digital kiosk and walked to the opposite side of the hall for check-in. The phlebotomist called her name and my mom proceeded slowly toward the lab. I never watched the blood draw, but I was well-accustomed to the process. Assorted vials of varying sizes and lid colors were deftly laid out, the rubbery tourniquet applied, a fist made, the prick of a needle, and voilà, you were done. After a quick Band-Aid application she was back in the waiting room. Despite my mother's slow pace, our efficiency left us an hour to spare.

My plan was working. We headed towards Di Bruno's. But first we had to traverse the scary Chestnut Street crosswalk. The illuminated "walk" signs in Center City Philadelphia never stayed lit long enough to allow my mother to cross. I had gotten into the habit of putting myself between the oncoming traffic and my mother. She never seemed to notice. "Focus Mom. Keep going." Once safely on the other side, she wanted to know how many more steps. She was tired. She remembered she was cranky. I pointed to Di Bruno's signage halfway down the block. She started screaming at me. Tears in her eyes. *I don't understand how hard it is. How tired she is. She can't go any further. She won't go any further.* Tired of arguing, of cajoling, I called my husband. He drove the car over, picked us up at one busy intersection, and dropped us off at another a block away.

What my mother hated more than anything was that I *did* understand. I understood complete exhaustion and mind-numbing pain. I understood endless blood-draws and waiting in over-air-conditioned rooms. I understood how one block, one flight of stairs, could feel like an endless mile. Perhaps she hadn't realized what I myself had been through while battling leukemia. How could she? She hadn't been sitting next to me back when my fatigue grew daily as my life became smaller and smaller. As I emptied my calendar and sat in one place all day, watching life happen around me. Despite me. The sleepless nights full of sweat and unexplained bone pain.

My leukemia journey started long before I told my mother, who was blissfully unaware until the day after I was officially diagnosed on my forty-eighth birthday. Because my mom had already been through great loss, I knew my job was to reassure her, even though I was terrified. I had walked to the edge of the cliff and looked down. Was this the end? I protected her from that. We never discussed the ugly bits. That's not what we did.

Yet my leukemia journey was instrumental in opening the door to inviting my mom to come live with my husband and me in our South

Philly row home. She had grown weary of being the widow who tended her garden and an empty suburban house. She was attracted to becoming the "city girl" she'd always dreamed of; and we would have an extra pair of hands and additional income to keep our household running. My illness allowed her to enter "our" household as an equal. Something we both needed. She would have never moved in otherwise. It's only now, looking back, that I can see what transpired. As my mother slowed, I gained speed. The fewer steps she took, the more determined I became to go further. It was the final challenge in our complicated mother-daughter relationship.

In the beginning our steps matched. We walked to dinner. We walked to a movie. We could slow-walk just about anywhere we wanted. I took her to the opera, the orchestra, and the theater. She was a lifelong bridge player, so I found her a group of ladies to join. Our neighborhood is touted as a "walker's paradise" by real estate agents and guidebooks alike. The Italian Market is a big draw. A few blocks from our home, the curbside market became a favorite walk. She befriended produce vendors and store owners who set aside her favorite items. She gossiped with the neighbors along the way.

Before my mother moved in, we knew she required knee replacement surgery. Not a big deal, we told ourselves. After all, from our home, it's an easy walk to both the world-class Rothman Orthopaedic Institute and Jefferson University Hospital. Still, there were some things we didn't think through. Like the fact that when you live in a row home, there are zero bedrooms, and often zero bathrooms, on the first floor. We had to factor a staircase into her recovery. My mother also had an issue with using a cane. Canes were for old people, she thought. In her late seventies, she wasn't ready to look old. Even our definition of an "easy walk" was unrealistic, and ultimately not helpful. For her, those five blocks to her outpatient therapy office were four blocks too far. In due course, though, we regained some semblance of normalcy. If the walk to therapy appointments didn't motivate her, her eagerness to get back out into the neighborhood and reconnect with the gossip on the street and cookies from Isgro's bakery did.

And then came the cancer. Uterine cancer. In the final days of December 2017, my mother had a complete hysterectomy and a bladder lift. It was an almost eight-hour robotic-assisted surgery performed by two specialists. Despite our post-knee-replacement experience, we were still learning how to navigate a senior citizen's medical care. We didn't understand she could benefit from a rehabilitation facility. Before the pain meds had worn off, she was back in her second-floor bedroom. There were other things my husband and I were unaware of back then. And subtler things that I, the daughter, had not yet caught onto. My mother's ability to act, to deflect, and to pretend would reveal themselves in the coming months.

My mother's resistance to using a cane after her knee surgery had been traumatic enough. Now the introduction of a walker, post-cancer surgery, brought on an entirely different level of stress. She believed public use of a walker to be simply impermissible. My husband and I and our wonderful physical therapist coaxed her into walking with varying levels of success. The promise of Taco Tuesday with a margarita might work one week. But not the next.

Days turned into weeks. And suddenly it was June. A significant milestone for my own cancer journey. Despite being told I would remain on life-long leukemia drugs, suddenly the protocols changed, and I was taken off them. Both leukemia and the cancer-fighting drug had similar side effects, the major one being extreme fatigue. Through the years I had learned to conserve my energy and move around as little as possible. Going off the drug changed everything. The fog lifted. I realized I had many survival skills to unlearn. I realized how much I'd missed moving freely around my walker's paradise.

By December 2018 my body really wanted to *move*. I asked for a Fitbit for Christmas. I was on a glorious new unexpected journey. In January 2019 I was wearing my Fitbit 24/7 and tracking my "step" progress. Little by little my daily steps increased from 3,000 to 4,000, then 5,000, and by April I could easily manage 6,000 steps a day. I caught a sunset on the Schuylkill, a lightshow at City Hall, and reintroduced myself to my favorite people-watching spot behind Independence Hall. When it was cold and rainy, I would walk the stairs in my house. Up and down, from the basement to my third-floor bedroom.

"Health is movement," my husband wrote in large letters on the kitchen chalkboard, a message for both my mother and me. But my increased step count had become a counterpoint to my mother's immobility. Despite that encouraging message, my husband and I were struggling to keep my mother walking. She wasn't motivated in the least. She sat at our kitchen table and watched as I diligently tracked every step up and down the stairs.

I recognized this inclination to sit in one place all day. I had done the same thing years earlier in my not-yet-diagnosed leukemia stage. Something was wrong, and my mother was in great denial. Despite her protests I took her to her primary care physician. During the visit, the doctor took me aside and told me to steel myself. With the marked change he witnessed, he assumed the cancer had returned. *She may not have much time,* he told me. I said nothing to her as we awaited the results from all the tests. They came back negative. No cancer. The primary had no answers. He sent us to a cardiologist. We waited another week for the appointment. In the meantime, my mother fell and shattered a glass-front cabinet. She tried to hide it.

The cardiologist's office was in the same building as both Rothman and the gynecologic oncologist. We'd been here before. The same drill. Elevator. Waiting. Tests. Waiting. My mother complaining of feeling cold in one of those too-thin gowns. The doctor arrived. *Houston, we have a problem,* he said by way of introduction. My mother was immediately admitted into the hospital. She'd suffered a "silent" heart attack. Who knows when? My best guess was sometime in early April, when I was celebrating my 6,000 steps a day. Her ten-day hospital stay was followed by two weeks in a rehabilitation facility. We were learning. My mother was never an easy patient. She wasn't self-motivated. She looked to me for acquiescence. She wanted me to join her in the alternate world she was creating in her head. That place where she didn't have to do anything differently, and it was all going to be okay. She wanted me to protect her from the challenges and expectations of the PT and OT staff. I gave her the opposite. I didn't know how to be that soft person for her. "My mother didn't raise me that way," I teased her.

While she was rehabilitating, I was processing. I wrote in my journal and I walked. I wrote. And I walked. Mostly I walked. It turns out I walked 58 miles in the first 15 days of May. Back and forth from home to the hospital, and from home to the rehab facility, each one-way trip less than a mile. I wrote down what I couldn't say to my mother.

Earlier, right before I took her to the cardiologist, when I already believed she was full of cancer and short on time, I attended my weekly meditation group. Before we began, we each picked an "Angel Card" from a basket. The card holds a single word, that week's mantra. That night, my card said "Clarity."

Yet it would take weeks before the clarity came.

That's what I wrote in my journal, where I said all I couldn't say directly to my mother.

16 May 2019

. . . I've tried to have faith in the fact that I am not in control. This is your life. How do I make this okay for you? Less scary? I know you are scared. How does it feel to see your options narrow? We can do this. Or that. But your choices don't include the life you imagined for yourself. You never pictured yourself old, restricted, unable to get around. Yet here we are.

I was troubled by something else too, something deeper, that I couldn't discuss with her. Before we learned the severity of her health condition, before she was admitted to the hospital, I'd felt the veil grow quite thin. That veil between life and death. I'd felt my father's presence. My grandfather. My aunt. All those dear ones I imagined would be waiting for her on the other side. I told my husband. He understood. But I couldn't tell my mom. Even though I wanted to comfort her, to say "you are not alone," I knew from previous conversations that she'd accuse me of just wanting her to die.

Of course I did not want her to die. But she couldn't continue to live in the untenable dreamworld she was constructing. I needed her to be realistic about the road ahead. That road would be difficult, especially after the doctors discovered an underlying kidney condition. She was actually in both heart *and* kidney failure. Movement, especially walking, would be key to her recovery.

Meanwhile, my own road to recovery became smoother. In June 2019 I celebrated one year "in remission" with no cancer drugs. The first big hurdle overcome. By the second week of July my Fitbit died and needed to be replaced. By the end of that month, I was walking more than 10,000 steps nearly every day. My mother, though, was not walking. After the in-home care folks completed their scheduled sessions, she got stubborn. She would argue and claim it was too hot to walk. *I will do it tomorrow*, she'd say.

Tomorrow. How many did she have left? Exasperated, we arranged outpatient PT sessions. Twice a week, my husband drove her the eight blocks there and back. He also printed up "Daily Walking" sheets to help track her exercise. Though, really, the charts were an exercise in proving our point that she wasn't even trying. Which we did: for *one* week in June, she filled in three days of information.

Along with her failing heart and kidneys, I started to notice her brain was faltering too. People would tell me how spry my mother was. So cute. So charming. Yes, I thought, a brilliant actress. I had never before realized her particular talent for pretending. She'd regale a friend about taking me dress shopping in downtown Philly when I was getting ready for kindergarten. A great story, except we lived in Los Angeles at that time. She would conflate time and place and get angry if I tried to correct the memory.

In August I took her for geriatric testing. After hours of testing, two doctors informed us that her loss of brain function went well beyond the typical aging process. She didn't listen to a word. They handed me a bunch of pamphlets on things like Alzheimer's and instructed me to get her to a community center for activities. They also asked me to take her for an audiology evaluation. They thought hearing aids would help slow her now-quickening decline. My mother was pissed. The indignity of it all was too much for her to bear.

By Labor Day she refused to get out of bed. I made an appointment with her primary for September 4th. That day, my husband wasn't home and I could barely get her dressed and down the stairs. It was as if her batteries had run out. I ended up calling an ambulance. She was readmitted to the hospital. It wasn't another heart attack. It was a bleeding ulcer. They changed her meds and sent her back to rehab. She ended up staying almost six weeks. This time, I'd really learned. I was adamant that she couldn't return home until she could walk a flight of stairs three times a day. Our kitchen was on the first floor, her bedroom and bathroom on the second. If she wanted three meals a day, she was required to walk downstairs. House rules. The PT folks at rehab responded with amazing patience and firmness. They learned my mom's tricks—her avoidance tactics—and got her moving. They upgraded her to the rollator. I attended as many PT sessions as I could to cheer her on and perhaps learn some tricks to keep her motivated. She seemed finally to be embracing the fact that her days of walking freely were gone.

Progress? Perhaps. Yet I was grappling with loss too. "This is not my mother," I wrote in my journal that September. "I don't want her to live a life full of all the things she always said she never wanted."

19 September 2019

. . . What is here for me to hold onto? What lesson am I supposed to find? I wanted peace for you. Simplicity. A nodding off in the garden on a breezy afternoon. Not this. Ugliness. Anger . . . Is the lesson that I cannot do anything? I cannot help. I cannot bring peace to the moment. She lives in a dream world thinking about some magic time when she'll be well again. I don't see it. I can't see it. Am I the one with no vision? Or a realist? I want her to find peace. It's all okay, mom. Let go.

My step count kept rising, some days topping 14,000. Back and forth to rehab day after day. A perpetual cycle: pick up mom's laundry, take it home, wash it, fold it, and deliver it back to her. There was one day in October, I walked 18,282 steps. I began to loathe that walk. On hot days there was little relief from the sun. My arms were always full of laundry. The days blurred as I tried to hold together some sense of my own life and work schedule.

She finally came back home after forty-two days—it was now mid-October. She promised she'd keep working hard. She promised she'd walk daily and work with PT. A week later I picked the "resilience" Angel Card at meditation. Okay. Here's where I will focus. Resilience.

Between Thanksgiving and the New Year we all pretended. I made sure my sister came for Christmas. I decorated my mom's favorite sugar cookies. I kept taking steps. "One step at a time" became my December mantra. I was averaging 10,000 steps a day. We made it through the holidays.

And then, 2020. By mid-January it was obvious my mother was not improving. She was taking no responsibility for her recovery. Now it was too cold to go outside. She worried about "ice" during our snowless, unseasonably warm winter. My husband and I were determined to bring in a home health aide. My mother refused to allow it. We needed help. She claimed we simply needed a house cleaner. We butted heads. But her 83rd birthday was coming up in February. I would make it nice. My husband would make her dinner and we would bake her favorite cookies.

As I had the entire past year, I sat and waited. And watched. I watched her through the heart attack, ulcers, failing kidneys, and brain failure. The craziness, the increased OCD, the manic behavior after midnight. The constant need to check her bank balance despite the fact I had taken over her financial management long ago. The falls she'd suffer trying to get out of bed. The falls I never knew about. Two days after her birthday I called for an ambulance. She was back in the hospital.

I wondered how long this could continue. I walked. I wrote. I tried to process where we were now. Writing it down didn't make me feel any better.

12 February 2020

. . . is this grief? Right now it only feels like anger. <u>ANGER</u>. I need to go to the hospital. What does she need? What do I need? Are we back on this fucking hamster wheel? . . . Has it become my job to break her will? That's what it feels like. I need for her to see reality. What is reality? Where are we? Really?

I walked to the hospital, where the doctors reported that everything was great. Really? I channeled my best Shirley MacLaine *Terms of Endearment* moment. I yelled at the doctors. I cried through my frustration. *Someone needs to be real here. You are going to tell me that my mother is suffering from all these failing systems and all is well? Just another medication adjustment and she'll be good as new?* I asked if I could talk to someone from palliative care. A lovely palliative specialist promised she'd work with the doctors and get someone to have an honest discussion with my mom, to tell her how bad things had gotten.

The next day my mom was discharged back into rehab.

Two days later, on February 17th, I texted a friend:

. . . I keep praying for some grace somewhere. But it never appears. I need to fight to get her some. I am fucking exhausted.

Grace was nowhere to be found. My faith that I could find dignity for my mother wasn't that strong to begin with. I was in the room when both my father and my father-in-law died. One was quick and gruesome. The other was slow, painful, and gruesome. Neither was peaceful.

The next twenty-three days were no better.

I must have repeated "one step at a time" to myself a thousand times. PT did get my mom out of bed and walking. But she would never be able to return home. The stairs to her second-floor bed and bathroom were now beyond her. I was the one who had to tell her.

Don't leave me, she said. She was terrified. Even though she had always told me that she never wanted me to be her caregiver, that she'd rather have a stranger take care of the private things. Her worst nightmare had always been being abandoned in a nursing home. Something she often reminded me. *Don't leave me.*

I reassured her that we'd found a luxurious assisted living arrangement. She would have a private room with 24/7 nursing staff. The dining room had beautiful views of the Swann Fountain at Logan Circle. I could meet her for Happy Hour and join her for dinner. It was less than two miles from our home.

I reassured myself too. I envisioned this as my daily exercise—walking back and forth to visit my mom. I pushed her to work harder with PT. To realize this dream, she had to be able to walk on her own with her rollator. She had to be able to perform some very basic functions without help, or else she wouldn't be allowed in. We paid a large down payment and started to move her belongings. And then she took another downturn. Unexplained. Wednesday, March 11th, I had a late-morning appointment with staff to discuss what might happen if she couldn't make it into assisted living. I stopped by my mother's room. It was completely empty. All her belongings had been cleared out. Except for her top dentures, which sat naked on the bedside table.

The staff was in a panic, preparing for COVID-19. After the initial confusion and much redress I was taken to my mother's new room on the long-term nursing floor—the place you check in but never leave. I was told to spend time with her now, because after today I wouldn't be allowed back in the building. Pandemic protocols were now in place. Even in her haze, my mother knew a big decision had been made. She knew she was in a different room. I called my sister for a video chat. It was painful. I tried to explain this COVID crisis. Nothing I said registered. My mom was simultaneously in denial, terrified, and pissed off. I said my final goodbye. I don't even remember what I said. What could I say? I didn't know when I would be coming back.

All of my mother's worst nightmares had come true. She was abandoned. Alone. The next morning, she had an aide call me from her bedside landline. *Where was I? Was I in the building?* Fury. Tears. There was nothing I could say. Nothing short of my showing up in her room was going to soothe her. She hung up on me.

Less than twenty-four hours later, at four in the morning, March 13, I got a call from her nurse. My mother was dead.

In those weeks before her death, while pushing my mom to get up and walk, I found myself trying to recall the circumstances of my own first steps. By the time I got around to thinking about it, the one person who could have filled in the blanks had already lost the memory of it. Her mind had gone. And now she had too. Of course, she was there when I took that first step. Chances are, it was likely just the two of us in the room. Yet I don't recall my mother ever mentioning it. According to the information she recorded in my baby book, I walked at eleven months.

I was the second of my mother's two children. My sister was six by the time I started walking. She remembers nothing. And truthfully, her memories of childhood overlap very little with my own. Our father was a huge presence in our lives, yet he wasn't present for many of the everyday things. What I realize now is that my mom and I spent a lot of time alone together. I have a sense my mom was impatient for me to learn to walk. It wasn't that my mother was uncaring or cold. It's just that she liked to be left alone. She had things to do. She had flowers to tend. She usually had a book she was in the midst of reading.

A few days after my mother died, we walked out of the funeral home. A box of ashes in hand. A fancy wooden box with a brass plaque. We didn't ask for such a box, since we were planning to spread her ashes. Eventually. I think the funeral director needed to do something nice, given the times we were headed into.

What I needed was to go for a walk. To be purposeful. We were officially in pandemic lockdown, yet people were still out and about. Picking up supplies for the unknown storm ahead and trying to figure out what it all meant. It was sunny and warm for mid-March. A perfect day in our walker's paradise. We decided to go pick up lunch, so my husband and I, along with my mom in her new earthly form, headed to a place known for its pork sandwiches. By the time we arrived, the sandwiches were sold out. But the bakery side still had treats. Which seemed right, given my mom's penchant for baked goods. Suddenly I had a craving for a nice flaky croissant.

We had walked a mile in the opposite direction from home. During our slow meander back, I pondered stopping for cheese. But it was getting late and I was hungry for my croissant. Once back home I pulled the butter dish from the fridge and poured a glass of red wine. I moved a bouquet of flowers and my mom's ashes to the kitchen table. It was time for rest.

The Body Resistant

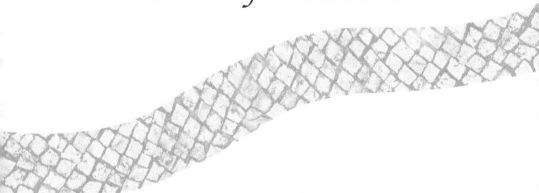

Incremental Man

Jay Heinrichs

ON THE EVENING of December 31, five hours before the year ticked over into 2019, I stood in our backyard with my wife and grown son and watched my sparkler fizz its last. "Well," I said. "Happy New Year." I turned to go inside, and my right foot skated on a patch of ice while the left stayed in place and torqued a perfect spiral up the two main bones from ankle to knee. My wife, Dorothy, swears she heard the crack. In an instant I went from holding my spent sparkler to lying crumpled on frozen ground. And at that moment my life began improving in tiny steps.

Oh, but trust me, this is not a broken-leg story; though, when you get to the end, you might legitimately label it a how-I-walked-with-my-hands story. In any case, the moral has to do with increments—"steps" if you like—and how they might offer a slow, meandering path in the general direction of wisdom.

To test that moral, we need to go twenty-five years into the past, before a moment that may well have been my life's apogee. It was when I found myself in mid-air, momentarily suspended over a couple making love.

IN THE LATE 1980s, I became a trail runner before I even knew the sport existed. Dorothy likes to believe I invented it. We had bought a house on the Appalachian Trail where it wanders up Moose Mountain in rural New Hampshire. I began running up the trail in late spring, when the frogs and woodcocks peeped and *peent*-ed their love songs and the ferns formed their perfect fiddleheads and the light stayed hopeful like a toddler who wouldn't go to bed.

Dorothy had blessed my evening escapes, sort of. I worked long hours at Dartmouth College while she cared for a two-year-old and a new baby far from her idea of civilization. When I finally came home from work, all she wanted was some adult company and help with the kids. But I had yearned all through my suburban childhood for the woods and lichen-covered ledges of northern mountains. And here I finally was in paradise; a buggy paradise, with thirsty blackflies and changeable weather, but my own ideal North Country, one that bent the Appalachian Trail around my very own yard.

Dorothy agreed to forgo adult company for a quarter hour each evening while I walked up the trail into the woods, checking my watch. The first few times, I turned back after seven and a half minutes. After a couple of weeks, we extended my time to twenty minutes, then half an hour.

The trouble was, every time I was supposed to turn around, something up the trail would tempt me: a giant boulder covered with bright red fruiting bodies called British Soldiers. Three baby raccoon faces peeking from an ancient oak. A muskrat sliding down a brook. More morsels lay farther and farther up, and I lacked the discipline to resist them. I would walk too far and then tear back down the trail to get home in time. After some weeks, I began running *up* the trail so I could see what lay beyond the point I had reached before—and discovered that I liked not just the exploring but the feel of flowing through this lush green tunnel.

In the years that followed, when both kids were in school, my routine extended to running up Moose Mountain two or three times a week and exploring every trail wearing nothing but soccer shorts and basketball shoes. Along the way I experienced first-rate adventures. I startled numerous bears and once almost ran into a moose; the animal blinked myopically and pondered my place in its universe while I plunged off-trail through a patch of thornberries.

It was while bombing down a narrow old logging skid road on the side of Moose Mountain that I reached my apogee. Turning a tight corner at full speed, I spotted a young couple lying a few feet ahead in the middle of the trail. They were locked in the missionary position, the man fully clothed but for a bare heedless bottom, the woman gazing ecstatic at the sky. Entwined in their tight loving world, the two gently heaved amid a pure blue sky and a susurrating stream and a rising, pounding rhythm that sounded like seismic passion but came from basketball shoes as they hit the rocks just above. With no time to think, I hurdled in a graceful arc over the man's backside, soaring through the woman's airspace. Her huge eyes looked like they were tracking an incoming asteroid. Raising my back foot a centimeter to avoid catching on their booted feet and forming an awkward threesome, I vanished down the trail.

That was my peak. In those days I trail-ran with former Olympians. My career was going just as fast; recruiters were talking about my running one of the big men's magazines in New York someday. I wrote two modest-selling books, launched an airline magazine, and commuted eight hundred miles to an office in Greensboro, North Carolina. I wasn't the best at anything, but I was *fast*, knocking out acceptable first drafts of magazine stories, dashing through pre-9/11 airports with just enough time to catch my flights, sketching out lineups while holding staff meetings, then squeezing in fast-hiking quality time with Dorothy and the kids up the four-thousand-foot mountains in New Hampshire. We finished all forty-eight before our youngest turned ten. And I ran mountains on my lonesome.

Was I really happy? Did it matter? I was fast. I was rising. I saw myself as a late-blooming jetsetter ground-truthed by the granite ledges of New Hampshire. Tucking a cigar and matches into a fanny pack, I liked to run to a mountain summit, descend for ten minutes, and sit on a ledge to watch the rising sun. I lit the cigar, took a luxuriant drag, and let the combination of endorphins and oxygen deprivation hit me like the world's biggest bong.

Was I a bit of an asshole? Did it matter?

On a trail-run, your feet perform a repertoire of balletic moves. You stretch your legs out on every relatively flat part, and on the steeps you increase your "turnover," the pace at which your feet hit the ground, to 180 beats per minute, the rhythm of Billy Idol's "Dancing with Myself." When descending from the summit, your gait tightens to tiny, dainty steps to lessen the risk of torquing a leg and snapping the fibula. I was slower on the downhill. The better runners said my technique sucked, but really I was just afraid of falling.

WHEN MY SPARKLER and I hit the ground, I heard a man yell. He kept on yelling, and I realized it was me. I looked at the end of my leg: the foot faced in exactly the wrong direction, Judas-like.

"I'll be back," Dorothy said, and took off. I began doing the Lamaze breathing we had learned in birthing classes—*hee hee haaww, hee hee hawww* . . .

"How you doing, Daddo?" George, thirty, peered into my face and looked at my eyes. He had training as a wilderness EMT.

"Not going into shock. Yet," I said, forcing a smile.

Dorothy steered the car into the backyard and stopped a couple feet away. George threw the door open, picked me up bodily, and laid my 165 pounds as gently as he could on the car seat. My foot hit something and I screamed, then Lamazed like I was birthing quintuplets. "Freezing rain," Dorothy said, gripping the steering wheel hard. Then she looked at me and smiled. "I called Dorothy Junior while I was shutting things down. She's getting others to take her shift and she'll drive up first thing tomorrow." Our daughter, a rapid response nurse in the largest hospital in Washington, D.C., has always been rapid and responsive.

I spent three nights in the hospital, getting a fourteen-inch nail down my leg and feeling ridiculously happy. It wasn't the drugs, which proved disappointing. Dorothy Junior says morphine is fun only when you're not in pain. It was something else. But it would take me many slow weeks of recovery to discern just what it was.

SOON AFTER my glorious suspended moment above the lovemakers on Moose Mountain, after thirteen years in New Hampshire, we moved to Santa Fe, New Mexico, so I could work at a prestigious magazine and avoid the long commute. I ended up seeing my family less than when I was working in North Carolina. I would homeschool Dorothy Junior at six in the morning before getting to work at eight, rarely getting home before eleven at night. Worse, I came to realize that I did not want to be a bigshot magazine editor in New York. The job would entail dashing around to advertisers in the day and attending parties sponsored by booze conglomerates, all while wearing fashion advertisers' clothing— the oil-slickest of fast lanes. Suddenly I no longer saw my future as a brilliant series of accomplishments but as a foreign country, a place that would never seem home. New Hampshire was home.

Dorothy calls that time our diaspora. We wanted nothing more than to get back to the familiar mountains and comforting woods. Mean-while, we bought a house in Connecticut and I took a job with an internet startup at the height of the dot-com frenzy. Then came the 9/11 terrorist attacks and the loss of our funding. I found myself unemployed, without health insurance, paying a ridiculous mortgage. A loser, by definition. I now know the clinical term for what I felt: "toxic shame," a compo-nent of clinical depression. Psychologist Bernard Golden describes the feeling as "a paralyzing global assessment of oneself as a person." In my case, the self-assessment seemed pretty accurate. After schlepping my family back and forth across the country in pursuit of my—I was going to say ambition, but call it what it was, pure ego—we were living where we didn't want to live, burning through our savings. When I managed to get off by myself, on long runs along the coast, I would find myself crying. Nothing in particular would trigger it; I would just feel this ter-rible rage, and this overwhelming shame. I remembered that I had cried a lot as an unathletic, overly dramatic kid; my siblings, in justified if cruel exasperation, called me Fat Baby. Now doubled over and sobbing while pretending to examine a horseshoe crab on the Fairfield beach, I flashed back to those times as a kid and realized exactly what I felt: rage and shame. Dr. Golden, an anger management specialist, says the two often go hand in clenched-fist hand.

My income got rescued by a job offer, overseeing five magazines in Emmaus, Pennsylvania, and New York City. I shuttled among three states, worried about newsstand sales, and schmoozed advertisers. I got up early every day to train for a marathon, resuming my type-A life, doing what's expected, running through the pain.

The pain: life actually hurt. While my restoration to breadwinner status relieved the financial anxiety, the depression stubbornly stuck with me. I forced myself to get up in the morning twilight, made myself run intervals in a park across from my apartment, and told sobbing laid-off editors that they no longer had a job. I had no real idea of what depression was, except that other people had it, but I had lost interest in everything. The pain grew increasingly hard to bear, and I began hearing a persistent argument in my head: Which was the greater act of cowardice—making my family suffer living with a miserable, angry, mostly absent father? Or stepping away from this life, leaving them with no father at all? My journalistic instincts stepped in, and I dealt with the question by obsessively researching it. Squirreling myself away in my office after hours to find more and more effective forms of suicide, I found a number of painless ways to stop living. This obsession made me feel more ashamed, which made me more depressed, which led to more research in self-offing, until one day I walked into the office of my close friend Steve, a colleague at the publishing company.

"I have something to tell you, but I need you to swear to keep it to yourself."

He nodded. "I swear."

And I told him what I was thinking about.

He said, "I'm going to break my promise. I'm calling Dorothy." She immediately arranged an appointment with a doctor and had Dorothy Junior drive me to it, knowing that I couldn't duck out from my indomitable twenty-year-old daughter. The doctor put me on medication. I stopped thinking about suicide and went back to work.

What helped me most, though—what made me better—wasn't so much the meds but the decision to tell Steve. Of *course* he would break his promise. All along I knew which was the more cowardly of my life-or-death choices; I'd just been too much of a coward to tell my wife directly. From that point on, I figured every day was a sort of lagniappe, an extra. I had seriously contemplated the worst. Compared to that, the rest of my life, with all its disappointments and failures, seemed positively blessed.

Dorothy told me to quit. She said it was time I moved back to New Hampshire and wrote a book I had been talking about forever. We moved into an 1810 farmhouse at the base of bald Cardigan Mountain, and I wrote the book. Dorothy went back onto the job market and within two years was vice president of development at a law school. The kids graduated from college, fell in love, and took on careers of their own. I hiked, skied on my own land, wrote a couple more books, and Dorothy and I settled into our empty nest. I was happy, probably happier than I had ever been; but I don't think I entirely realized the fact. My ego stepped in again, reminding me of the young man who considered himself . . . not awesome, but future-awesome. Someone his high school classmates would hear about someday.

So I kept running. Figuring that maybe I could make myself the athlete I'd longed to be, I spent nine months training to be the first recorded person over fifty to "run my age" up Mount Moosilauke, a classic trail-running peak an hour from my house. That meant running to the summit in fewer minutes than I was old in years. Only a dozen people had run their age on that mountain, and none of them was over fifty. During those nine months I lost twenty-eight pounds, trained up to four hours a day, read books of physiology, and stalked experts. On my fifty-eighth birthday, I ran the mountain in less than fifty-five minutes, getting virtually younger by several years.

The only thing was, I had run the mountain ten minutes faster back when I was forty. I had reset my apogee by cheating, using a different measurement. Still, it was satisfying to know that I still had enough type-A in my character to succeed in a goal so gloriously, dramatically pointless. I called my feat a *hyperbole*, a trope that comes from the Greek for "throw beyond." I wanted the rest of my life to be like that: to project my mind or ambition beyond what seemed possible and then dash after it like a dog after a ball. Sprinters say that to win a race you must accelerate through the finish line. I wanted to accelerate through to the end, somehow. And then came New Year's Eve and the downward acceleration to a dead stop.

As I sat in the car that New Year's Eve, everything pulled in. I had no peripheral vision. No thought about whether I'd ever be able to trail-run again. Everything focused on the pain.

The car lurched and bumped on our mountain road, which at that time of year becomes more frost heave than road. With every sway and wobble, I felt a wave of electric pain travel up my leg and into my heaving stomach. Doctors later told us the bone just missed bursting through the skin. The car's movement sent bone scraping against nerves. I Lamazed and Lamazed and thought, "Stay on top of it," meaning the pain. "Stay on top of it."

"That's right," George said. "Stay on top of it."

"You heard that?" Apparently I had lost my internal monologue. "We almost there?"

Dorothy grimaced. "We're at the end of our road. We've been gone five minutes."

"Hee hee haaaawwwwww," I replied.

This was, in some weird way, a challenge. All my worries traveled down to my left leg, compacted into bursts of pain. This was physical, purely physical, and it felt . . . liberating. The last time I had felt this way was some thirty years before, when my sister called, saying our mother had died. Mom and I were close, and while the news wasn't unexpected, I wasn't sure I could bear it. This was pain I didn't know how to stay on top of. After getting off the phone, I got on my bike and rode down a long steep hill to a lake, then turned around and climbed back up. I stood from the saddle, pumping hard, and thought: *This is physical. The pain is just pain.* I had never felt this degree of grief before. But grief is pain. I knew how to deal with pain. At that moment, I knew I could bear Mom's death.

A broken leg? This was nothing. Not grief-pain, not shame-pain, not depression-pain. Just pain.

Everything after that was a series of tiny accomplishments. I managed to joke with the E.R. doctor. After surgery, I almost succeeded in getting out of bed before the nurse caught me. After that, a series of even greater firsts: Wheelchair speed record. First time sliding on my butt from car to house after Dorothy drove me home from the hospital. First time using a walker. Every day a first. I had become the world's latest-blooming toddler.

Have you ever tried to use a walker? You wonder how elderly people manage it. In this gadget-filled age, when robots run up stairs and drones deliver packages and our watches tell us when to breathe, a walker seems like a cheap steampunk movie prop. Four legs, a pair of handles, that's it. Feel free to accessorize with tennis balls. Even the name is misleading. The walker does no walking. You have to pick it up or slide it to go anywhere. Proper form does not mean hunching over it like Harvey Weinstein; instead you should stay upright, lift the whole contraption off the ground, swing it legs-first ahead of you, then catch up. I kept my bum leg cocked behind me and used my good leg to push off in a hopping motion. Once or twice I hopped too far and almost did a walker Endo, toppling end-over-end. After a successful hop, I would put all my weight on the handles, working my triceps, then swing my good leg forward and repeat the process. A wholly challenging, athletic, fast-twitch, high-intensity exercise, and every day I got better at it.

Soon after, I started walking with my hands. Crawling Marine-style into our mud entry, I maneuvered myself onto a plastic sled, sat up facing forward, and used my hands to push out of our mud entry onto a snow-covered ramp that a friend had built for me. I savored the sweet cold air. The day after that, I pushed myself partway down our snow-covered drive. The day after that, I paddled two hundred feet to the cabin behind our house, where I have my office, sliding backward up the steps and opening the door all by myself.

At the end of each day, my face hurt from smiling. My mother had once told me I was the happiest toddler, and I was beginning to see why.

Toddling is a series of small, silly, brilliant triumphs, each lurching step a miracle.

Next day, I paddled a quarter mile to the top of our meadow and a quarter mile back.

Next day, I paddled down to the brook, got trapped in deep snow between low spruce branches, and lay wet and cold and laughing with the knowledge that I could still do something stupid outdoors.

Next day, I told my wife how grateful I was for her.

Next day, I told her I loved her.

Soon after, I graduated to crutches. I bought spikes that fit onto the tips so I could walk outside. With microspikes—a sort of crampon—on my one shoe, the devices let me walk down our long drive and up a country road. Every day I walked a little farther.

After six weeks, the surgeon gave his reluctant okay for me to fly to Seattle. Pre-break, I had booked a Nordic ski trip with my son to the legendary Methow Valley, four hours' drive from the city. Now, instead of skate-skiing on some of the most beautifully groomed snow in North America, I spent eight days on George's couch. But on the way over, strangers in airports showed a degree of kindness I had never seen directed at me. Case in point: I had to switch planes at DFW, and my wheelchair attendant pushed me onto the monorail between terminals. It was Presidents' Day weekend, and the airport filled up with leisure travelers. At one stop, more people got on, packing the car. My leg was propped up sticking straight ahead. A woman carrying a heavy bag with long straps on her shoulder stood beside me—early seventies, an infrequent flier judging by her luggage and the way she wielded it. I eyed her bag, preparing for the worst. The car lurched forward and she swayed into me, gripping the rail overhead. Her bag swung and I grabbed it, steering it away from my leg while unintentionally pulling the poor woman down. Using my other hand to keep her from falling onto me, I unconsciously formed a fist. And so I yanked an elderly woman to the floor while punching her in the ribs.

And she apologized to me.

Part of my happiness came from all that kindness—from my remarkably resourceful family, from their unquestioning willingness to drop everything for an imperfect father, and from the altruism of strangers like that poor lovely woman.

Post-break, it occurred to me that true gratitude—a term that has become so self-helpish that it makes my teeth hurt—comes not so much from counting your blessings as from thinking that you don't deserve any of them. Your blessings come from having your sins forgiven and your past lives rewarded; from your hard-working ancestors; from dumb, heedless luck.

But it wasn't just the kindness that made me feel happier than I can remember. It was the realization that every day was a tiny improvement over the last, and that if I acted on this awareness, it could continue to improve in exquisitely slow time, in small steps, at walking pace, until my very last day.

When the snow melted that spring, I got back on the mountain for the first time, walking partway up on deer-thin legs. A few days later I managed to walk a third of the way up. A week after that, I summited with Dorothy. Standing on the mountain's bald top, I turned to her and quoted Ed Hillary: "Well, we knocked the bastard off." This did not sound grandiose at the time.

I came to realize that the trope of sprinting through life's finish line makes little sense when you get older. Not that you have to forgo a toddler's experience of succeeding triumphs. You just need to reacquire the toddler's joy of walking, advancing, exploring. Getting better somehow. This idea has come to me later in life than it probably does to wiser people. A few studies seem to show that those in their sixties are experiencing their most joyful decade. My older friends say that happiness often continues well into the seventies until loved ones die and the body begins to give over. Maybe that sweet spot, the golden era, results from giving up the climb. With some strange exceptions (recent presidential candidates), most of us have less to prove. We don't have to be sexually attractive, or display our wealth, or gain power. We need not run; we can walk.

Which leads to another trope. When you walk, you shed where you have been. Your progress—time itself—is Heraclitus's river. Turn around, and it's a new path. I sometimes get gloriously lost on my own land, despite having covered every square foot of its hundred and fifty acres. Beavers build a new dam and flood a trail. A tree falls and changes the flow of a brook. Wildlife comes and goes and comes again. Rocks from 200-year-old walls get tossed by insect-hunting bears. A patch of snow reveals itself in May below a glacial erratic boulder, never to be seen again. Each time I stop, the clock stops with me, then starts anew. Every break allows an entirely new set of firsts: newly revealed kindnesses, new discoveries of my aging body, new ideas. Losses, gains—these are all steps. Forward, backward, all steps.

My leg won't let me trail-run just yet, maybe never. It's been a year and a half since the break, and while walking up mountains seems a breeze, running them sets off a chain of WTF reactions in the nerves of my leg. My surgeon says that titanium is less forgiving than bone; it makes running feel like driving with bad shocks. But then, my life no longer revolves around running. Last July, for the fifth year in a row, George and I made our annual hike up the Falling Waters Trail to the Franconia Ridge in New Hampshire's White Mountains. As always, we hit the trailhead at four-thirty in the morning, walking up the sides of cascades in the dark, and, at six, getting one of the world's great ridges to ourselves and covering three beautiful peaks before reaching the Greenleaf Hut, a high-mountain hostel, for breakfast. The first time we did it seemed like an achievement. The second through fourth times, a tradition. This last time . . . this last time was the first of its kind. It was the first time I felt I didn't deserve any of it—my health, a son who flew across a continent to hike with his dad, the mountains, my titanium-rod-enabled leg. I had thought we would never do this again.

Even the most familiar path seems newer than ever, because I have faith in every novel delight hiding around the next turn. If the time comes when I can't physically walk, I now know to make it a break, a reset, when everything becomes new. And when my body quits entirely it will be the ultimate break, and I hope I'll be ready for that biggest step of all.

The Effort in the Image

ON SEEING CÉZANNE'S *THE LARGE BATHERS* FROM A RENTED WHEELCHAIR

Victoria Reynolds Farmer

In the days before my first-ever trip to London, many friends and acquaintances asked me if I was excited to go. I responded that I was; my husband and I had planned this trip to celebrate our having finally paid off the loans incurred on the way to my earning a doctorate in British Renaissance literature. But now, I confessed, I was apprehensive: How would it feel to be in buildings and spaces that I had spent so much of my life studying, like Westminster Abbey and the Tower of London, and to walk in the footsteps of some of the writers and thinkers that had most shaped my work, like Elizabeth I and Virginia Woolf? Or roll in them, as the case may be. As someone with spastic diplegic cerebral palsy, I generally get around without aids. Since vacations require a lot more walking than everyday life, I had decided to use a chair while sightseeing. That wasn't the source of my apprehension, though. "There's a part of my brain that thinks these things don't actually exist," I said, over and over, to my friends, "so seeing them might be kind of surreal."

It wasn't until we got there that I fully understood how London, an old city, was not built with accessibility in mind. My husband spent

"The Effort in the Image" is adapted from an essay published online in *Plough*, August 10, 2020.

lots of time lugging the wheelchair up and down Tube station steps as I walked behind him. I felt betrayed by a place I had wanted to be in for so long. In our first couple of days touring the city, I thought often of Virginia Woolf. The majority of my academic research as a Renaissance scholar incorporated feminist theory, and Woolf's writings in that vein had influenced me deeply, especially her hypothetical musings on the life of "Shakespeare's sister" in *A Room of One's Own*. My first experience reading that text as an undergraduate taught me that looking closely for the stories that *don't* get told is just as important as being able to argue intelligently about the stories that texts do tell—sometimes even more important.

I was thinking about Woolf's invisible stories one morning when we were on our way to tour the Victoria and Albert Museum. We could not get on the first bus that stopped for us because each bus had room for only one wheelchair-using passenger at a time. The driver opened the door and yelled this explanation out to us. Because the bus had stopped without picking anybody up, some of the passengers near the door stared out at me from inside. I felt conspicuous and embarrassed, simultaneously invisible and too visible. I remembered a bit of Woolf's essay "Street Haunting," in which she offers snapshots of what it is like to walk unaccompanied in London:

> A fine spring day. I walked along Oxford St. The buses are strung on a chain. People fight & struggle. Knocking each other off the pavement. Old bareheaded men; a motor car accident, &c. To walk alone in London is the greatest rest.

I was used to viewing Woolf as an ally against the oppressive norm. In that moment, though, I felt unmoored. The boisterous, noisy norm she described literally didn't have room for me. I was between the links of the chain—walking alone, but neither walking nor alone. Greatest rest didn't enter into the equation at all.

This trip was mostly mine—the capstone to my experience of earning a doctoral degree. Since I was picking most of the things we did and saw, while my husband pushed or picked up my wheelchair, I didn't feel right questioning the one thing he really wanted to experience while on our trip: dinner at Dans le Noir? He had heard about this restaurant, where you eat, as its name suggests, entirely in the dark, years before. A musician he likes had mentioned eating there, and he had wanted to visit ever since. The London restaurant is one of only ten of its kind in the world, and who knew when we would have the opportunity (or the budget) again?

All perfectly reasonable, and yet I was still deeply hesitant. I don't do a great job at walking in crowded restaurants when I *can* see where I'm going, much less in total darkness. I called the restaurant in advance to ask about accessibility, and was reassured that I would be well taken care of. Even so, I still worried. When reading reviews, I noted that to walk from the restaurant's lit antechamber into the dark dining room one places one's hand on another diner's shoulder—as if in a sort of conga line—and moves slowly to the table. Walking in the dark while touching strangers was not something I looked forward to.

The evening of our dinner reservation came. It was time to face my fear. We lined up with the six other couples who would be seated at our table. I was behind a man named Emanuel who was there celebrating his girlfriend's birthday. I placed my right hand on his right shoulder, as instructed. We followed our server, Nadeen, at the head of the line, who, like all servers at Dans le Noir?, was blind. I was heartened by the restaurant's commitment to inclusion, which is in keeping with the social model of disability. As opposed to the medical model, which frames disability as something to be overcome by the disabled person individually, the social model places the onus of change on society. Even though I was initially anxious, I was heartened to spend some time in a place that reinforced my own view that disability is not an inherently negative state of existence. Rather, we disabled people can positively experience the world in a way others do not. Dans le Noir?'s waitstaff are especially suited to navigating the restaurant due to the work they have already done to adapt to a seeing world, and the restaurant recognizes this.

As a sighted person, I found that I had to reinterpret my own experiences with disability in that context. I was surprised at how difficult it was for me to judge the distance from my plate to my mouth. A few times, I stabbed myself with my fork, then struggled to stay silent and hide that I was having trouble. Meanwhile, one woman announced that she was just going to eat with her hands; no one could see her anyway. That made me feel better about my own ineptitude with the fork—momentarily. I quickly shifted from being comforted by her remarks to feeling frustrated. That she could just decide to do away with table manners without being judged spoke to her privilege. She was free of the pressure that disabled people often feel not to stand out, not to be a burden, not to take up too much space. I became determined to learn to use my fork in the dark.

Another thing that gave me pause was a joke that Nadeen made during dinner, one that she had obviously made many times before. When a couple told her that they were there on a blind date, she quickly responded, "*Every* date is a blind date for me!" I laughed along with the rest of the table, but I was disoriented. In this circumstance, I was passing as an able-bodied person, when what I really wanted to do—and couldn't—was connect with Nadeen in a way that showed I understood the need to make such a joke first, before someone else does it at our expense. And that was a huge reframing of a central facet of my identity relative to those around me.

OUR DINNER at Dans le Noir? shadowed me later that week as we toured Westminster Abbey and I searched for the tomb of Aphra Behn. "All women together ought to let flowers fall upon the tomb of Aphra Behn," exhorts Virginia Woolf in Chapter Four of *A Room of One's Own*, "for it was she who earned them the right to speak their minds." Women ought to do this, says Woolf, because Behn is the first woman in British history to support herself with money earned by writing. I'd wanted to experience this place since the first time I'd read *A Room of One's Own* as a precocious high schooler. Behn's memorial isn't in Poet's Corner proper, but off in a side hallway. One of Woolf's central questions—who gets to tell their own stories and why—weighed heavily on my mind. When I asked a tour guide where to find Behn's grave, she remarked, "That's not one we get asked about often." I knew that somewhere, the ghost of Virginia Woolf was smiling knowingly, or maybe rolling her eyes. Anonymous was a woman, indeed. I couldn't get the wheelchair down the corridor, so I hopped out and walked, all the while hyper-aware of the discordant echo my slightly uneven steps added to such a sacred space devoted to people who seemed so much larger than me.

My husband stayed behind, partly to guard the chair, and partly, I knew, to let me have a moment alone with one of my feminist foremothers. Though I didn't dare actually bring flowers, I did manage to snap a quick (technically forbidden) picture of the monument itself to commemorate the moment. In the picture, you can see the inscription on the black stone inlaid into the floor if you look closely. It reads, "Here lies a Proof that Wit can never be Defence enough against Mortality." Not only does this quotation reflect the kind of wry humor that pops up frequently in Behn's plays, it also undeniably hammers home the fact that Behn was, in addition to being a groundbreaking artist, a mortal human—an embodied person whose time-transcendent intellect was, for better or worse, tethered to a body that was subject to age, pain, decay, and death, as all bodies are. Looking at Behn's monument, I thought again of Nadeen's easy joke at her own expense, and of the many times I had made similar ones to ease the discomfort of able-bodied people. If you look even closer at my picture of the gravestone, you can see my reflection, too.

While at Westminster Abbey, I had one more experience that made me reconsider my relationship to the women who came before me. I was able to spend a minute at the tomb of Queens Mary I and Elizabeth I. As is typical of feminist scholars of sixteenth-century British drama (and lots of feminists of the Anglophilic variety in general), I've always been fascinated with Elizabeth I. In 1588, when speaking to the troops at Tilbury in advance of the defeat of the Spanish Armada, she famously said, "I know I have the body but of a weak and feeble woman; but I have the heart and stomach of a king." Most readings of that statement focus on the gendered juxtaposition Elizabeth sets up, and argue that she is claiming power in a publicly acceptable way by playing to commonly held stereotypes about the inability of women to rule the way men could. I agree with these readings, but because of my own experiences in a body that the world often tells me is inferior, and that I feel is disconnected from my larger spiritual or intellectual experience, I also feel that statement in a different way. I relate to the fragmentation the statement identifies when bodily weakness is connected to emotional strength.

The tomb itself is in a small marble room, and to enter it, you have to walk down a couple of stone steps. I needed to brace myself on the stone walls a bit to get down them, but felt guilty that I had to disobey the markers warning against touching anything in the chamber. Once again, I felt like my body couldn't act in a way befitting the space. I knew that the two queens lay entombed next to one another, and that their side-by-side graves make a powerful political statement. Elizabeth was Protestant and Mary Catholic during the Protestant Reformation, a time of deep religious unrest in England and in all of Europe. Though Mary goes down in history as "Bloody Mary" for ordering the execution of thousands of Protestants, Elizabeth largely escapes blame for anti-Catholic violence. Her public position claimed that she didn't care what people believed in their hearts, only that they outwardly assented to the Church of England. I was not prepared, though, for two inscriptions I read in the crypt—and how strongly they would move me.

The first inscription, at the base of the queens' monument, reads, translated from Latin, "Partners in throne and grave, here we sleep Elizabeth and Mary, sisters in [the] hope of the Resurrection." As with Aphra Behn's epitaph, this brief inscription, ordered by Elizabeth's successor, King James I, helped me think of these towering political and historical figures as actual people. They were sisters, bonded to one another in family despite their differences, and because they were also partners in the throne, they had a commonality of experience that very few other people could know.

In the same small room is another monument—to the martyrs of the Protestant Reformation, installed much later, in 1977. Its inscription reads, "Near the tomb of Mary and Elizabeth remember before God all those who divided at the Reformation by different convictions laid down their lives for Christ and Conscience' sake." The stone is just large enough to be noticeable in such a crowded place and not very raised. It's much easier to miss, and much less recognizable than the ten modern martyrs over the western door, and maybe that's why it affected me so strongly.

Those words on the martyrs' monument touched me in a deeply personal way. I grew up Protestant, but at the time of my trip to London was early in the process of converting to the Catholic Church. It was a years' long theological journey, and one that I undertook primarily because of an attraction to sacramental theology and the ways that performing the sacraments is both physical and spiritual at once. In the sign of the cross, the anointing of the sick, and the consecration of the host, there is a unity in body and spirit that I did not feel from the tradition I was brought up in. I welcomed that unity as I sought to develop my own theology of disability as an adult. In that moment in front of that monument, I was struck by the enormity of the sacrifice of those martyrs, and was grateful for the self-knowledge that my own spiritual journey was bringing me.

More than anything else I saw in the city, I wanted to see Paul Cézanne's *The Large Bathers* in the National Gallery. Since I can remember, I have preferred the work of the post-Impressionists to all other styles of painting.

There's something about the paint on the canvas that connotes all the work that goes into the creation of a beautiful piece of art. Up close you can see the brushstrokes, and in some cases, the texture of multiple layers of paint. That layered mixing of colors is the evidence that this beautiful thing was made by a person. Someone made decisions about color palettes and techniques. The painter probably got frustrated at one point or another, maybe even letting a few swear words slip out during the process.

These clues to the work that went into the art run counter to the idea that if you're a really talented artist, your effort should not be apparent to observers. Art theorists call this concept *sprezzatura*, a studied carelessness or nonchalance. The word first appears in a 1528 text by Baldassare Castiglione called *The Book of the Courtier*, which was important to court culture in Renaissance England because it laid out a lot of rules that were instrumental to getting and maintaining the right kind of reputation as a courtier. Like *sprezzatura*, a number of these rules center on creating an ethos of effortlessness that itself takes a great deal of effort to construct. There are tips on how to choose clothes that are becoming, but not too showy, advice on how to praise oneself in public, but not too much.

I've always been a little annoyed with this book, and with *sprezzatura* more specifically. I am not a person who can really hide the effort it takes me to move around in the world. When I walk down the street, people stare. Children point and whisper. Sometimes they even turn their heads backward to keep looking at me as I pass. Once, a child doing this lost his balance and fell down, and I'd be lying if I said I didn't relish this poetic justice just a bit. My body doesn't allow me the luxury of forgetting it exists, and, petty though I know it is, I am sometimes jealous of people who do get to experience that. To me, these messy complexities, both of movement and of emotion, are the very things that make us the most human. To deny them, and especially to paper over them with the moderation of existence demanded by Castiglione and his social-climbing adherents, is to sacrifice the things that make our experiences and perspectives truly our own.

I don't remember the first time I saw an image of Cézanne's *The Large Bathers*. Maybe it was during the overview of how different artists interpreted bodies in art camp the summer after sixth grade. Maybe it was during a college art history seminar, or flipping through art books during a boring stretch volunteering in my hometown library. Whenever it happened, I do know that that painting sticks out as the culmination of my fascination with the visible effort of the post-Impressionists. There's something unexplainable about the combination of cool, calming colors and the way that the thick, curved brushstrokes unify the unabashedly nude, undeniably beautiful bodies of the bathers with the shrubs and trees behind them. They are all artifacts of the same miraculous creation—trees and bodies alike are reflections of the *imago dei* in the world.

At the National Gallery, I sat in front of the painting for several minutes, taking it in, trying not to think about the way my rented wheelchair was blocking other museum patrons. "It looks the way that moving without effort must feel," I said. "That's really sad and beautiful," my husband replied. It was the first time I had ever put my love for the painting into words, and I realized that I loved it because it let effort and smoothness coexist in a way I didn't feel I ever could. The painting and the way I felt looking at it seemed to cause all the other noteworthy moments I experienced moving through London to coalesce. I started to understand why I couldn't feel entirely represented by the works of the writers and thinkers I came to London to feel closer to, why I was feeling connected to those people either spiritually or physically, but never entirely both at once.

Sitting there, in the middle of the city that I had loved from afar for so long, a city that didn't seem built for my existence in the world, I began to think deeply and intently about my life inside my body. I thought about all the ways I've struggled to let this body belong to a conception of the *imago dei* in the way that Cézanne's bathers belong with the trees because they have the same brushstrokes. I knew logically that the relationship between Creator and created was just as strong in both cases, even that it had just as many physical manifestations. Why, then, was it so much easier for me to believe in one relationship's existence than the other's?

I remembered the jolt of pain and unworthiness I felt as a child every time my congregation sang "Take My Life and Let It Be," and reached that second verse: *Take my feet and let them be / Swift and beautiful for Thee.* My feet, I knew, would never be swift or beautiful, not for God or anyone. I remembered the shame and embarrassment I felt every time a stranger stopped me on the street and asked to pray for God to heal my disability, never pausing to ask whether that's what I wanted. I remembered the joy and wonder I felt when I first started attending mass at

St. Gabriel's near our home in Minnesota, when I realized that all the aisles were ramps and one of the Eucharistic servers used a wheelchair. In that space, seeing him serving as he could in a space made for all its members, I felt a part of the family of God in a way I never had before, like I was holy in body *and* soul.

I bought a postcard of *The Large Bathers* for a pound sterling. I cried on the Tube back to our hotel—for myself, for my dinner companion eating with her hands, for the wheelchair-using Eucharistic minister, for Virginia and Aphra and Elizabeth and Mary, for the way Christ's incarnational crucified body and miraculous resurrection make it impossible to separate beauty from pain. The station didn't have a lift, of course.

Tread Lightly

Lena Popkin

THE FIRST TIME I went to therapy, my therapist remarked that it seemed like walking was meditative for me. She had just asked me what I liked to do. I was confused; I wasn't walking in order to meditate. For me, walking has proven time and again to be both the most reliable form of transportation and the most exciting way to learn about new places. Without a car, and when public transportation is hard to navigate, my feet and a map have never left me without a way to get home.

Before, when I'd been told to meditate, mostly by my mother and other people who care about my mental health, I had merely rolled my eyes. To suddenly learn that I had been meditating all along, that my mile or two-mile or three-mile excursions were demonstrations of a search for internal peace and balance, made me question what role these walks really served for me, not to mention wonder if I even understood what meditation is supposed to achieve.

For some people, my therapist explained, meditating is painting, or writing, or actually sitting quietly and letting go of anxiety. When I thought about it, I had to agree that walking does allow me a space and time in which I'm not obligated to the place I came from or to the place I'm going, and it connects me to all the fascinating places I've been lucky enough to explore. Maybe then I shouldn't have been surprised that, when I told my therapist I would often choose to walk the six miles from downtown Boston back to my college campus in Medford rather than take the Red Line, she framed my choice back to me as meditative. Why else would I often walk the twenty minutes across campus in the snow when I could just take the shuttle? Why was I always trying to convince my friends that we would benefit from the fresh air on the walk back from a restaurant?

My therapist understood implicitly: These long strolls have become for me a way to combat anxiety and uncertainty. When my friend got alcohol poisoning that turned to travel sickness and left me alone in Madrid for several days, I found myself wandering the city's café-strewn streets, walking fifteen miles or more each day that he was sick. And during the months-long shutdowns from COVID-19, as I bounced back and forth from my childhood home to my adult life, walking was a way for me not only to get out of the house, but to get out of my head and to feel connected again to the communities that seemed to have disappeared.

When I was born, my dad, rather than bring the car to pick up my mom and newborn self, half-jokingly encouraged my mom to walk us home from the hospital, six or so blocks. My dad and I have walked together in many cities across the world, ranging from our home of Philadelphia to Jerusalem to Guanajuato, Mexico. Every time I come home from college, even for a few days, we set aside time for a walk, usually a long one, across the city.

My dad also taught me to be fearless. When I was scared of something as a kid, which I often was, my dad would tell me that the fear was in my head. Whether I panicked at a flu shot or a spider or a bad dream, my dad was always there to remind me that fear is only as powerful as I allow it to be.

And although I am fearless, I am also cautious, in many ways. It is important not to confuse the two, or we risk undermining the power of courage. I grew up in the city, taking the subway to and from school, and walking home from various places after dark, just as so many other kids across the country and the world do every day. When I was eleven, though, I became abruptly aware of how the sense of freedom that walking gave me was qualified by my gender. I was sexually assaulted and forced to reconcile the relationship between myself, my actions, and the way others saw me far before most of my peers. In the years before I turned eighteen, I learned to keep a sweatshirt in my backpack that I could wear when I felt uncomfortable on the subway or the street in my summer clothes, to walk in zigzags across the city when I thought

I was being followed, and to carry my keys between my fingers when I walked anywhere alone.

It is difficult to characterize this kind of walking, a kind that many women are familiar with, as meditative. Unlike painting or drawing or reading, walking takes you somewhere, and often without pleasure. And so walking instills in me two conflicting, almost clashing, emotions. When I walk I feel both apprehensive and calm, often in the same walk and sometimes at the same time. Is it possible to feel these two things at once? Is something that elicits fear necessarily a bad thing? And what if it's only fearful for some of us? I find myself trapped in a liminal space: those who love to walk, often men like my dad, are too immersed in their own experiences to see my apprehension, and those who are too scared by what they might encounter on a walk, unfortunately most women, just never do it.

In late May, still in the early stages of the pandemic, in the period between having to leave college and moving back to some sort of ghost version of it, my dad, my seventeen-year-old brother, and I took a walk after dinner, a time at which few people were outside and risk of COVID-19 transmission was low. It was about eight in the evening, and probably half an hour or so before sunset. I had assumed we would stroll around our sleepy neighborhood. But my dad, like many others during quarantine who had been forced to slow down or nearly stop, had become captivated by the previously ignored life of birds. He wanted to walk to a park to hear their sound in as much darkness as the city could offer.

It was a short walk, only about a mile or so. I was comfortable, listening to my dad and brother chatting and enjoying the relative emptiness of the evening, which meant I could take off my mask and breathe easily. The night was hot, and so I was wearing one of my tiny little shirts, the kind that often makes me feel powerful and sexy when I go out with my friends, but that produces a certain kind of melancholy during the pandemic. The purpose they used to serve for me is no longer relevant, so they've fallen by the wayside, worn only on nights like this one when everything else is just too much fabric. The park was on the other side of a highway overpass, the kind of place I would usually avoid. We had to cross underneath it, and I instinctively crossed my arms over my chest as I fell in line behind my dad and brother. No other people were around us, but my flimsy little shirt suddenly felt very exposing under the orange glare of the underpass lamps.

A block or two later, we crossed a wide road and I let my arms fall to my sides. As usual, I convinced myself, I was reacting to nothing. Yet just a moment later we passed a couple of guys, around my own age, walking in the opposite direction. I'm sure they had no real obnoxious intent. Still, they looked at me. Or rather looked at what they supposed my clothes might reveal of me. "I love summer," one nonchalantly said to the other, just a step or two after walking by.

I wrapped my hands tightly around my torso. I clutched my phone in my hand. We kept walking. My dad and brother were laughing ahead of me, probably about the birds in the park. They hadn't even registered that we were passing anyone, let alone heard what the guys had said.

So, on the first humid night of a summer that started off strange and only got stranger, I opened my mouth and begged my dad and brother to consider how uncomfortable their choice of a walk had made me. Their incessant talk of birds and their quest to find a place where they could hear them more clearly had drowned out any noise they didn't want to hear. They had become deaf not only to their surroundings, but to me. My stomach sank as my dad, my radical and environmentalist and feminist dad, the kind of dad whom my friends absolutely love to talk to, who taught me to carry myself through the world without fear, shrugged and replied that it shouldn't really matter. Because I was walking with men.

He then continued to walk into the park, my brother beside him, alert really only to the birds. I sighed, resigned and frustrated, and followed them into the park, where I waited anxiously to be allowed to go home.

On the walk home, I tried again. My whole life, I said, we had been walking places together. And my whole life, I had been a child. He chose where we walked to and how we got there. And often, because he so deeply wanted to teach me to be unafraid, that meant wandering through strange neighborhoods, along edges of highways, in construction zones, where he felt like a visitor or an explorer and I felt like a spectacle. My brother shuffled a few steps ahead with his head down and his hands in his pockets, having signed up for a nice evening walk, not a feminist rant. I wanted to scream, to blow up my argument and just be angry at them for making me feel unsafe. But to be a woman responding to the actions of men is to reduce your anger to language that they understand, that won't make *them* want to blow it all up.

How could I explain to my father, who had raised me to be fierce and independent, that he had ostensibly just told me that I would never be safe without the presence of a man? When I'm fifty, as he is, and I want to take a six-mile walk across whatever city I'm living in, will I have to find a man to accompany me? The thought upset me: I love walking with people, but mostly I love walking alone. I thought about my therapist's suggestion that my desire for solitude and space to think and to process was a form of meditation. Does my choice of setting in which to sort and think imply some inevitable and unspeakable ending? Does my fearlessness, assumed of me by my father, and quite often embodied by my own actions, mean that I must endure situations and contexts that actually do scare me? This night was just a small moment, not one that will really stick out to me going forward, but one, I realized, that was typical of so many just like it. Would I have to stop walking to stop feeling fear? Could I walk through that fear, or would doing so force me to act brash and stupid?

As our sacred father-daughter ritual became an occasion of critical reflection on my part, my dad expressed his own frustration. He told me that he had taken me, and would continue to take me, to all of these places in Philadelphia and around the world to teach me to be fearless. Somehow this conversation proved to him that he had failed.

But to that, I say that he had missed the point. As the COVID pandemic tore through our communities and sent university students home, I mourned not only the loss of my college years and my early twenties, but also the loss of some of my former fearlessness. Some might just call it naivete. Though I had never before been afraid of eating food off the ground, for example, or of touching something dirty like a park bench or a door handle, suddenly the conditions had drastically changed. Similarly, the conditions of my walks with my dad changed too. Although walking had at times brought us together, that night, when I expressed my sense of danger, it was clear to me that my dad and I would never really walk as equals. To his credit, though, he sees this essay as constructive criticism, and usually lets me choose where we walk now.

In my therapist's office, during an appointment for which I arrived ten minutes late because I'd insisted on walking, I couldn't really argue with the fact that walking has a special power for me. What I struggle with is how to reconcile the reality that something so powerful and significant to my life and well-being can also give rise to a unique kind of wariness and fear. But as I write this, as hundreds of thousands of Americans have died at the hands of a mishandled pandemic and millions of others take to the streets to call for racial and economic justice, I have learned that we must be able to hold multiple truths in one space. And such it is with walking: it has taught me both real danger and real peace.

Along MLK

Kabria Rogers

My body is always in an oversized and uncomfortable state, exhausted by sitting on super-soft couches and looking at screens. On top of that, there's the perpetual reel inside my head, the list of things I should be doing. Don't feel too much. Don't think too much. Don't sit too much. Movement is the only way to stave off the uncertainty, the blues, the humanity. I find myself both yearning for and dreading the walk and its consequences. I feel a joint discomfort in anticipation of a walk. But like everything else, freedom starts when you begin.

In my case, the beginning starts before my feet touch the sidewalk. In summer heat, my oversized body sweats and sticks to every article of clothing. So, of course, the beginning must be a shower, to defy the sweat and discomfort. After, I make sure my body is perfectly dry and apply body glide to all of my winding curves. When the sweat returns, I know it will be coupled with the persistent chafe between my jelly thighs. I can't allow for deterrents. My mind runs away with me again— I should be eating better, cutting carbs, standing every hour, bending, twisting, and moving always. I should be perfect with all this time on my hands—after all, I'm working from home. I shake off all the never-ending demands inside my head. I need space outside my head, outside my apartment, outside myself. Next, deodorant, for when the summer sun bears down on me. Then clothes: I must suit myself up for such an event. My chest lets out a sigh; nothing ever quite fits right, too snug on my larger-than-life-size body, not quite breathable and not quite right to be outside in the world where other people can see me. As I shuffle between yoga pants and sundress, I'm at it again, inside my head preparing for battle, even if only in the form of a walk.

Eventually, I choose some washed or dingy fabric to cover me. Finally, I am acceptable to be seen and to see. Now let's triple-check.

I've applied my body glide.

Check.

My thighs are covered up.

Check.

The roundness of my stomach is covered up.

Check.

My saggy arm fat is contained and covered up.

Check.

I opted to wear a bra because panties in this heat are completely optional.

Check.

Glasses.

Check.

Cell phone, in case my loving pooh bear worries or I see a horrific crime.

Check.

Keys, so I can lock the door behind and have a weapon in case someone jumps out of the bushes.

Check.

It is summer, so sunglasses.

Check.

I head downstairs from the second floor onto the indoor porch reeking of trash until trash day.

Damn, I forgot my mask. So back up the fifteen stairs and through the door into my kitchen.

Hot, black nonbreathable mask.

Check.

Then I'm out the front door and the nuisance of getting ready is forgotten. It's almost as if I am not that stubby, round Black girl going for a walk. I'll take a walk to the dam today, away from the cracked sidewalks, the stench of trash, and the scattering waterbugs. The humidity sticks to me but finally I'm outside, leaving the self-imposed expectations behind me. So when the sweat comes, my ability to bear the dripping moisture is a defiance.

I cross the street through the parking lot of the School of the Future. No noisy Thunderbirds this year, only an empty beige and gray building. I look for any cops sitting in their stylish car, poised to take the long way around to avoid them. There's no room for them today, no room for talking, no room for tickets, no room for my fear or their authority—not before my walk. Lucky for me today, the coast is clear. The school, its adjacent parking lot, and the two-lane asphalt street that runs behind it are my last portions of the city grid before I cross into the green and overgrown wild of Fairmount Park. Instantly, my back and shoulders straighten. With my head up, I focus on extending my duck-like gait. For when I am going for a walk I am not some clumsy duck. I am an ambassador of my city and of myself.

Down the incline of Lansdowne Avenue, on the concrete sidewalk amid the Fairmount green and leading toward the highway. Sidewalk always feels better on my feet and ankles than asphalt. At least that's what I tell myself. I've only been walking ten minutes when I begin to feel the heat and tingle. Starting in the ball of my foot and climbing up my ankle, up my calf, to my hips, settling in this ring around my lower back and lower abdomen. If I did not feel these things, it would not be a walk. The heat of a walk far surpasses the entropy of being still. It's as if the building heat in my limbs and joints is burning away my tortured idle state, replacing it with the familiar discomfort of progress.

My glasses fog as I follow under the expressway overpass. Above me cars jet to I-76. I turn left and continue until I reach the T intersection of Sweetbriar Road and Martin Luther King Drive. This drive runs along the west bank of the Schuylkill River, and is often confused with Kelly Drive. Once the roads were known simply and less confusingly as West River Drive and East River Drive. I stand at the intersection, where a traffic light flashes yellow. MLK Drive has been closed to cars for months to allow people space outside—in light of stay-at-home orders. Despite the street's being closed, I look both ways for a runaway car, speedy cyclists, a running pair, or a family not fully six feet away. Then I dash across and land as always on the far sidewalk. Maintaining my steady pace, I see, on my left, shady trees, rickety wood benches, and the Schuylkill River. On the opposite side, grass replaces the sidewalk and a flimsy diamond metal fence separates grass and interstate. I still can't bring myself to walk in the street. In my mind, the street is always for cars and my fellow outdoorsmen with a sense of urgency. You know the joggers, the rollerbladers, the triathlon trainers.

My walk follows a slow and steady pace that builds over time, as a burning ache spreads through my lower joints and muscles. The air and openness expand my chest, my view, my horizon—allowing my mind to wander, free from the nagging consequences of reality. Each step brings out of me confidence, clarity, and peace of mind. Heat and moisture collect in my mask. In a regular act of defiance, I remove the cloth and loop it around my wrists. As people approach, my now pandemic-wired body will jump and put my mask on quickly. Or not. I'll walk past them, like I used to when the world made sense and time bombs weren't ticking above everyone's heads.

All of gritty Parkside lies behind me as I walk the long stretch along the river toward Boathouse Row. With gravel underfoot, I can see across the Schuylkill two frisbee throwers and picnics on Kelly Drive. The world feels peaceful here, and the Philadelphia smog is cleaned away by the effervescent dam that lies ahead.

I walk under one more overpass with a sidewalk shifting between cement and gravel. The shaded trees in my view start to clear away and reveal the boathouses on Kelly Drive. The slender two-person sidewalk now expands into a carved-out landing, impeccably paved with pink terracotta and beige brick, with room for twenty people to stand. This is my stop. Grateful no one is here today, I stand in the center of the pavement. I prop my elbows on the rail looking across at Boathouse Row. Today I count ten boathouses. Have there always been ten? I manage to remember only two, when I walk away from this view, Malta and Vesper.

From my chosen spot looking over, there are two distinct pathways. One leads down to another landing extending further over the water. Another path leads down to a rocky water line for the adventurous fisherman. The first landing is equipped with two hanging orange life preservers. A shush fills the air, as the churning section of the Schuylkill drops into a small waterfall with white rapids and bubbling foam. Even ducks avoid this waterfall. No swimming. No wading. Laughter and cell phone conversations pass behind me, as fellow walkers continue on toward Center City. The wind picks up in this spot and all I smell is salt, water, and earth. No amount of heat or sweat can withstand that breeze. My forehead is dry and my body belongs. The built-up burning in my muscles is mild, a friendly reminder of what was necessary to bring me to this point. The inner reel is quiet now. I am allowed to be still as long as I'm looking at my persistent dam.

To the far right, I can see the inspired architecture of the Philadelphia Museum of Art. I can never tell which is the front of the building. Although when tourists ask, I say the gazebo side, that I'm gazing at now, is the back and the iconic Rocky stairs are the front. The building is glowing peach under the sunset rays. To my left is the route back home, with its unswept, cracked sidewalks and trash that's been sitting out for two days too long in the Philadelphia summer heat.

I shift between my left and right feet, humming *Summer, Summer, Summertime*, with a smirk. Will Smith left out the stench, the roaches, and the incessant waft of marijuana. I guess that doesn't matter, only this feeling of freedom that comes with Philadelphia summer. Freedom separate from the sweat and the heat. I stand dead center between the two complexions of Philadelphia.

At my dam, somewhere between Center City, a tourist colony, and the summer-steeped stench of everyday life, there lies this churning resolve of possibility. The dam pulls me in with majesty, as an island by itself, in between these two stark realities and beholden to no one. Never weary, despite the season, the climate, the people, always churning and steadfast. A beautifully controlled force of nature.

How do you do that? I ask it. I wonder how anything so individually purposeful can keep going without being weary. How anything can belong solely to itself with no expectations or questions, just purpose and perpetual motion. If only in your churning, I ask, you could help me find my purpose, my path, my course. Perhaps another day and another walk. Right now it's enough to watch you.

A Subtle Magnetism
in Nature

Walking

(VARIATIONS ON THOREAU)

Sharon White

I HAVE MET WITH *but one or two persons in the course of my life who understood the art of Walking, that is, of taking walks—who had a genius, so to speak, for* sauntering, *which word is beautifully derived "from idle people who roved about the country, in the Middle Ages, and asked charity, under pretense of going* a la Sainte Terre," *to the Holy Land, till the children exclaimed, "There goes a* Sainte-Terrer," *a Saunterer, a Holy-Lander.*

Once I woke at first light. A young man was washing his face in snow-melt. A braided stream in the north. In the cabin were the children I was leading on a bike trip. I was almost a child myself. At night I opened the tiny bottles of brandy my mother had packed for the trip. I'm bending now over the stream close to his face. He has long black hair and blue eyes. He tells me he lives in the forest on Haida Gwaii. The trees are thousands of years old. *Do I want to follow him into the forest?* he asks, and I do. Leaving the children squabbling in the cabin. Cooking eggs and potatoes on iron skillets. Later I'll jump off a bridge into the coldest water and think my heart's stopped beating. The milky

The extended quotations in this essay are from Henry David Thoreau's "Walking," as published in *The Atlantic Monthly* in June 1862.

glacial silt running off my arms as I break the surface of the river and take a deep gasp.

I'm in the woods with my brother and his friends. We've been climbing over logs, jumping across stones. I must be nine or ten. The leaves soggy under my sneakers. We have canteens and sticks. The wood's full of interesting things—old houses just about to crumble into the ground, trees split in half, singed by lightning. Cellar holes with busted doors and old pails. These were fields once. Farmers and their families lived in the squat houses. Stone walls intercept the woody fields, piled in haphazard zig-zags on the outskirts of the city known for clocks. My paternal grandmother grew up on a farm with eleven (or twelve) brothers and sisters. I knew two of them. We're supposed to be back by dark. I can smell spring in the air. The stream at the back of our lot is rushing with snowmelt. The tiny tree in the middle of our lawn has tight buds.

I was trotting away to the neighbor down the street from our first house. My dog sniffing along behind me. Getting out of the small house with mother and father and brother and then sister. But this was when I was two. The screen door flapped back and forth when someone went out to the miniature backyard. Years later I sell all my Golden Books to a neighbor who gives me candy.

I run away sometimes when the dinner table is laden with turkey and cranberry sauce and white onions in silver bowls and crescent rolls in a basket. The table is rectangular and each parent sits at one end. I'm shouting now and everyone shakes their head and thumps the table. "You do-gooders," my father says, "you never think about what's practical, do you?" They're drinking wine and laughing. I know if I walk down the narrow road past the place where there used to be a two-hundred-year-old tree in the middle of the road and along the edge of the field with remnants of corn stalks and dark brown furrowed soil I can squeeze through the farmyard on a track past the manure pile and the ramshackle house where white shirts flap in the wind and another family is just sitting down to eat after milking their cows.

The mirror is leaning against the cabin wall. There's a box of cookies for me and a bed to sleep in. The ranger who owns the house is gone. She's out in the field. I'm looking at myself in the mirror at twenty-one. My pale breasts, my pale thighs. My arms and face tanned from weeks in the mountains. Am I very different from the person I thought I was when I went into the mountains? Can I be different from who I was when I went into the mountains?

I'm running up the hill across the main road into the forest. I know reindeer are on the vidda eating curly lichen, suckling their calves. Sometimes the women go up to the forest to pick cloudberries. Once, two women got lost circling the tents where their families were camped. It's easy to get lost on the vidda. Everything looks the same, Harald tells me. His aunt cuts the tall grass with a sickle, sharp and curved, bent to the long sweet grass around her house. On the track through the forest the moss gives way under my feet. I'm running as fast as I can. Past the bog where the tiniest of orchids grow, white and pink with curled lips.

How WOMANKIND, *who are confined to the house still more than men, stand it I do not know; but I have ground to suspect that most of them do not* stand *it at all. When, early in a summer afternoon, we have been shaking the dust of the village from the skirts of our garments, making haste past those houses with purely Doric or Gothic fronts, which have such an air of repose about them, my companion whispers that probably about these times their occupants are all gone to bed. Then it is that I appreciate the beauty and the glory of architecture, which itself never turns in, but forever stands out and erect, keeping watch over the slumberers.*

Did I have to be edging into old before I started to wonder what Thoreau really thought about women? Does it matter? I knew he was prickly and choosy when it came to his friends. I knew there was something about a lost love. I read his journal when I was in college in Maine. Each of his observations about flora or fauna matched something I'd seen on one of my walks into the woods. I know, too, that if I'd read his work then as I hear it now I wouldn't have liked him very much. As it is, it doesn't seem as if he pays attention to my wants, my visions in any sentence in "Walking" except to close the door in a room in the village as I sleep and then take the key.

I'm hiking across the scree field. My first time walking in the mountains. I want to be fierce like the women I've met on the way. Women with strong arms and long braids and tanned faces. My instructor says, you want to be a writer. Yes. A children's book writer? he asks. Yes. Behind us one of the group starts to throw up on the trail. A boy with thin blond hair and a round face. The wind is howling across the steep slope. We've been taught how to self-arrest on snow and talus. We've been taught how to rock climb. I'm ecstatic and want every day to be in the mountains. Later, when we swim in the cold mountain stream, my instructor looks straight into my eyes. His body twists in the frigid water as he moves his arms to stay put.

Once I was living alone in my own kind of woods close to beavers who played in the pond nearby and deer who left their prints in the yard. I answered an ad for someone to hang syrup buckets in the woods. It was late winter, just about the time when the sap begins to run, and the farmer had a beautiful team of horses with fancy harnesses pulling his wagon full of tin buckets and spouts. My job was to hammer the spouts into the bark of the maples. He watched me carefully for a few minutes and then said, "Some girls can get the hang of a hammer and others aren't so quick. But you'll do." It was a magical day, the sound of the horses' bells, the smell of moss and running pine under the snow, little streams thawing all over the forest.

I'm a widow stung by nettles in the mountains on a wide trail. I've seen women haying in the fields that lead up to the peaks. Their heads wrapped in kerchiefs, their rakes combing the ground. My thighs sting, the palms of my hands itch. How could I be so stupid to wade through plants I knew would cause me pain? The slopes of the mountains are still white and in the gardens in small towns on the flank, lettuces line up on terraced steps.

A family adopted me for a day not long after you died. I was staying in a narrow house on a narrow road in Aberystwyth in a narrow bed in a narrow room. I walked along the sea. I was killing time. My friends were away and I was at loose ends. The next day I went to a hotel in the Brecon Beacons and slept in another small room with a bright red Indian bedspread. The family who adopted me was the perfect shape. A mother, a father, a boy, and a girl. We hiked up to the ridge where the slope dropped off so steeply I could hardly catch my breath. There were flat black lakes with solitary ducks and miles of green ridges going off to the north. The boy took care of me. He told me funny stories and pointed out birds I didn't know the names of. The rest of the family was friendly too. I didn't know why I thought all of this would make me feel better, but it did.

THERE ARE SOME intervals which border the strain of the wood thrush, to which I would migrate—wild lands where no settler has squatted; to which, methinks, I am already acclimated.

I wanted to shed every inch of who I was. So I walked out from the college on the hill on roads that turned to dirt, once I was far enough away into the woods. It was easy to be gone a whole day then as I passed the small village with the white church and then the barn with the singing swallows and bales of hay and the field with saplings protected by flutes of plastic. Sometimes there were sheep in fields, the lowing of cows, the warming sun making me so hot, I'd take off my sweatshirt. I knew I was far enough when I came to the field bordered by thick forest, so deep you could hardly see through the trunks of slender pines. And, then, the long way back across the train tracks down the hill, my mind erased by the hours alone.

It was not always idyllic. One Halloween a woman I knew left a party at a house of a friend of mine who played the piano and wore two black hats, one on top of the other. The woman, a dancer, was dressed as a butterfly for the party with glittering wings. It was a pretty long walk in the dark under the highway and up the steep hill to the dorms. I never walked it at night. The cops think someone drove off the exit a few miles down the highway and found her walking back to the college, her costume tucked under her coat. Then he bludgeoned her to death and took off.

In the pine forests it's not a handicap to be alone. A group of fishermen give me a map. A ranger says I should have had an ice ax, but I don't. I take a day or so to reach the ridge and then it's splendor wherever I look. The chime of the wind crashing against my ears. In the morning I can't see, my eyes pinned shut by bees. My first-aid kit is useless. But I make it down to the series of clear sandy streams emptying into pools where I strip off my clothes and soak my bites in the water.

Later, I drive a friend's car to the Middle Fork of the Salmon and wait a day picking apricots in the heat by the river until a guide tells me Paul is days behind schedule. A man, his hair tied back in a ponytail, offers me a ride to the only town around and I take it. By this time, I'm covered in poison ivy. His wife and daughter are at a hot spring miles away for the night and he wants to sleep with me. We've been looking at the stars as we float in a hot tub. When I say no, he laughs. He's got a gun, he says, he could shoot me. The stars fill the sky from stem to stern. I'm not afraid. The next morning, I hitch a ride to Ketchum.

My son and I are walking in the wild north of Sweden. He takes my hand and swings it back and forth, like when he was younger. The slender birches and scruffy willows poke up through the melting snow. "We should have skis," I say. "Forget it," he says, "I hate cross-country skiing." "Yeah, I know," I answer.

The reindeer are moving up the slopes of the mountains to calve. He's hundreds of miles away from his girlfriend. We live in a summer house. A painter's cottage. He has the studio with the high ceiling. I sleep in the ancient past of the house. Two bunkbeds stashed against the walls, kitty-corner. Every day we go out into the wild mountains. One day we ride our rented bikes down from a church village at the edge of a northern river. We can see ice breaking up along the edge of the water. A huge shudder and then the foaming shards of ice scattering and sliding. I was lucky to be so far north, I thought. And lucky to sit on the little bench in the sun looking at the lake, my son on FaceTime with his girlfriend. The swollen buds of Icelandic poppies bent above their leaves, just now clear of snow. If we wanted to, we could walk for days and not see anyone else.

WHAT IS IT that makes it so hard sometimes to determine whither we will walk? I believe that there is a subtle magnetism in Nature, which, if we unconsciously yield to it, will direct us aright. It is not indifferent to us which way we walk. There is a right way: but we are very liable from heedlessness and stupidity to take the wrong one. We would fain take that walk, never yet taken by us through this actual world, which is perfectly symbolical of the path which we love to travel in the interior and ideal world; and sometimes, no doubt, we find it difficult to choose our direction, because it does not yet exist distinctly in our idea.

Why did I want to go off into the woods? I was a suburban girl who wore uniforms to school. I was a banker's daughter. There were always woods somewhere in my backyard but it was the mountains that seduced me. Craggy, ice-sheeted, thick with pine. And the north. Hudson Bay, Labrador, Greenland. When I could I went as far north as possible to a farm perched on the wide shallow Tana River. I don't know why I wanted to scour out whatever was folded in my brain. I didn't believe in a soul. I wanted to be free from ordinary days. When I got to the north I squandered my freedom for affection. Who wouldn't? There was a waterfall that took a few days to walk to across the vidda along the rutted tracks of the reindeer herders and fishermen, the women and children who picked berries in the bogs. Once there was a farmer who harvested bog hay like wind but when I was there we used tractors.

We slept in sheds piled with reindeer hides, heavy against my skin as I dreamed. Mostly the land was wide open, rivulets of miniature birch trees with tiny leaves. The wind had nothing to block its way and scoured my face and hands. Somewhere there were reindeer off on their own, bedded down at night on moss. Sometimes when it was cold I couldn't feel my hands and could hardly see your back as you found the way across the little hills. By the time we slept at the waterfall it was day all night. The water crashing against my heart as I slept on the lip of the fall.

I first saw the wild goats when we were lost in Rhinogs. It was my fault. I thought we should follow them from the stone wall leading up to the peak. It's the most difficult place in Snowdonia to hike, a friend told us later. Terrible footing, tussocks and rocks. The goats were huge and jaunty as if they all wore red bandanas, heading off in a line south. "Aye, it's the wild goats, don't follow them. They'll lead you astray," a man said when we stopped for cold juice at a store. But isn't that the point, to be led astray, off a cliff through the fog to a lake, your hands covered with brambles. Astray, a kind of adventure. Just like in love. How could you not love the wild goats heading off in a line to the south? In the land of an old road said to be Roman, large flat stones climbing up the ridge and down the other side. The tarn at the neck of the climb. The dark pool filled with secrets. Mine bubbling up without me.

How could you not think this was eternal, this day, this second, as the goats split and then ran away. We saw them again years later lounging on the edge of a cliff, their whorled horns medieval, regal, bandanas gone. We were taking the easy way to the top and the track went straight up through sod and then across an escarpment, black and narrow.

Now that the world's shrunk, the goats were seen in Llandudno, eating lettuce in gardens, tearing up bushes, roaring through the empty town like the plague.

When we went to the island we just wanted a bit of summer, somewhere not over the international dateline or hours away by plane. How could we know that the island we landed on was more than just a pretty beach? We'd been living in winter in a small house with a log burner for months. Who would blame us if we got away for a few days of tropical paradise? One day we walked from our hotel to the Intercontinental Resort just down the beach and caught a ride up to the golf course on the top of the hill. A man who told us he was learning to be a pro said we couldn't walk on the course, but he'd take us as far as the old rail line in his golf cart. His village was half an hour away, he said. We'd seen trucks full of harvested sugar cane packed tightly. Our bedroom was roofed with thatch, swept by women whom we'd seen lining the main road waiting for a bus on their way home.

"You can walk that way," the slim man with the pink golf cap said, and pointed downhill. "Not that way," turning to face the opposite direction in the cart. But I could see two women walking toward us, frangipani blossoms tucked behind their ears. The track was muddy after fierce tropical rain the night before. We walked through trash on the rutted grass until we came to the village. Along both sides of the path children were saying, bula, bula, and waving their hands. A man came up behind us. He was very tall and had on soccer shorts and a T-shirt. "Those are my pigs," he said. "Two are pregnant." In the wooden pen on the side of the track the two huge pigs were on their sides, their skin mottled pink. A third pig rooted in the straw. "They're beautiful," I said. He smiled and told us he played football for the Israeli league.

Up ahead a man gestured to the children. The village houses were cinderblock and corrugated metal painted blue and purple, trimmed with lime. In the middle was a bure, conical and thatched. There was no electricity, no running water. As the track narrowed though tangled trees, we could hear music and the thwacks of a machete in a coconut tree.

At the edge of the lagoon two boys pushed a paddle board, and men pulled nets from the water. Goats foraged on the bank. On the other side of the gate to the resort people were drinking around the pool. On the beach a woman in a white thong straddled a pony as her companion proudly held the reins. Behind her one of the boys from the village tapped the pony's rump with a switch.

The buses are running empty past our house down the street. The sidewalks are empty too except for one, and then another person, carrying a plastic bag full of food or walking their dog or running, huffing and spitting. We find a path above the river that's been hidden until now. Along the edges of the path golden star blooms, winsome flowers the size of a fingernail sprout from heart-shaped leaves. All the trees are expectant, it's spring after all. The Lenten rose blooming white. Churches are empty, stores are empty, highways almost stripped of cars and trucks and buses. In the swamp birds gather on their way north. Bodies are stored all over the world in strange places, refrigerated trucks, ice skating rinks. They can't bury them fast enough. All this death is news to some people when often it isn't, depending on where you are. The lengthening days remind us that yes, summer is just around the corner. Yesterday I watched a robin enthusiastically slurp down a worm. Dark brown, wiggling.

I BELIEVE IN the forest, and in the meadow, and in the night in which the corn grows. We require an infusion of hemlock, spruce or arbor vitae in our tea. There is a difference between eating and drinking for strength and from mere gluttony.

Sometimes I feel as if I've lost everything I was. Is that so bad? Isn't that what I wanted so many years ago: to strip myself down to basic elements, to pay attention until there was nothing left of who I was? I wanted to be strong enough to live alone in the woods. To not feel anything except the elixir of the wild. I was happy when I was walking anywhere there was a patch of forest or mountain or lake and filled small notebooks with descriptions of the light, the shape of a leaf, a bird's song. I was too romantic, my dance teacher in college said. I'd keep hitting my head against a wall. Did I learn this from Thoreau?

Laura Dassow Walls, his most recent biographer, paints him as a lovelorn misfit in his twenties. Or rather, he appears like a misfit to some people. He just about burns the town up playing campfire—he kindles a fire on a stump to cook "a nice mess of fish" and the fire takes off, he loses the woman he loves to a richer man, and his brother to tetanus. He learns many years later from farmers clearing the woods with brushfires, "You must burn against the wind always & and burn slowly." On the other hand, by his mid-twenties he's perfected the pencils his father makes so they're as fine as any English drawing pencil. He's been published in several literary journals, started a school with his brother, fallen in love with a woman who said no to both Thoreau and his brother (because she loved Henry), walked all over Massachusetts and New Hampshire, been invited to travel the world and said no, been wracked by illness, hollowed by loss, "struggling with sickness of heart."

He wanted what he wrote to be new, a little rough. In *A Week on the Concord and Merrimack Rivers*, he writes about climbing Mount Greylock. At one house on the way up, he met a young woman, "busily and unconcernedly combing her long black hair while she talked, [giving] her head the necessary toss with each sweep of the comb, with lively, sparkling eyes, and full of interest in that lower world from which I had come."

Walls writes, "He drank dry the tiny puddles pooled in horse tracks, 'a pure, cold, spring-like water.'"

I don't walk along the river now because there's a march of people two by two, six feet apart, clogging the path. But we return to the dirt track through the woods bordering Lemon Hill where spring is blooming. Red-winged blackbirds have been back in the trees for almost a month and the studious robins listening on the grass. Two woodpeckers scattered as we bent under white blooms on scraggly trees. I was going to walk the pilgrimage route from France over the Pyrenees across Spain to Santiago Compostela this spring. But today we walked past silver bells rising up in pale lavender spires above matted leaves. The golden stars, like miniature buttercups, continue to fill the woods. You could see the river below us shining, empty. No rowers out when the river would usually be full of them. By the end of the path the woods reeked of pee. But there were apple blossoms hanging over the road on our way home. Dense, sweet, a bit foreign above the pavement.

Thoreau built his house on Walden Pond on the bones of other houses, the remnants of the lives of people who'd lived there and furrowed the fields with clamshells and sold herbs and built the railroad. By the time Emerson bought the land where Thoreau built his shed, the Irish were moving on. Thoreau bought the boards he used for his experiment from a family moving away from Concord for work somewhere else. His furrowed beanfield was on land cultivated for hundreds of years, though the woods had grown up to cover the fields. The first time he planted the beans a woodchuck ate his crop.

All I can think of this morning, Easter Sunday, is the image of Potter's Field and the hundreds of boxes lined up in ditches dug on the furrowed graveyard. Wooden box after box, waiting for the layer of earth to bind those who died alone back into the soil.

WE HAD A remarkable sunset one day last November. I was walking in a meadow, the source of a small brook, when the sun at last, just before setting, after a cold, gray day, reached a clear stratum in the horizon, and the softest, brightest morning sunlight fell on the dry grass and on the stems of the trees in the opposite horizon and on the leaves of the shrub oaks on the hillside, while our shadows stretched long over the meadow east-ward, as if we were the only motes in its beams. It was such a light as we could not have imagined a moment before, and the air also was so warm and serene that nothing was wanting to make a paradise of that meadow. When we reflected that this was not a solitary phenomenon, never to happen again, but that it would happen forever and ever, an infinite number of evenings, and cheer and reassure the latest child that walked there, it was more glorious still.

In the once upon a time there were two winters and spring coming twice. Four women who greeted the dawn with an old song sung by their ancestors. A track churning through mud on the bones of an old railroad carrying the bodies of tall trees on their way to the mill. On the rocks along the beach I saw a giant cormorant. Just sitting, a bit down the beach from the cluster of oystercatchers, orange beaks aflame. We'd been walking for hours, past the four singing women stretched out on another beach in view of the waters near Antarctica. Near the top of the ridge succulents held fat fluorescent leaves up to the sun, even in winter. I was not in possession of sadness here. Everything, even the muddy track and the margins of the beach near the hut where sandflies bit my ankles, was singing out *here, here, here.*

Ah, Ifrane

Ruth Knafo Setton

"No DAWDLING OR DAYDREAMING," warned the mother of a school friend. "Go directly to school and come directly back home."

Her words filled me with horror. To walk back and forth from school and not stop to notice the cornstalks bursting through sheets of ice. Not stand beneath a tree and puzzle at the cottony gray veils spreading between branches—a witch's shawl, I thought. Not crouch over a brass key found on the sidewalk, and shiver, knowing it was a clue dropped by a spy who was watching right now to see who dared pick it up.

Each day was an adventure, a treasure hunt crammed with fascinating characters and wondrous sights, and how on earth could I get to the heart of the mystery if I didn't dawdle, daydream, and step off the path? At nine, I already knew I'd be a writer and accepted my destiny: to always be late, to go off the clearly marked, brightly lit path, and to make it to my destination via the most winding route imaginable, and afterwards, to spin tales about it.

Today, I see my friend's mother's warnings echoed and transformed into time management software, templates and graphs offering short-cuts that speed you through life—and the creative process. No pain. No wasted minutes. No blundering in the dark. Someone has already mapped your journey for you and connected the dots.

It may not be fair, but I blame Little Red Riding Hood's mother for our obsession with racing to our destination while ignoring the bypaths that tempt along the way. Go directly to Grandma's house, she told Red. Don't go off the path or talk to the Wolf.

Even as a kid, I loathed this tale and its cheerless message: Complete your mission and do not stop to smell the flowers or acknowledge the danger that lurks at the side of the road.

Luckily, I had Maurice Knafo, my father, to show me another way.

MY FATHER WALKED outside every single day of his life—until he couldn't anymore. In parks, along rivers or the sea, down city streets. Journeys without goal or destination, not the inn at the end of the road, but the path itself. The act of walking was its own goal, the reward the discoveries made along the way. Although I accompanied him on many walks during our travels, I didn't completely understand the joy of walking until the summer he turned eighty-nine, and we decided to walk together every morning. We chose Covered Bridge Park, one of my favorite places in the Pennsylvania countryside. Bordered by two peeling red covered bridges, the heart of the park, and the heart of our walks, is the thirty-four-mile-long body of water officially known as Jordan Creek, which, for all of us who walk, fish, and hike there, has the mystery and seductive promise of a river.

EARLY SUMMER MORNINGS, there were only a handful of people in the park: dogwalkers, a stray fisherman or two, and our harmonious trio: Maurice, my dog Ginger, and me. Ginger was a Blue Heeler, a breed of Australian Shepherd, with one blue eye and one brown eye. Warm and wise, a natural herder, he was a magnet to every dog in the park, rounding them up the way he had my kids when they were small. He ran ahead and returned to alert us of the arrival of suspicious humans and animals. He adored my father, who teased him by throwing sticks and rewarded him with treats he kept in his pocket.

There was me. Wife, mother of three, writer, teacher, dreamer, and daughter of a man who had crossed the Atlantic Ocean with his wife and two small daughters. At the time, he did not have a job or speak English, but he had a dream to create a secure future for his children.

When we walked, my dad set the pace. I could never keep up with him, not even in his eighties. A former soccer player and tennis player in our native Morocco, as well as a math teacher and owner of Galeries de Safi, a successful store that imported French goods, he was always bursting with restless energy. Even in photos, he stood with one foot up on a rock, as if ready to leap off in an instant. Slight, with a gargantuan appetite for food and experiences, he never gained an ounce. He devoured fruits, a kilo at a time, the way he'd told me his father, grandfather, uncle, and the farm workers ate hard-boiled eggs on their farm near Mogador, the colorful sea-town now known as Essaouira. The men sat in a circle on the ground and reached toward a basket heaped full of eggs, at least a hundred eggs, hatched from their own chickens. The eggs had been boiled and salted and were still burning hot when the men grabbed one and cracked open the shell. One egg after another, swallowed in a single gulp.

That appetite for life was reflected in the way he walked, arms crossed behind his back, a posture I find myself unconsciously imitating. It symbolized his eagerness to embrace what lay ahead and a curiosity that never ceased. As we walked, Dad noticed everything and everyone. A sharp, witty observer of people, he often made me laugh to tears, and strangely, he even made Ginger smile. Neither one of us knew the names of plants, trees, birds, but we noted minute variations in the water level, the immense girth of a tree that had fallen during a storm, and after heavy rains the mushrooms sprouting around tree roots, pale freckled squatters that spread to monstrous proportions.

That August, after weeks of drought, the river dried up, baring its secrets, and released a sour, bitter smell. Ginger stood back with Dad and me. There was something wondrous and terrible about seeing what the water hid. Fissures and craters, stirring between the cracks, rustling beneath the ground. Dad listened intently when I told him that I heard a whisper on the back of my neck and felt fingers brush my arms. Our walks that week were haunted by a premonition of loss and death. When the rain finally came and the river filled again, we sat for a long time on the bank while Ginger joyfully plunged in and bolted out to spray and splash us.

As if we were doctors, we paused to examine the red bamboo, a fragile yet sturdy traveler on her own, far from her native China. She'd staked her claim and stood solitary and proud by the river. Dad and I puzzled over her existence. What was she doing here, a lone red stalk growing on a riverbank in Pennsylvania? I imagined her at night, as the water swirled past, and the grasses and leaves rustled and chattered. She didn't speak their language. They didn't speak hers. And yet she was here, an intrepid trespasser, and I wondered if she believed the voyage had been worth it. It wasn't till I wrote a poem about her that I realized she reminded me of myself, an immigrant girl growing up in small-town America. Others had stared at me as if I too were a burst of feverish, incomprehensible color in a black-and-white world.

We always stopped at a curve in the river where my father breathed the green air of trees leaning toward the river and watched the sparkle of water splashing over rocks. It reminded him of Ifrane, the mountain resort in Morocco where he'd camped in his twenties, and where he may have felt freer than he'd ever felt before or since. Each time we passed, he said, "Ah, Ifrane," as if those two words captured the memory of youth and freedom.

After the Ifrane bend, the honeysuckle bush announced its presence by exploding a burst of dizzyingly sweet scent. We stopped to breathe it in and show we appreciated the gift.

The walking path culminated in our favorite area. A sign warned, "This Path is not Maintained." We hoped it frightened off the timid. For us, this winding, unpaved path of dirt, leaves, mulch, spreading roots, and fallen trees was the high point of our adventure. As soon as we entered, a hush surrounded us. We walked along the river, sheltered by the leafy boughs of ancient trees. We felt like explorers in a new land—maybe we were—discovering our America, a land of transcendent beauty and promise. The path ended abruptly at the edge of a steep hill. And we reluctantly turned back toward civilization.

In the center of this untamed, unmaintained area was the most mysterious place of all: a natural clearing surrounded by trees that released a scent as unmistakable as the honeysuckle bush. A scent that mingled magic, history, and pain. I called it the Witches' Circle. We always paused inside the hushed circle. Even Ginger stood silent. Something powerful, mystical, dangerous had happened here. I felt it in my bones. A coven had met here, a magical group had gathered around a fire, spells had been set. When I tried to explain to my dad, he said, "The land remembers."

The land remembers. This, from the man who prided himself on being down to earth, who loved to do calculations on torn envelopes, adding and subtracting lists of numbers, creating eternal budgets for me. A man who read only the news, never fiction, and who worried I would lose myself in stories while the real world passed me by.

ANOTHER SUMMER, DECADES earlier, Dad and I traveled back to Morocco. I went in search of Suleika, the legendary Jewish martyr whose story formed the backbone of my first novel, *The Road to Fez*. Dad did not want me to go alone. This was his first trip back since we'd sailed from Tangiers to New York twenty-five years earlier. I'd returned once before, at seventeen, with my mother. After a week of travel and research around the country, Dad and I went to Safi, the stark little town on a cliff that loomed over the Atlantic. Known for its pottery and sardines, Safi was the town where we'd both been born. During one unforgettable July day, we walked back through time.

The smells, tastes, and caress of the North African air were all familiar, as if they'd been waiting for me to return. I was pregnant with my daughter, and I felt as ripe and heavy as the fruits hanging from trees. While Dad recaptured his youth, I followed—absorbing, listening, remembering what I didn't know I'd forgotten. *This town remembers me.*

We began at the Jewish cemetery of Safi. The caretaker of the cemetery rode down the hill toward us on a white donkey. His broad face beneath a large straw hat was red and seamed like a cloth doll's. Gnarled brown fingers loosely held the reins. He greeted my father like an old friend, then rode past us. We were alone with the notorious Safi wind and the graves.

The dirt path leading up the steep hill was too narrow for two. The higher we climbed, the fiercer the wind. No regular plots or planned rows of tombs, not even an attempt at taming death, at rendering it civilized and acceptable. White tombs—nameless, unmarked—like the doors of Safi—tilted forward precariously, as if one more ferocious gust would force them down the hill. This was death's true face, not regimented and organized, neatly marked and prepared for, but brutal fury shrieking in my ears.

At the top of the hill, amid graves packed helter-skelter and choked by weeds, I paid my respects to my mother's and father's ancestors, generations of Knafos, Leks, Cohens, Cabessas, Ohayons. My father wept at his parents' and grandparents' tombstones. From the highest point I looked down at the glittering Atlantic Ocean and imagined my ancestors fleeing the horrors of the Inquisition in Spain in 1492, crossing the Strait of Gibraltar and finding refuge in Morocco. As we left the cemetery, I brooded over the rusted gates, weeds, scattered stones, and fading inscriptions, and wondered what would happen to the tombs after a few more years of neglect.

From the cemetery, Dad and I walked to a small square building.

Inside, a young man in a navy-blue suit looked up from his desk. Dad spoke in rapid Arabic, gesturing toward me. With a smile, the man rose and led us into a back room. Two men, working at their desks, nodded and stood. The first one brought out a bottle of chilled mineral water and five paper cups, filled them and passed them around. Dad and the three men raised their cups to me and drank. Baffled, I looked around the small, airy room. A square window opened to a great tree with heavy, hanging branches. Glistening sun cast light and shadows on us. I edged nearer to my father, perched on the edge of a desk. "Why are they drinking to me?"

"You were born in this room. The midwife, Sultana l'Haoud, known as 'The Horse,' delivered you. She had six toes on each foot, and she delivered everyone in Safi for generations."

I took a deep breath and went to the window, stared out at the big tree. Tears burned in my throat. In this room, maybe on the exact spot where I stood, my mother had screamed, the tree had blown outside the square window and urged her on, the palm tree had danced in the wind in front, the ocean had raged below.

From death to birth, and in between, Dad and I continued our emotional zigzag of a path through town and time. After lunch at the port—fresh-caught sardines grilled in olive oil—we went downtown, to the site of Dad's former store, Galeries de Safi, at one time the most popular store in town.

To the spacious white villa surrounded by lush flowering bushes, where we'd lived until we left Morocco.

To the Alliance Israelite, the French-run school for Jewish students, where he'd studied as a boy and later taught math. The site of the tales he told my kids when he took them on walks along the river in Pennsylvania.

To the famous *pôterie* of Safi, where potters extract red clay found nearby and mold, dry, shape, paint, and fire it in traditional domed wood-fired kilns. Safi pottery, all made by hand, is famous throughout Morocco for its distinctive geometric and arabesque patterns. The clay is glazed in green, turquoise, and black, often against a cream-colored background. I watched Dad bargain with skill and charm, and gift me with a green and turquoise ceramic bowl I still have.

To the house where he'd grown up. A family lived there and did not invite us in, but I peeked at the black-and-white tiled floor, the narrow corridor that led to the back, and the small faces peeking back at us.

To a family gathering that evening, where my father received a shock from which he never recovered. He'd never received a birth certificate, but a nephew of the town mohel, whose job was to circumcise Jewish boys eight days after their birth, found the book in which his uncle had recorded every circumcision. The notation for my father was clearly marked. He was two years older than he'd been led to believe. He discovered his true birthdate as well: the last day of August. When he arrived in America, he'd adopted June 16th, our first U.S. Father's Day, as his birthday. August 31st, he accepted, but the extra two years tacked onto his life? Never. Did I mention how stubborn my father was?

And our final stop, the town bus station. A shabby street corner, where buses came and went. He told me that, as a boy, he used to sneak onto a waiting bus, set a stone on a seat, and whisper, "Go and see the world for me." Then he'd dismount and watch the bus roar off in a cloud of dust and gravel and imagine he was the stone, beginning his voyage. Oh, Dad, you pretended you weren't a poet, but your soul was free and wild, never completely tamed.

WHEN WE RETURNED to the States, I understood both of us better. My desire to become a detective—linked with my desire to become a writer—began with him. He was my first mystery. A man who kept secrets and hid great portions of his life, who transformed himself when we arrived in America, a cautious adventurer, a pragmatic dreamer— who was he, this puzzle of a man?

No one frustrated me more. No one infuriated me as much or moved me more deeply. I rebelled against his lessons and warnings to structure my life, and even to get a job at the U.S. Post Office so I'd receive a regular salary from the government. One day I wrote him a letter, outlining my grievances. Days passed without a response. Finally, I asked him what he thought.

"To tell you the truth, I don't know," he said. "The writing was so beautiful I didn't pay attention to the meaning."

That glorious summer—his eighty-ninth, or eighty-seventh (as he passionately insisted)—we were past all that and could simply enjoy each other's company. And watch people. I inherited his endless curiosity about everyone. During family trips, the first thing Dad and I did was wander through town to explore the customs, landscape, and inhabitants. We walked through outdoor (and indoor) markets to see how people in that area ate, checked theaters to see what entertained them, peered in store windows to see what they wore, and read local newspapers (if we could) to see what concerned them. Often, we sat at a sidewalk café and people-watched, commenting on those who sparked our interest and creating stories about them.

That summer in the Covered Bridge Park, we got to know the regulars—the smarmy mustached dog-walker who talked to Dad as he ogled me up and down . . . the handsome pony-tailed man whose small stable adjoined the park and who brought out his horses, to Ginger's delight . . . the furtive woman who wore a headscarf down to her eyes and hurried past, gaze lowered . . . the fisherman who aimed and thrust his line into the river as if he were going to shoot the fish . . . the young man who wore his shorts so low and long they brushed his ankles like a skirt. . . .

After the daily morning walk, we stopped for coffee and his weakness, a sticky bun, and continued our conversation, often recounting memories of different walks. Walks we'd taken together down busy streets in Paris, Jerusalem, San Francisco, and New York, and along beaches at the Jersey shore, in Tel Aviv and Torremolinos, where he'd always wade in and splash salt water over his face. Walks with my children in the same park along the river, when he entertained them with stories about the ducks who paddled in the water. He named the ducks after the kids' friends and created fabulous adventures in which the ducks needed to look out for that notorious scamp, the Duck with the Hat. He recounted tales of his schooldays in Morocco, when his desk was between those two troublemakers, King Kong and Queen Elizabeth, and he, age nine, was the one who tried to keep order. My kids laughed, but believed him, of course. And till the end, none of them could keep up with him either.

THE LAST WALK with my father was the walk that wasn't. After our dazzling summer of daily walks, fall crept in, leaves teasing us with traces of vivid color. We set off on our familiar path, and I'd taken only a few steps when I realized he hadn't advanced. I turned in time to see him tipping forward, arms flailing, but his legs motionless. I reached out and caught him before he toppled face-down. But he was so strong that he pushed me, and I tilted back toward the ground.

Luckily, a man saw us and pushed behind me, holding me up, and keeping us both from falling. But my dad, who had walked every day of his life, through rain and storm and snow, for whom the act of walking was sacred, his daily journey through life, had lost control of his legs.

After that day, he still walked, but in limited doses, and never alone. Dementia had also begun its insidious, destructive track through his brain—like the harshest winter, blasting at colors and tearing down memories, slicing through the heart of the man.

The world is still the grand mystery it always was. I am still a trespasser walking to explore and discover not just where I am, but who I am. But I'm not searching for definitive answers anymore: there is no one true solution to the mystery. And there is no one walk that will tell me: this is it, the final border, no more to see, nothing left to explore. There will always be more. Many great travelers have said that we travel in order to understand the landscape of ourselves. My father taught me that walking is the greatest way to understand the world by becoming part of it. Walking *is* seeing. We acknowledge the show the world has put on for us—weather, nature, creatures—two-legged, four-legged, winged. Walking is an act of gratitude for our ability to perceive, to move with our bodies, and to see and absorb with our senses.

Is there anything more subversive than walking, step by step, through the world and discovering secrets about people, nature, and perhaps most of all, about yourself? Each time you set off on a journey—physical or imaginative, whether you go on foot or scrawl with your pen or tap across keys—you are on a voyage of discovery. The world is filled with holy sparks and clues, and it's up to you to uncover its secrets, and not to turn back when you realize the deepest, darkest secret is your connection to the universe.

I DON'T FIND my father in the cemetery or synagogue. I feel his presence when I walk. It's been twelve years since Dad died, five since Ginger died, but each time I walk in Covered Bridge Park, I see their shadows next to mine. Since that golden summer I shared with my father, many more people have discovered the park. At times, it's even crowded. The ogling man and furtive woman have disappeared. The horse farmer closed his stable and moved away. The honeysuckle bush mysteriously stopped releasing its scent. The stubborn red bamboo finally admitted defeat and either sank into the ground or drifted down the river.

The untamed path is now maintained. They've chopped down many of the trees, obliterating the edges of the Witches' Circle so it's difficult to determine where it was, and as a final outrage, installed Disc Golf stations and wire baskets throughout the formerly wild area. Dad would be horrified. But as I walk along the path, pushing aside invisible lacy branches, I listen for sounds behind the trees, a faint rustling of leaves, the whispering river, and the hush beneath it all. I remember what the water hid. I stop where the Circle was. I feel it. *The land remembers.*

My father waits for me around the bend, the place he paused to breathe the air and watch water hit the rocks in sunlight, the place he dreamed of being free. I see him as a boy running onto a bus and setting down a stone to travel for him. And I often pick up a stone and throw it into the sparkling water. "Ah, Ifrane," he says in my ear. We share a moment of awe and wonder, and then he advances, hands behind his back, leaving me to follow and see what's around the corner.

Five Thousand Walks
Toward Thoreau's Journal

Christine Nelson

Henry David Thoreau (1817–1862) is the iconic American walker. He's on every list of those whose footsteps history remembers. There is even a scholarly journal, *The Concord Saunterer*, that takes its name from the word he liked to use to describe his slow, unstructured walks. Not only did Thoreau himself write memorably about walking, many folks in turn have produced essays about his legendary practice, inevitably quoting an 1841 line from his journal: "It is a great art to saunter." This will not be one of them. This is the story of a different lifetime of walks.

Every walk is fleeting: it exists in the moment and then in memory, while a journal (if kept on paper) is a physical thing that lasts as long as it remains safe and dry. While Thoreau ceased to saunter a century and a half ago, his journal survives. The bulk of it (in thirty-nine notebooks) remains safe, dry, and under continuous surveillance at the Morgan Library & Museum in New York. For more than thirty years, I've worked there as a librarian and curator of literary and historical manuscripts. Since 1990 (with a hiatus in 2020, when COVID kept me away), I've been taking variations of the same short walk, day after day, from my office to a secure underground collections vault where Thoreau's journal resides. My office location has moved seven times and the vault itself three times, so my route has altered. The destination, though, has remained the same.

How many times have I made the trip? I did some calculations. If I've worked about 220 days a year, that comes to 6,600 days across three decades. It's not unusual for me to go to the vault more than once a day, but some days I don't go at all. So to be conservative, let's assume I've made 5,000 visits. In the early years, I would spin a combination lock and lift a heavy lever to get in. Today, I hold a programmed identification card up to an electronic panel that recognizes my security clearance and releases a submarine door meant to keep water at bay in the event of a catastrophic incident. I don't handle Thoreau's notebooks every time I enter, but I'm always aware of their presence. Whether they belong on the cold, white, powder-coated steel shelves of the Morgan's vault is something I consider. Perhaps they would sit more comfortably on bookshelves made of driftwood, like those Thoreau once built by repurposing a twenty-foot oak timber he had found lodged in some rocks on the Assabet River? There is plenty of time for such musings over the course of five thousand walks.

It might seem that journal keeping has little in common with walking. Many of us do one sitting down and the other standing up, one indoors and the other outside. One act engages the mind, the other the body. One requires reflection and stillness, the other action and movement. Walking may be social; writing is often solitary. Even if we keep a journal of a walk, the writing tends to memorialize rather than constitute the central act, much like the essays in this volume record walks that were arduous, ordinary, transformative, or otherwise memorable. But walking and journal keeping can be fundamentally interdependent. They most certainly were for Thoreau. They were complementary ways of moving through life with openness and deliberateness. They were more than acts or duties; they were parallel practices. Each fed the other and was incomplete without its counterpart.

Thoreau's journal output was nearly continuous over the course of twenty-four years, from his first entry on October 22, 1837, when he was twenty, to his last in 1861, when he was forty-four and getting close to the end of his life. His early notebooks are full of meditations on lofty topics like heroism and truth; the middle and later ones are dominated by disciplined and joyous observations of natural phenomena. Now and then he wrote about the challenges of forming meaningful bonds with other people; occasionally there was an explosive outpouring about racial injustice and American hypocrisy. Here and there he added little sketches of plants, ice crystals, and animal tracks. Most of all, he wrote about what he saw, heard, smelled, tasted, measured, or otherwise observed on his long daily walks close to home in Concord, Massachusetts.

As a special collections librarian, I've thought about how Thoreau got special books into his hands. He couldn't just walk to a local library branch to find the works that fueled him. So I took special note of what he wrote in his journal one day in February 1852. He had skipped his usual walk and gone to Cambridge and Boston to look at some old books. As a Harvard graduate he had lifetime privileges at the college library, and as a citizen naturalist he liked to take advantage of the holdings of the Boston Society of Natural History. Thoreau was by no means averse to a twenty-mile walk, but on that particular day he presumably rode "the cars"—the Fitchburg rail line that ran close to home.

Many of us have an idea of Thoreau based on what we've heard about him or what we remember from reading *Walden*. He wasn't all about beans and ponds. He read a great deal—and in quite a few languages: Latin, Greek, French, German, and Italian. He could get by in Spanish and Portuguese, and he read key texts of Hinduism, Buddhism, and Confucianism in translation. When he was at home in Concord, he did his best to split his days between intellectual and physical pursuits—sitting at his small green desk to write in the mornings, then walking all afternoon. And yes, he worked for a living as well—first as a teacher, then as a pencil-maker and graphite entrepreneur, and ultimately as an accomplished land surveyor, a profession that called for a great deal of walking, though not of the sauntering kind.

But on the days he went to Boston, he lost the sense of balance—physical, intellectual, spiritual—that he cultivated at home in Concord. He sometimes felt that the libraries he visited were altogether the wrong kinds of places to house the works of writers who, like himself, were intimately engaged with the natural world. The day after that 1852 excursion, he began an entry in his journal:

> I have been to the Libraries (yesterday) at Cambridge & Boston. . . .
> How happens it that I find not in the country, in the field & woods,
> the *works* even of like minded naturalists & poets – Those who have
> expressed the purest & deepest love of nature – have not recorded it
> on the bark of the trees with the lichens – they have left no memento

of it there – but if I would read their books I must go to the city – so strange & repulsive both to them & to me. . . .

Extracting a single entry from a lifetime of journal writing can give a skewed impression. Here Thoreau expressed disgust with the city (and don't we all have places we don't feel at ease?), but on the whole his journal is full of expressions of wonder and even ecstasy, which for him meant a sense of profound communion with the universe. On this day, however, he was irritated, and he dealt with that feeling by letting his mind run in unexpected directions. He conjured a Borgesian fantasy about what might constitute a truly suitable repository for the old books he loved:

> I have sometimes imagined a library i.e. a collection of the works of true poets philosophers naturalists &c deposited not in a brick or marble edifice in a crowded & dusty city – guarded by cold-blooded & methodical officials – & preyed on by bookworms – in which you own no share, and are not likely to – but rather far away in the depths of a primitive forest – like the ruins of central America – where you can trace a series of crumbling alcoves – the older books protecting the more modern from the elements – partially buried by the luxuriance of nature – which the heroic student could reach only after adventures in the wilderness, amid wild beasts & wild men.

Unlike the Prussian naturalist Alexander von Humboldt, whose work he revered, Thoreau never went to Central America. Though he embarked on a few extended excursions (notably to Maine and Cape Cod), he remained mostly close to home, walking the land around his home in Concord, Massachusetts, time and again, finding endless fascination in close observation of the world at hand. "Pursue, keep up with, circle round and round your life as a dog does his master's chaise," he told a friend who had asked for advice. "Do what you love. Know your own bone; gnaw at it, bury it, unearth it, and gnaw it still." He never felt he had to travel far to experience abundance. Walking in circles, the usual metaphor for futility, could be fruitful instead.

In that 1852 journal entry, Thoreau envisioned a fertile reward for the true student of nature: a fantastical library that took the form of a verdant dugout, fully integrated within nature itself. "That to my imagination," he continued, "seems a fitter place for these interesting relics, which owe no small part of their interest to their antiquity – and whose occasion is nature – than the well preserved edifice – with its well preserved officials on the side of a city's square." To reach this imagined library, a student-reader would have to turn their back on conventional, buttoned-up bibliophilic bureaucrats—people, perhaps, like me. They would have to eschew catalogs and hushed study rooms like those of the Morgan Library. They would have to commit to a long, hard walk. There would be beasts along the way, to be sure, but at the end of the trek there would be a great reward: a lush library of glorious books.

WHEN I DISCOVERED this journal entry (possibly around my three-thousandth walk), I was not exactly charmed. I was horrified. It was then that I began to doubt whether the Morgan Library & Museum was a fitting storehouse for the notebooks of someone who had "expressed the purest & deepest love of nature," as Thoreau had described his naturalist forebears. After all, the architectural heart of the institution is a luxury library created for the American financier and collector J. Pierpont Morgan. Though it looks much like an Italian Renaissance palazzo with its elegant exterior of Tennessee pink marble, it sits right in the middle of Manhattan, on Thirty-sixth Street off Madison Avenue. It resembles, in short, the kind of library Thoreau described in his journal: *a brick or marble edifice in a crowded & dusty city – guarded by cold-blooded & methodical officials – & preyed on by bookworms. . . .* Did Thoreau's works belong inside?

I first reported for work there in 1990, perhaps destined to *become* one of those cold-blooded and methodical library officials Thoreau had so disparaged. (Despite his harsh language about my profession in that one journal entry, it should be noted that Thoreau did value his relationship with Thaddeus William Harris, the entomologist who served as Harvard's librarian for a time.) Robert Parks, my new colleague and boss, showed me the East Room of Morgan's Library. There were floor-to-ceiling bookcases of fine, polished cherrywood, hidden staircases that allowed access to the upper tiers, and ceiling murals depicting such European cultural luminaries as Dante, Caxton, and Galileo—hardly the crumbling alcoves Thoreau imagined as a suitable home for the works of true poets, naturalists, and philosophers, let alone his own.

Over the mantelpiece hung a sixteenth-century Brussels tapestry depicting one of the seven deadly sins in the Christian tradition. Known as *The Triumph of Avarice*, it is marked with a Latin motto that reads, "As Tantalus is ever thirsty in the midst of water, so is the miser always desirous of riches." Many find it ironic, if not hypocritical, that J. Pierpont Morgan, the leading American money man at the beginning of the twentieth century, should have chosen to crown his library with a mural communicating a warning about the dangers of greed. Surely Thoreau—our nation's quintessential simplifier—had no proper place within this temple of wealth?

It is true that Morgan never seemed to have enough rare books and manuscripts—those tangible artifacts of history, creativity, communication, ideas, and, of course, power and privilege. Like King Midas, depicted in the tapestry, Morgan was always desirous of more. Today many of his precious volumes are housed in a series of collection vaults; the East Room cannot contain them all. On my first day of work all those years ago, Robert took me into one of them and introduced me to some of the riches held there. This was the first of my five thousand walks.

First we passed through the Library's elegant Rotunda and into a long passageway then known as the Cloister, then down a tight spiral staircase that led to the manuscripts vault. We passed a hand-lettered sign that read QUIET, SCHOLARS AT WORK. There were no howling beasts or rustling tree limbs, only the sound of our heels on the cold marble floors. This was not the heroic trek Thoreau had envisioned for the true lover of books.

Inside the vault, Robert showed me the only surviving portion of Milton's manuscript of *Paradise Lost*, the manuscript of Dickens's *A Christmas Carol*, and miniature manuscripts written by the teenage Charlotte Brontë, born the year before Henry Thoreau in a different small town an ocean away. And then we came to something completely different. It was a pockmarked wooden crate that looked strangely out of place. This box didn't proclaim power and privilege; it embodied utility and simplicity. Robert lifted the lid, and inside was a long row of notebooks. Affixed to the inside of the lid, a bronze plate explained what this humble thing was doing in such august company. It read, *The Complete Original Manuscript of the Journal of Henry D. Thoreau in the Wooden Box Made by Thoreau Himself.*

Well, that explained it! I later learned that there were a few problems with the words engraved there. The manuscript of the journal inside the box was not exactly complete (though it was pretty nearly so), and as for the words *Made by Thoreau Himself*? It was a reasonable assumption, but probably untrue. But one thing was certain: the box had served as a simple storage container for most of Thoreau's journal notebooks for a very long time—a century, maybe longer—and, over time, this ordinary container had taken on the air of a reliquary. But unlike a renowned Byzantine triptych also in the Morgan's collection, it did not hold a spurious fragment of the true cross; it held the absolutely *real* written traces of one person's life.

Robert pulled out notebook number eight, which opened very naturally to A Particular Page. I now know why. The notebook had been opened to That Particular Page so many times that the volume had developed a sort of muscle memory. It was clearly considered the most important one of the several thousand inside the box. It was headed *Walden Sat. July 5th 1845*, and the narrative entry began in a nice, bold hand: "Yesterday I came here to live."

Here were six words that a young man had written the day after the Fourth of July, starting a fresh page in his notebook as he started a new phase of his life in a small house he had built by Walden Pond. He was grieving after the death of his beloved brother, John. He needed time and focus to write a book about a trip they had once taken together. He wanted to try a fresh way of living, upending some of the usual expectations about what matters most. He had no intention of retreating into solitude, living entirely off the grid, or divorcing himself from family and society; he just needed some clear space. He was excited about this new start, but he couldn't begin to know all that would unfold beginning that summer day in 1845.

After his Walden sojourn was over, Thoreau would give lectures in town, describing to his neighbors how he had lived for two years, two months, and two days in that small house by the pond. He would spend several years writing and revising a big book about his time there. That book would be published and sold, and it would grow in influence in the century and a half after its author's death to the point that a bunch of nails—pretty much all that survives from the house he built—is carefully retained within a museum in his hometown. People would make pilgrimages to the site, placing stones on a cairn in the author's memory. Some would revere him; others would disparage him. Many would gather in classrooms, conference centers, and protest sites to talk together about how one young man had lived, thought, walked, and resisted.

But when twenty-seven-year-old Henry Thoreau wrote that sentence in his journal—*Yesterday I came here to live*—he didn't know all that was to come. It's an entry that resonates with some of us now because *we* know how the story turned out, but young Thoreau did not. The Page reminds us that Henry Thoreau was simply a young person, holding a quill pen, seated at his desk, marking a moment in time that felt momentous to him and has come to feel momentous to many of us. But on the day he filled The Page, the rest of the notebook was still blank. A good deal of living was still ahead of him. He couldn't have anticipated, for example, that nine years later, on a different Fourth of July, he would deliver the fiery address known as "Slavery in Massachusetts." Sharing the speakers' platform in Framingham that afternoon in 1854 were several other ardent abolitionists, including William Lloyd Garrison, Lucy Stone, and Sojourner Truth. One of them, the Rev. John Pierpont, had a seventeen-year-old grandson, J. Pierpont Morgan, who would ultimately purchase the journals Thoreau was filling with a lifetime of moments.

And now, a confession. When my colleague opened Thoreau's journal number eight for me that day thirty years ago (when I was about the same age as Thoreau when he moved to Walden Pond), I didn't feel any of that. I could tell I was supposed to feel awe, and I did. It would've been hard not to. There I was inside the splendid library of one of the world's most powerful bankers and collectors, J. Pierpont Morgan, a space *designed* to make you feel you're in the presence of greatness. Within that exclusive library, I was further ensconced in a secure underground chamber that was such a privileged space that I wouldn't be allowed to go in there alone for months, until I'd been through a probationary period. Valuable manuscripts were being flourished before my eyes as if they were trophies. So yes, it was a treat to see that page on which Thoreau had written about moving to Walden; everything was conspiring to make me appreciate what a treat it was.

But where was my heart? It wasn't with Thoreau, the author, or even the icon. In college I'd been made to read something about ants and something about beans, I think, in the *Norton Anthology of American Literature*, and neither of those *Walden* passages, presented out of context, did much for me. I just didn't get it. His writings had been *assigned* to me. I hadn't yet come to *Walden* on my own to discover that it was about much more than insect communities and vegetable gardens.

I certainly hadn't yet immersed myself in Thoreau's journal. I hadn't embarked on my journey of five thousand walks. What I saw that day remained primarily a thing I was expected to bow down to. And so I did.

What I was really looking at with curiosity and true wonder were all the *other* notebooks—not just number eight, not just the one that contained The Page. I'd never seen anything like it—the physical record of so many days, so many miles of walks. Something had driven Thoreau to fill all those notebooks. I was looking at forty of them that day, and I later learned that he'd kept still more. Why did he do it? What was he after? I began to look at the journal closely not because Thoreau was famous, but because he was human. Here before me was a record of that humanity, a library of the self. But where was it housed? Not in the crumbling alcoves of Thoreau's fantasy but in precisely the sort of place, a "marble edifice" in the heart of a teeming city, he had deemed unsuitable. Could this grotesque discrepancy possibly be reconciled?

In one of his earliest surviving entries, Thoreau started with a heading, "Discipline," as if it were a classroom essay: "I yet lack discernment to distinguish the whole lesson of to-day; but it is not lost – it will come to me at last. My desire is to know *what* I have lived, that I may know *how* to live henceforth." As his practice deepened over the ensuing years, that principle remained the same: he was keeping track of things in order to know how best to live. The handwritten marks on the page would be like footprints in the earth—tangible records of a walk that could otherwise never be revisited.

Writing was a discipline—but one of self-renewal rather than self-denial. And Thoreau was keeping track of things incrementally, in the form of a journal, because he knew he was not equipped (as few of us are) to distinguish the lesson of today. He committed not just to marking the day but to a lifetime of patience, building up a record of expressions of joy, rage, gratitude, and surprise without knowing what they would amount to over time.

When he first got started, he wasn't sure he had the patience. "But what does all this scribbling amount to?" he asked himself during that first year of journal keeping. He felt happy with the words he put down in the ardor of the moment but sometimes found them "stale, flat – and unprofitable" the morning after. He quickly realized that wasn't the point. A couple of years later, he had begun to turn a profit—but not the sort J. Pierpont Morgan would later go after. "No day will have been wholly misspent," Thoreau told himself, "if one sincere thoughtful page has been written." Instead of entering well-honed passages into the journal, he was starting to loosen up, to see the marks he made on paper as something like the traces ocean waves leave upon the sand. "Let the daily tide leave some deposit on these pages," he wrote, "as it leaves sands and shells on the shore. . . . This [the journal] may be a calendar of the ebbs and flows of the soul; and on these sheets as a beach, the waves may cast up pearls and seaweed."

So Thoreau kept at it, and he got used to trusting in the process, embracing both jewels and dross. He accepted the thoughts that came to mind, even if they were contradictory or strange—like his vision of a student's heroic trek. When I look at Thoreau's well-worn notebooks I'm reminded that the journal was, for him, a dynamic document—one that accommodated new entries while accumulating layers of meaning. He handled each notebook countless times—as he opened it to make an entry, dipped his quill pen into his inkwell, blotted each page with a blank sheet and moved on to the next, then closed up the notebook for the day and opened it again when he had more to say. He would return to old notebooks from time to time, rereading old entries to get a sense of how life had progressed or to organize his documentation of natural phenomena. Such was the value of making tracks.

Thoreau used his journal in parallel with other written records, such as a series of notebooks dedicated to his extensive readings about North American geography and Indigenous peoples. He was deeply engaged in this self-directed program of study that day he went to the libraries in Boston and Cambridge in 1852 and on subsequent visits. He described his encounter with some of the volumes in sensuous terms: "Those old books suggested a certain fertility – an Ohio soil – as if they were making a humus for new literatures to spring in. I heard the bellowing of bull frogs & the hum of mosquitoes reverberating through the thick embossed covers when I had closed the book."

Time and again Thoreau described the books he was reading *and* the journal he was writing in such voluptuous language. He found Cato's ancient farm records "as fresh as a dripping dishcloth from a Roman kitchen." Thoreau felt his hands in an ancient washtub just as surely as he heard frogs and insects resounding within the leather-covered boards of an old book about Canada. So naturally he felt grumpy when forced to confront what he considered living documents—the writings of his comrades across time and space—in an urban setting he found stifling and confining.

Two of the books he checked out that day in Boston and Cambridge were Linnaeus's famous work on plant taxonomy and Lindley's *Natural System of Botany*, and though he loved them he found them limiting. He sought lore among the facts. A manual of botany, he felt, should be "the most poetical of books" containing the "beauty & the fragrance of flowers" and even "some of their color." He started out trying to keep science and art separate in his personal reading notes but soon realized he perceived the world in a more integrated fashion. "I have a common-place book for facts and another for poetry," he wrote, "but I find it difficult always to preserve the vague distinction which I had in mind – for the most interesting & beautiful facts are so much the more poetry and that is their success."

All of these notebooks—his journal and his research records and reading notes—along with a series of detailed phenological tables he created late in his life, were linked elements in Thoreau's lifelong practice of self-education, self-documentation, and self-development. He had taken to heart the advice of his early mentor and lifelong friend Ralph Waldo Emerson, who had challenged his contemporaries to confront God and nature face to face. We should seek truth in many forms, Emerson said, through meaningful engagement with the writings of the past as well as direct engagement with the universe. It was Emerson who had suggested to young Thoreau that a journal would be an essential tool in that quest, and he was right. Even as Thoreau was fantasizing about an epic journey to a living library, he was busy writing the volumes that would constitute his own.

IN THE YEARS since I first peered inside that pine box that Thoreau probably didn't build with his own hands, I have continued to resist viewing his notebooks with the reverence that seemed to be demanded of me. I have regarded the notebooks from a more intimate stance, person to person, with frank human curiosity, compassion, and yes, even love. If Thoreau had days when he expressed frustration or arrogance, I accept those along with the many days when he challenged himself to live rightly and well.

I have even come to believe that Thoreau's journal is very much at home in J. Pierpont Morgan's Library, crowned as it is with a tapestry entitled *The Triumph of Avarice*. Here's why. In 1851, Thoreau wrote these words in his journal:

> It is not in vain that the mind turns aside this way or that. Follow its leading – apply it whither it inclines to go. Probe the universe in a myriad points. Be avaricious of these impulses. You must try a thousand themes before you find the right one – as nature makes a thousand acorns to get one oak.

Thoreau was exhorting himself to practice avarice, but not like the miser depicted on Morgan's tapestry, whose greed comes from a place of moral emptiness. Thoreau's avarice came from a place of openness, a desire for a different kind of riches. *Probe the universe in a myriad points*, he said, *Be avaricious of these impulses*. This kind of greed is good.

In the early 1860s, as Thoreau wrote in what would be his last journal notebook, he maintained that avaricious spirit. He kept on living: building a fence, dissecting a crow's stomach, and interviewing his old aunt about her memories. On his final pages, he wrote about walking—but not his own. He'd been watching a litter of kittens, noting their physical characteristics in the first weeks of life—the closed eyes, silent mews, the folded ears—and paying special attention to their first unsteady steps. "At 3 weeks old the kitten begins to walk in a staggering & creeping manner – & even to play a little with its mother," he wrote, "& if you put [your] ear close you may hear it purr." As Thoreau was nuzzling kittens and observing the dawn of their lives, he was coming to the end of his own. Some months later, after he succumbed to tuberculosis, leaving his final notebook half empty, all those volumes—that extraordinary physical record of thousands of days and miles and miles of walks—passed into someone else's hands.

That is the handwritten library that Thoreau created, and bequeathed, in a sense, to all of us. Many people have held the notebooks since he closed his final one: Sophia Thoreau, Henry's sister and first literary executor; his friends Ellery Channing, Ralph Waldo Emerson, Bronson Alcott, and Harrison Gray Otis Blake; and the editors of the monumental 1906 edition of the journal. In our own generation, the journal notebooks have been handled with care by my friends Beth Witherell, the editor of the ongoing Princeton edition; David Wood, my curatorial co-conspirator at the Concord Museum; María Molestina, head of the Morgan's Reading Room, who issues the journal to visiting scholars; Frank Trujillo, the book conservator who rescued one of the crumbling volumes; and artist Abelardo Morell, who lovingly photographed all their covers. All these readers and many others have kept the journal opening and closing, the notebooks' joints and edges wearing down little by little from all that human contact. All these people have been latter-day companions on Thoreau's lifetime of walks.

On thousands of days throughout most of my adult life, I've been physically close to Thoreau's journal. I've taken that easy walk across the Morgan Library's marble floors to the manuscripts vault time and again, much as Thoreau circled the same paths close to home in Concord, on the alert for fresh insights. My relationship to the journal is one that no other living person shares. I've lived with it in the way we keep our favorite books physically close to us even if we're not reading them every day. I am, for now, one of the journal's keepers. The notebooks were entrusted to me that moment I first saw The Page and all the others, just as they were entrusted to Sophia Thoreau when Henry died in 1862, and then to a few others before J. Pierpont Morgan and his librarian, Belle da Costa Greene, became their keepers in 1909. Since then, a succession of curators and librarians has kept company with them. For the last three decades, it's been my turn. I've watched over Thoreau's journal as it sits in the Morgan's vault within a well-preserved edifice in a crowded city, mindful that, for him, it properly belongs among the lichens and the fungi—in an overgrown alcove we reach after a good, hard walk.

Lost and Found

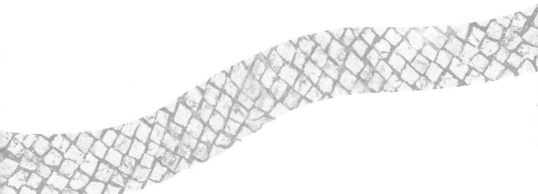

Across the Harbor

Hannah Judd

FOR MY FATHER'S BIRTHDAY, shortly after he moved to New York, we walked across the Brooklyn Bridge.

At least, I proposed the outing that way. It's something people do when they move to New York, something on the list; we didn't go up the Empire State Building or to the Statue of Liberty but we did this. I was home from college for spring break. At first we were going to take the train from the Upper West Side to the Lower East, but it was a nice day and so I said, why don't we walk it all. Across Central Park, down Fifth Avenue, where I made fun of the ugly outfits in the Gucci window and he said he didn't get fashion. To the bridge, crowded and sunny, and across it. We talked about Leonard Nimoy reading Hart Crane's *The Bridge* and looked over the water at the downtown skyline. We stopped just over the other side in Brooklyn at a café with onigiri and coffee, and when he was ready to turn around I told him there was actually another place, just a little further, that I wanted to take him.

The walk was another forty minutes. I led him as part of the birthday emphasis of the walk, a month after his real birthday but a gift that could only be had in person. I implied a gift that waited at the end, and he patiently kept walking with me from the café near the base of the bridge to the corner of Classon and Dekalb, Clinton Hill, to an unassuming storefront filled with enormous white buckets, door open and fan blowing in the heat. Surveyed by an unsmiling woman who watched us peruse our options, the only two people in the store, we browsed the kimchi and fermented ginger and spicy dill and half sour.

It was nearly impossible to buy gifts for my father. When you asked him what he wanted, he would say: "Get rid of all this junk!" He was concerned about the problems of excessive waste and consumption, and how to push against them in everyday life. He liked tiny houses and minimalism; he insisted his sneakers were fine and put duct tape over the holes; he insisted his shirts were also fine and put on sweaters to hide the coffee and ink stains. If you pushed back on his wish to have less and his insistence that he owned too many things and didn't need anything new, the only gift advice you were left with was that he wanted to be surprised and delighted.

"Surprise and delight" is something that my dad did for everyone in my family, often. The last gift he sent me was for my half-birthday: a tiny green frying pan that you can use to cook a single egg. He built wood footstools and a sled and an entire playhouse and swing set for my sisters and me in our backyard; he cooked dinner and made pickles from the vegetables that my mother grew in the garden. He taught me how to do too many things to name; more than that, he taught me—and modeled—how to approach anything that I wanted to do: he was patient, slow, exacting, and methodical, unwilling to cut corners and insistent on the time and care needed to make something that was good.

This was the ethos of the pickle shop, which was an offshoot of Guss' Pickles, on the Lower East Side. Guss' was a pushcart first and then a storefront on Hester Street in 1920, one of a collection of more than eighty stores in "pickle alley," run by Polish immigrant Isidor Guss. The store outlived the others in pickle alley, in part because of Guss' reputation as the Botticelli of brine. After his death, in 1975, the business passed on to Harold Baker, who then handed it down to his son, Tim; he and Andrew Leibowitz, Guss' cucumber supplier and self-described "pickle maven," opened another arm of Guss' in Cedarhurst together.

Baker decided to sell the business in 2004 and Leibowitz did not buy it; Guss' then passed to Patricia Fairhurst, but when she chose to stop using Leibowitz as a supplier he sued her for the name, claiming he had purchased it from Baker in the course of their previous business relationship. When he won the lawsuit, Fairhurst was forced to surrender the name and left the Lower East Side location: she opened Clinton Hill Pickles as a result. She had the true Guss touch, and the real recipes, or so the rumor went: the Guss name stayed on the Lower East Side, but the authentic pickle was gone. I didn't know all of the story when I found the shop, but the tangled lineage belies the strength of the final taste, as clear and true in my memory as the image of my dad savoring his first bite—the scrunch of his nose as he chewed, his wide grin after he swallowed, the pickles crunchy and saturated with flavor, and the understated store with six-dollar quarts and no air conditioning in the unexpected March heat.

After my father died, I bought the ingredients to make miso in my apartment. I was thinking about the act of pickling. I wanted to have faith that letting something ferment for a year or two wasn't leaving it to rot; that I was allowing magic to happen, growth and flavor to emerge in the secret dark. More than that, I was doing what he taught me: making more with less, making things with my own hands, taking things one step at a time, waiting for something to be ready without hurrying it, learning patience that I didn't—and don't—have, making something to share. Passive creation was all I could do. Fermentation became my medium.

Pickling is a heavy-handed metaphor. I know. I was swimming in bathwater and tears, steeped in resentment and pain, marinating in guilt, drowning in sadness. At the same time, my mouth was puckering from the vinegar brine of the mushrooms and carrots and onions and cucumbers and beets, cold from my fridge. *You are what you eat*, I thought, *and I'm eating what's preserved in the hope I too will be saved. I'm a pickle myself, putting my faith in salt and time to cure me.*

Except I'm animal, not vegetable. I had to move. Footsteps became my medium too.

When he died I couldn't stop walking. Pacing at the airport before mercifully collapsing on the plane; at home I couldn't sleep, a gnawing dread in the pit of my stomach, and in the night I paced the suburbs, five miles, eight, ten. Bees buzzing inside my head. Back in Chicago, still insomniac, roaming my neighborhood at night, aimless during the day, waking up each morning before the sun rose, under a lead weight, nauseous, anxious, heartsick. I was signed up for the New York City Marathon and it was too late to pull out, but I stopped training; all I did was wander, not tracking the miles or the times, miles adding themselves up under my feet.

Walking filled the space of the day when I couldn't bear to do nothing but couldn't stand to do anything more. Picking random destinations—my friend's house a few neighborhoods over, a German specialty store I thought might stock Club-Mate, the lakeshore, my therapist, downtown and through the industrial underpass dividing my neighborhood, the art museum, the Korean grocery, the park, the TJ Maxx for tchotchkes I wrapped up and gave to friends who didn't want them, the Nordstrom, buying slip dresses in a daze, the Sephora, the bodega for a can of wine I drank by the river—anything far enough away to give some purpose to the wandering, to set a single task for the day that I could meet. Spending money and forgetting what I'd bought while I was buying it, walking until my feet hurt and my shoes turned dirty and wore down at the back of the heel, anything to feel exhausted, anything to feel numb for a while. Sobbing open-mouthed on the sidewalk by the highway, walking in the rain to hide that I was crying.

I can't stand to be where I am (I can't stand to feel how I feel), so I'd better go somewhere else. But when I get there I'm still the same, everything is still the same. The substitute destinations attempting to serve as proxy for the aimless, endless drift. I can't get to where I want to go.

I ran the marathon but I walked across the bridges. The Brooklyn Bridge isn't on the route. The marathon starts at the tip of Staten Island, then goes across the Verrazano through Brooklyn and north over the Pulaski to Queens, across the Queensboro to Manhattan and north again on the Willis Avenue Bridge to the Bronx. The Madison Avenue Bridge turns the runners back south to Manhattan, and the race finishes in Central Park. I wasn't thinking about the walk with my dad when I was running the marathon; mostly I chose to walk on the bridges because, terrified at my own lack of training, I was afraid there was no way I would finish if I tried to run the whole route.

Walking across, surrounded by runners, I found the uphill and downhill slopes manageable, a slowing of the blurred course. They allowed me to see the city more slowly than I usually did from the passenger windows of cars and buses: expanses of water going out toward the horizon, concrete and steel in any direction. The bridges eliminated the cheering crowds at the sides of the streets; the other runners thundered by while I paused, and watched, and remembered, and walked.

That walk with my father was the only time I've walked the Brooklyn Bridge, somehow, even as I learned the rest of the city avenue by avenue and step by step, retracing the other walks we took and the ones I took alone, finding my haunts and visiting my memories. I'm afraid to go back. I know if I do I won't find what I'm looking for.

For my father's birthday we walked across the Brooklyn Bridge and we went to a pickle shop and he was surprised and he was delighted, and I cling to the memory because in my twenty-four years with him I know that at least once I gave him what he gave me; I got it exactly right.

We listened to Hart Crane once we were home, tired, looking back at the day.

> And Thee, across the harbor, silver-paced
> As though the sun took step of thee, yet left
> Some motion ever unspent in thy stride,—
> Implicitly thy freedom staying thee!

For my father's birthday we walked across the Brooklyn Bridge and we went to the best pickle store in New York and bit into crisp kosher dills, tangy and vibrant after the long journey, travelers' ambrosia, and we bought sauerkraut and pickled garlic and more dills for the road, and we took the train home, sweaty and content. Now the pickle shop is closed, and he is dead, and I make my own pickles and I walk and walk and walk because I don't know what to do. If I stop moving, what's going to catch up to me? I don't know where I'm going, but I'll know when I get there. I can feel it waiting.

Crossing to Jordan

Yasser Allaham

"WHAT ARE YOU coming to Jordan for?" the border guard asked, right after I handed him my brand-new passport.

"I'm going to see my family," I answered.

I was eighteen years old, one of the youngest people riding on the bus from Damascus. I tried not to act like a refugee, to talk more like a tourist. I was a college student going to visit my family, I claimed. I gave them the names and the villages of those I would see on the Jordanian side.

The guard stamped my passport, took it, and disappeared. I waited. A group of guards came back. They'd lost my passport, they told me. At first, I thought they were playing with me. That didn't make sense.

Outside the border patrol station, the bus to Jordan was waiting. Everybody's passport had been returned but mine. I was kept sitting in the waiting room for more than seven hours.

The men finally came back with my passport. They said they had found it under the desk.

A guard stamped it again. A cancellation stamp over the first stamp. I was no longer allowed to enter Jordan. I had to wait another month, they said.

They asked the bus to leave.

Later, they put me in a minivan and dropped me off in the Free Zone, the no-man's-land between Syria and Jordan.

I didn't know exactly where I was. I wasn't sure what to do.

That was the beginning of my forty-days' walk to get to my family in Jordan.

BACK IN 2013 in Damascus, the capital of Syria, my family and I had a very important meeting to decide our future. Everything at that time was getting worse in our country. Kisweh, the town where we lived, sat below the mountains where the army launched their rockets, straight for Aleppo. The rebel forces fired back. Our house was in the middle. Day and night, rockets screeched overhead, bombs boomed. After the fire stopped, we would go up to our roof and pick up the mortar shells.

My family discussed the situation and decided to leave Syria as soon as possible. I was eighteen years old and a student. I was the one who helped the family to move out of Syria to Lebanon. Our ultimate goal was to move to Jordan. I got everyone their passports and found us a place to stay, as we prepared for our next move. There was one problem. I didn't have a passport. But I wanted my family to be safe and out of the war zone our country had become.

We took a car from Damascus to Lebanon; the driver was a family friend, and he was very helpful. He gave away, at every single checkpoint, a packet of cigarettes to the soldiers. He was trying to make everything go smoothly for my family, and it worked out. We all made it safely to Lebanon, which has an open border with Syria.

After being in Lebanon for a month my family got ready to move to Jordan. After they left Lebanon, I went back to Syria to obtain my passport. I would then join my family in Jordan.

Getting a passport was not easy at all. First, I had to pretend I was going to continue my college studies, even though I knew that I was not going to graduate. As a student, I would be allowed to leave the country—and come back again. If I wasn't enrolled in college, I'd have to do mandatory army service. So I took my final exam, and I told my professor honestly what I was going to do. I was leaving the country to join my family in Jordan.

I took my final, then I went to apply for my passport. The government building was a scary place, secured by armed guards. When I arrived at 6:30 a.m., there was already a huge line outside. While I waited two or three hours out on the street, the day kept getting hotter. I helped people out by writing their queue numbers on their hands so they could sit and relax until the doors were open. One of the employees asked me what I was doing. I told him I was trying to help. Nobody had asked me to. I'd just volunteered in order to make people's long wait easier. Like me, they were trying to leave the country.

The employee took my paperwork and led me inside, before it was my turn. I was shaking. But he quickly processed me through. "Because you did this good deed," he said. It was magical. The process usually took between three and six months, but I went in and signed the paper and got my passport in two days, all because I had volunteered to help people out. I was so lucky with this process.

I left Damascus secretly, without telling friends or anyone else. I was concerned that if anyone knew, they would tell the government I was leaving the country. And then I wouldn't be able to. I took only my summer clothes with me, not expecting to have to say goodbye forever to my house, thinking I would be back soon. I boarded the bus with only two suitcases; the big suitcase was filled with a lot of items for my family and the small suitcase was filled with my items.

I took the bus from Damascus with my third cousin and others from my extended family. I was the only man. I had no place to sit, so I sat on the floor next to the driver. It was about 100 kilometers. A couple of hours' drive. We had to detour to avoid the war. The roads were bad, and what I saw on the way was scary—cities and towns destroyed, the houses just heaps of stones with pebbles scattered all around.

We drove through the city of Daraa, where the revolution began. We were stopped at multiple checkpoints—some manned by the regime, others by the rebel militia. It was impossible to tell the difference. They all wore the same army uniform. They all carried machine guns. They asked for IDs and passports. They checked our bags. The militia were looking for supporters of the regime. The regime were looking for secret militia—and also for people like me, who were planning to skip the country. Surprisingly, though, everything went smoothly. I was feeling lucky.

Then we got to the Jordanian border, and the officers claimed they lost my passport, and the bus left without me. While my cousins and my suitcases crossed the border and headed to Amman, I was put in a minivan and dropped off in the Free Zone between the two countries, the one I was fleeing and the one where my family was waiting.

What one of the soldiers had told me inside the border control, to explain my rejected passport, was not the truth. He told me that somebody with Jordanian citizenship who had the same name and date of birth as me was wanted by the government. Only later, after we crossed into that strip between the two countries in the small minivan, did they tell me the truth: Jordan could not take Syrian refugees. This was the reason I was not allowed in the country.

I SPENT FIVE OR SIX DAYS in the Free Zone. Syrians who were let into Jordan left their cars there. Some were open. I slept in these open cars and bought food from trucks. This was the only way to get food. There was very little food, though, and none of the medicine I usually took for my rheumatism. Without it, it was painful for me to stand or walk for a long time. I was in pain most of the journey.

In the Free Zone, I met a Palestinian, Ahmad, who lived in Syria. His mother was Jordanian, and when he left Syria to go to Jordan to see her, the Jordanians would not let him in, and the Syrians wouldn't let him come back. He was just stuck in the Free Zone.

We stayed together. We couldn't always find cars to sleep in. One night it was so cold. I was asleep outside on the ground, using my wallet as a pillow, sleeping next to my new Palestinian friend. The Jordanian police were patrolling the Free Zone. A small cat jumped on me when I was asleep. I woke up, panicked, grabbed the cat and flung it off me, thinking it was a snake, a scorpion, or something worse. A Jordanian policemen stood over me, laughing. He told me that a dog had jumped on me. He was trying to make fun of me. Then he checked our IDs. He told me my cancellation stamp was temporary, and I could try to cross into Jordan in a month.

But he must have told the Syrian police on patrol, because after that, a Syrian officer came to the Free Zone to find the Syrian who was hiding there. He told me I had to leave the Free Zone. Otherwise I would go to jail, where he could do whatever he wished with me, he said, and made a gesture like slashing his neck. "I'm going to kill you," he was saying, even if he didn't use those words. I freaked. I could not stay in the Free Zone.

I took a taxi to Nassib, a nearby village in Syria on the border. I knew there was no way I could stay in Syria for very long. I would be forced to serve in the regime's army, thrown in jail, or worse. My only option was to find a way out of the country. So I started asking the people there about illegally getting into Jordan.

First I went to the mosque. There I found food. I took a shower. And I was able to buy medicine from the pharmacy. The people in Nassib were so friendly, I was shocked. I didn't trust anyone, but they fed me—

real food. It was unbelievable, especially after having eaten nothing but bread and cheese in the Free Zone. I relaxed a little bit. I spent a couple of days taking walks around the village. Every day, I would take a walk around the school.

The people in Nassib got used to my presence. They treated me like a guest in their town. People started to tell me what I should to do to get out of Syria and into Jordan. One family tried to get me to take the identity of their missing Syrian son. He was around my age, and they offered me his documents to use to go to a refugee camp in Jordan. I decided not to do this because I didn't want to get stuck in the refugee camp. I knew that would be as bad as a jail, and once I was in, I would never get out.

IN NASSIB, I spent four days living in the mosque. One day a group of rebel militia showed up. They asked me what I was doing there.

I said, "I want to skip the country."

"Would you like to join us?" they asked me.

"I don't want to share in the civil war," I told them. "I'm just a student and I don't know anything about fighting."

Nobody from the militia bothered me after I said this. They were friendly. They made me feel positive about the revolution. They weren't pushing anybody to fight. But I realized I was wasting my time there. I had family to take care of. I had to go.

I walked over to the school, and a guy there told me who to talk to. An old man came over to me and said that the next day he was taking some people to a place where they could cross the border easily. Next morning, he showed up with a pickup. I got in the back with a man, his wife, and his baby. The baby was really tiny, just a couple of months old. We were stopped at multiple checkpoints, just like on the bus ride from Damascus. Some of these checkpoints were run by the militia and others by the Syrian regime.

At one checkpoint, the regime soldiers asked the husband to pull his pants down. I was thinking they were searching for something hidden in his underpants. But under his pants he had on Jordanian army pants, which the militia often wore. The soldiers grabbed him and his wife, and the baby too. They stuck a machine gun in the man's face. And then they took them all away.

That moment was the hardest part of my journey on my way to Jordan.

A WHILE LATER, the truck driver stopped. He said we were outside the village of Tal Shihab. He took our payments and left us in the middle of nowhere. I didn't see any people. Only trees. I walked for hours and hours. I was lost in what looked like a jungle. For hours I saw nobody. I still had a phone with a Jordanian SIM card, an old phone, and called my uncle in Jordan. I was screaming into the phone, "I don't want to come to Jordan."

Even today I don't know exactly where I was. But somehow after walking all night I found the village. I remembered that somebody had told me that I should go to the school there, though finding the school was also very difficult. The outside was surrounded by armed militia and their enormous trucks. There was a UN bus too, delivering food. Inside was a huge room where refugee families lined up for the food. It felt like what I imagined a jail to be. I walked around, looking into the classrooms. All the desks had been cleared out so families could sleep there. I had nothing on me but my phone and wallet. I found an empty classroom, and put my wallet under my head to use as my pillow. I slept like that all the time on my journey to Jordan.

Again I called my uncle in Jordan, and he called a friend he knew who lived in south Syria to help me out. That friend sent another friend to find me at the school, who set me up with the person who was going to help me get out of Syria. There would be a small group of us, nine in total.

We waited until nighttime, then the nine of us were picked up in a minivan. We stopped at a farm on the way and asked for food. The farmer gave us a whole basket of tomatoes. Fresh and free. It was the most delicious food I had on my journey.

The van dropped us far enough from the border crossing that no one would spot the vehicle. We set off walking in the dark, trying not to make any sounds or use any lights. Israel was on our right, Jordan was on our left. The only light came from the moon and the stars. I did whatever our guide said, *Go left, go right*. We walked for a few hours and then went down to the river.

Searchlights flashed through the dark. "Hey, Syrian guys!" we heard Jordanian soldiers call to us from the other side over loudspeakers. Our guide had assured us that he had made a deal with the Jordanian police. They were shouting across the river, scanning the area with their big flashlights, trying to catch us. They didn't really know where we were. We backed up and walked the rest of the night to a tiny village, still stuck in Syria. Nobody would give us food, except for old bread and watermelon. We went looking for a market, but food was so scarce in that village that nobody wanted to give us any, not even for money.

We waited there for three days. We were right next to a war zone. We could hear the gunfire and explosions.

Our guide insisted he always had another plan, but we ended up finding someone else to help our group get to Jordan. A young kid showed up, maybe around sixteen years old, younger than me. He said he would take us out of Syria. Once again, we set off in the night. This time we took a different route. It was worse. We had to walk in the mountains. I was hugging the side of the mountain in the dark. One wrong step and I'd fall down the hill. In our group was a man who had been shot in the belly and another who was shot in the leg. Also a mentally disabled guy. I was in charge of him and the man shot in the stomach.

Out of nowhere, Syrian militia showed up and demanded to see our IDs. They treated us well, though, and gave us some water and food. Then, without warning, the militia started shooting at the sky. Across the river, the Jordanian border patrol started shooting back. The sky was full of sparks. I was confused and scared. What was going on? I asked. The militia explained that they were pressuring the Jordanians to open the border to take people who needed medical assistance. That signal wouldn't help us though. Because the Jordanians were so close, we would have to wait another three hours to make a move. Finally, after the shooting stopped, we made our way down to the river. Once again, lights swept toward us from the Jordanian side. *We've failed again*, I said to myself, and prepared to turn back.

Instead, we waited in the dark until everything was quiet. At last it was time to cross the river. The water was up to my chest, then up to my neck. I was helping one of the men who'd been shot who was trying to cross with his crutches. He stumbled twice, but I held him from behind and made sure he didn't fall. The water was rising up my chest. I had to hold my wallet and phone above my head. I didn't want my documents to get wet. Fortunately, I didn't have any bag to carry and that made my movements lighter.

Jordanian police cars patrolled the other shore. I could see them while we were crossing. I told the guide that we should time our movements to avoid the patrols. Once the cars passed, he signaled for us to crawl out on our elbows like soldiers.

We crawled that way all the way up the mountain. We knew the Jordanian police were above us. Any stone that fell would give us away. I was last in line, so I could stop the tumbling stones. I kept praying as we moved up the mountain. There was no place to put two feet together. It was very narrow, high, and dangerous.

At last we reached the top of the mountain. It was still dark. Our young guide told us to stop. He had to call someone who would come to escort us to a safe house inside Jordan, but he couldn't get a signal there. He started walking away—to get the signal, he said. He left us in a kind of cave in the side of the mountain. We had no choice but to wait. I didn't know if we were stranded, if I was trapped in a setup after all.

He came back, discouraged. He told us he couldn't find the signal and didn't know what to do. I told him I had a phone with a Jordanian SIM card, and we walked together until we found a signal. He finally reached his contact with my phone.

Two hours later, our escort showed up just as the morning sun was starting to rise. He was wearing a Jordanian army uniform and carrying a gun. He urged us to hurry. We continued our journey on foot, passing by houses, through places where people lived. If anyone woke up and spotted us, they could call the police.

We walked for hours and hours. I eyed every house we passed, afraid that someone would see us. Of all the walking I'd done in the past forty days, those few hours walking in the early morning in Jordan felt like the longest journey of all.

We reached his house. He locked us in with a big lock and asked us for our money. He took all our possessions, including our cell phones. We had to renegotiate our deals. I bargained for myself and the two men I'd been watching out for, the one who was shot in the stomach and the one with a mental disability.

There were two Jordanians in that house. One of them drove us and the man who'd been shot in the leg in a truck to a place where a friend of two of the Syrians could get money to pay the fee. Once we paid, the Jordanians returned our possessions to us.

The friend we met took the wounded men to the hospital. Then he looked me over. I had a long beard and dirty clothes. He asked me to take a shower, get changed, and shave my beard. I was happy to take a shower. I hadn't washed for more than a month during this journey. Still, I didn't want to shave yet. I wanted my parents to see some sign of what I'd been through. So he gave me clean clothes and a fake ID, and he made sure I knew the information on the ID in case I got stopped by the police. We were still very close to the border. I was on my way to Amman, the capital, where my family was, still two and a half hours away by car.

Because I had helped his friends, he volunteered to drive me along with another Syrian who had just crossed the border. Just as we were leaving his neighborhood, a friend asked our driver for a ride. He was a cop. He asked the driver about the guys in the back seat. He said we were two employees working for him in construction. We were actually lucky to have the cop with us in the car, because no other cops would stop us to question us. We had an excuse not to be afraid of other cops. This cop had no idea who we really were.

At last I arrived in Amman. My family came out on the street to meet me. I could tell from their faces how different I looked from the last time they had seen me. My hair was curly, my beard was long, and the blue jeans I'd changed out of, now in a plastic bag, were completely black. I had lost a lot of weight. I was very sick and very tired.

None of that mattered. I was so excited to have hugs from all of my family. At last, after forty days of walking and driving and sleeping with my wallet as a pillow, and never being sure I could trust anyone, I had crossed the border.

I threw my clothes in the trash.

MONTHS LATER, before we prepared to leave for America, I went hiking in the mountains of Jordan, those same steep mountains I'd climbed on my knees in the dark. I was near the borders of Syria and Palestine. I noticed a change in the air. The winds blew up from across the river. I was breathing Syrian air!

I climbed up higher and looked down at the river, across to my home. I breathed the Syrian air for the last time in my life.

MY GRANDFATHER USED to tell me that a person who has two ears and a tongue will never get lost. I never forget my grandfather's words. I love to sit with people and hear them tell their stories. And I'm not afraid to speak up for myself. His advice has helped me out so much in my life, especially on my journey to Jordan—and after, when I came to America alone.

But that's another story.

A Walk with Hawk

Dwight Sterling Dunston

Dear Pops,

It dawned on me as I started writing this letter to you that perhaps the last letter I wrote you was when I was eleven years old. You may or may not remember this, but I was often too shy to ask outwardly if I could play Sega Genesis after finishing my homework, so I would come up with creative ways to ask your permission. On one particular day I tossed a paper airplane with the request from the top of the staircase as you sat watching TV on the couch. Maybe it was the request on the paper or the creativity in the ask, but you looked up and smiled when you opened the letter. And that moment has stayed with me.

Well, it is 2021 now and I am thirty-two years old and I don't really play video games as much, and I've almost gotten over the shyness that comes along with asking for things that I want (but sometimes I just can't help it). And my creativity these days mostly gets channeled into music and films. And you . . .

You have been gone for almost a decade.

There is so much to say to you. And there were so many moments— your birthday, holidays, the anniversary of your memorial service— that I could have taken a pen to a sheet of paper. But these thoughts below came to me unceremoniously while on a walk around the neighborhood. Our neighborhood. Over the years I've paid more and more attention to the practices that soothe and invigorate my spirit and body, and activate my creativity and imagination. Nothing does this for me quite like a walk around West Philly.

Our relationship to this city is intertwined. In West Philly, we were Black boys who became Black teens and grew to be Black men. Some things haven't changed much about the city. Market Street from 48th Street all the way down to City Hall is still booming first thing in the morning, with cars and bikes on their way to work, and young folks, sometimes with their parents right by their side, on their way to school. And I still know how to catch every light on Walnut and Chestnut like you taught me (if you're at the front of traffic, go 20 mph and you'll hit every light 'til 30th Street!). There are some new things though. For one, it feels like there is construction everywhere and always. The old West Philly High, a rival of your alma mater Overbrook High School, is being turned into apartments, which I know would be a big surprise to you. Oh, and the El has gone digital which means . . . no more tokens!

But you would be happy to know that the courts that you grew up on and I grew up on are still around. It feels miraculous to think that we played basketball in the same places, decades apart. Our shoes, our sweat, and our passion settling into the same asphalt on different sides of time. I sometimes imagine you as a young boy imagining me, dreaming me up, breathing life into my existence. It was a radically hopeful thing to do, knowing all you were up against.

You were sometimes very blunt with the realities a Black boy growing up poor in a major city faces on the daily. But you were also very open and proud about the ways that you and others figured out how. Through camaraderie and love from your community, you survived the racism, classism, and the other oppressions and systems built to erase you. As a child, I heard many people shout "Yo Hawkeye!" or simply "Yo Hawk!" as we walked up to basketball courts around the city, and I came to learn that those who knew you by that nickname (which you got as a teen for your ability to see things on the court!) were often wrapped up in your stories of perseverance and preservation.

I remember you telling me one time about starting a new job in a different part of the city and having to take many buses to get there. On the first day after work ended, you encountered a mob of angry white folks who were shocked to see a Black person in this part of Philly and they chased you for blocks. You laughed as you talked about narrowly escaping on the only bus headed back toward West Philly. You never went back to the job after that. This story has stayed with me for many reasons, but particularly because of the final lesson you shared with me. The lesson was this: Your Blackness is a blessing. For as long as I knew you, you were never confused about what it meant to be Black, even as others threw their own confused anger at you. You saw Blackness as a gift, a joy, an honor. And even when you would retell painful experiences you encountered while being Black in this city, your pride in your Black identity was evident. So when I would go on my own walks and the racial epithets were hurled my way by a group of white folks driving in a car—or when a police officer, looking to intimidate me and my friend, pulled up and after asking us where we were going told us, "You know you can't listen to hip-hop there"—though there was a sting, nothing could pierce the lesson you helped to etch into my core.

So today, as I walk around the city, I am prideful in walking in this Black body. And even in spaces outside of the city, like the Lake District in England or the White Mountains of New Hampshire, where I've gotten to hike many times over the last few years, I carry this joy. It radiates from me and supports me to not shrink in the faces that I pass and places that feel foreign, in Philly and beyond. I don't think you ever made it as far north as the White Mountains, but I think you would've enjoyed walking some of the Presidential Range together with me. We might not see too many other folks who look like us while up there (New Hampshire is 94% white!), but we could be bold and joyful and Black together up there. And while walking I could share with you about the summer of uprisings and George Floyd, and Breonna Taylor and Ahmaud Arbery, and share with you how walking for me is not only inspiring and grounding, but also an act of resistance.

And on our walk you could tell me about the parts of your life that were foreign to me. What did you love and remember most about Grandma? I've grown more and more curious about her because I was only four when she passed away, but I can feel the southern roots deep in me, and I know it is because they were deep in her. I would want to hear everything you remember about the life that she lived before you and your brothers were born. Was there anything she shared with you about her life growing up in North Carolina that stands out? What did she think of Philadelphia? I know how much you loved her, so I can imagine that these questions may bring a bit of the heartbreak back to the surface. But we could hold the heartbreak together. Laugh, cry, reminisce even more. Whatever felt natural and healing to do, we could do it together.

I can imagine us walking by Mill Creek Playground, crossing thru the stop sign on Aspen Street and standing in front of your middle school, Sulzberger Junior High School. (It now has a new name, but we would call it by its original name because that's how you knew it.) It's at this point that I would ask you who some of your biggest influences have been, and to tell me about some of the things that you are most proud of in your life. I have some ideas about how you would answer each of these questions, but just to hear these answers in your voice would make me more curious about your life. I could imagine you being pleasantly annoyed with my incessant questioning, but the fact that we were in motion coupled with my obvious excitement would make you more open to sharing pieces of your life. You would surprise yourself with the details of your own story that you had long forgotten. One of the gifts of getting to spend time walking with someone who loves you and who you love . . .

I could share with you the parts of my life that were just emerging before you passed away. I could tell you about becoming a Quaker and how it's different from Baptist church and how I've gotten really good at just sitting still. It is hard to imagine you sitting still for that long, as my memory of you was of someone who was always on the move. But I think you would've enjoyed the stillness. At least for a bit of time.

And you could share with me about what you remember of your lone summer connecting with our North Carolina roots. Was it quiet there? What was it like to live on the land? Do you think you could've grown up there, or do you feel like the city life is the only life for you? When I've traveled outside of Philly to more rural parts of the country, I have been surprised at how much I enjoy the slower pace of things. And nothing replaces looking up at the sky at night and seeing what feels like almost every star in the universe. Have you ever done that? Have you ever been taken outside of yourself by looking at something in the natural world? When do you feel most grounded? Most spiritual? Most connected to yourself or others?

If we had the chance to walk together, either in Philly or beyond, we could spend some time, or all of our time, dreaming together. I know you had a dream of building a center for Black youth, and I've had some dreams of building something with music and the arts for Black folks here in Philly. We could talk about what's been hard about working with young folks. And what's been life-giving about that work, too. We could talk about how we want to be remembered and the legacy we want to leave behind.

I think about that a lot, honestly.

Pops, though it dawned on me in writing this that I have not written you a letter for over twenty years, it is not lost on me all of the ways that you loved me and all the ways I feel you here, walking beside me. There is more to say and more to share, no doubt. (I haven't even had the chance to tell you about all the music I've made!) We'll be walking together again, I'm sure. I have more questions to ask, more of my own memories and experiences to sift through, and more stillness to rest in.

But for now I'll just say,

Thank you.

Love,
Dwight Sterling Dunston
a.k.a. Little Hawk

The Way Home

Justin Coffin

I WAS A KID of seven and my family were building a cabin on a small lump of a mountain in Appalachian West Virginia. It was going to be a humble structure, four walls and a roof in a clearing at one end of a logging road. My parents had bought a spread and then turned around and offered a parcel to their friends the Schnarrs, who by now had finished their cabin at the other end of the property. The sites were rustic, off a dirt road, over a little stream and up to the ridge that ran from a meadow at the Schnarrs' end to a gentle slope at ours. The road between the clearings wound through silver maples and blueberry bushes. A fork at the meadow end took you straight to the Schnarrs' campsite or by the meadow to bring you in the back way.

Others bought into the eighty-acre parcel, but this concerns the Schnarr site and my family's. We spent most Memorial Day and Labor Day weekends at our sites, and two weeks around the Fourth of July. During the longer summer stay, in mid-morning, I found myself at the Schnarrs'. Work had started on our cabin, but I was not very interested, nor, at my age, much help doing framing work. I don't know if I wandered up there myself or if the family had gone to visit and then left without me. But I was there as the Schnarrs were setting about their day and it was past time for me to go.

I didn't have a great sense of direction because I was a daydreamer. Like Ishmael in the *Pequod*'s mast-head, I was a "young Platonist," "given to unseasonable meditativeness," and I moved through the world absentmindedly. I strolled through the Schnarrs' campsite the front way, past the tire swing, shed, and shelter, down the driveway and toward what I expected was home, only to soon find myself approaching their cabin from the back.

I was momentarily confused but not surprised. I was used to returning from a reverie to figure out where I'd wound up. I just turned around and went back the way I'd come, a pleasant walk in the pleasant woods on a pleasant morning until I pulled up short, met again by the Schnarrs' cabin, now from the front. I started to worry. That worry turned to panic after I turned around and tried again to get home but again found myself approaching the now inescapable cabin from the back.

The world had grown terrifying in its tininess and inevitability—like the Little Prince's little globe, where walking away was only an early start on walking toward. I was flung off into an orbit that offered me no way to get back to my own family. Things felt too small and too large at once, tightly packed, impenetrable, and inconceivable. After I think the third time approaching the Schnarrs' cabin, I went to the door and knocked.

Kindly Mrs. Schnarr smiled through the screen door and opened it. She was tall to me, with an affable, gangly, loose-jointed way. She would sit in a folding chair by the campfire in her polyester pants, smoking a long white cigarette, making almost no impression on the chair's interwoven green nylon straps, legs crossed so that her one foot could tap distractedly against the ankle of the other. She spoke gently, smiled gently. And when I told her I couldn't find my way home, trying not to cry, she gently offered help. She said if I could quiet down and listen, I might be able to hear where to go. Could I do that? Could I hear what was happening?

I listened. The woods in midsummer offered layers of sound, rich and deep, the noises of wind and birds and bugs, a buzzing, a soughing, a singing. The breathing, fricative hush of serrated green leaves tickling the air as it breezed through their million fingers. What else? In the distance I heard hammering. The scream of a circular saw, occasional and sudden. That was the sound of cheerful work being done on my family's cabin. She told me to just keep listening and to follow it.

I did. I walked again through the Schnarrs' campsite and again past the shed and the shelter and the tire swing. And when I got to the place where the ridgeline road met their driveway, where I'd always gone left and found myself back at the same place, I heard the sounds coming from my right. Mrs. Schnarr had invited me out into the world, where I had a place in it and could reach out to find others in other places. I found myself when I placed myself in the world, and could find home. Feeling lost had driven me further inward, growing more frightened and feeling more lost in a familiar place. But the sound! It was so clear, coming from there! That's where my family was. That was home.

Mrs. Schnarr offered a solution to a little boy's problem. It was simple, and it was kind. But it also had a resonance. She helped me find my way home. Later, home would be harder to find.

When I was not much older than my son is now—I think of it as being at the end of a process that he, at twenty, has just begun—I made an impromptu ten-mile hike from the place I felt I had outgrown to the way station I was living in. Childhood had run out, but adulthood seemed to be taking its time in arriving, and I was in between things. One life had gotten me to that point, but another would need to begin before I could leave it.

My childhood world had been small, small towns, small communities, and schools that ranged from minuscule to small. And it had run out of things to offer me. I'd limped across the provisional finish line of an associates degree, having lost interest in school altogether. I had fallen out of love with being a student, being a kid, and I was focused instead on cultivating an earnest attitude of ennui and disillusionment with a world I had barely experienced.

My community was like a hall of mirrors where everywhere I saw limited, distorted reflections of who I was—who I should have been, who I was in danger of becoming. I felt constrained by an accepted, shared set of perceptions of me, a municipality-wide agreement about who I wasn't and what I hadn't lived up to. I didn't know what else might be possible for me, and didn't know how to get at it, but I wanted out.

So I had moved to a neighboring county and gotten a job as a landscaper, and then a construction site janitor, and then a cheese shop sandwich maker. I had run out of ideas. My life was spent at two ends of a ten-mile stretch between the place I couldn't quite leave behind and the place that had my futon in it.

Life was expensive. My parents were in no position to help, but they had offered me a car. Or, really, car trouble in the shape of a maroon Mercury Zephyr station wagon that might have driven to the polls to vote for Morning in America and to put an end to the Carter administration.

If you went to the gas station and turned the car off to put five bucks in, you could only start it again by sticking a pencil in the manifold. It soon blew the head gasket on a long hill and was towed away. Next, the '72 Dodge Charger with expired tags and inspection stickers that just cost too much to fuel and insure, which moldered in its space in the development parking lot until it was also towed away. One day, there was just the space where it had been, nothing left but a grease spot on the tarmac. Finally the T-boned Toyota pickup I had bought from a friend's dad for $300. When the cop who pulled me over asked me if it was my car, I answered, "Sort of." That one got impounded. I watched from the back of the police cruiser as the tow truck took it away. No title, no registration, no insurance, no nothing. The only way it could have been more illegal was if I'd stolen it.

To get around from then on, I was hitching, hoofing it, or hollering for help.

On one Sunday evening in the fall of maybe 1991, an evening that was shaping into a very Sunday-evening-feeling time, with the chill in the air, and the dark falling earlier, and everything feeling like it was winding down and turning inward, I discovered that I'd overstayed my welcome at my friend's house, or I'd overstayed something, either by an hour or by a couple of months.

But there I was, an interloper witnessing someone else's family putting away the weekend's convivialities and assuming a more domestic aspect—amber lit, flannel wearing, slippered. It was a time to prepare and to tidy, not a time for lingering visitors. I was ten miles from where I lived and no one seemed keen on giving me a ride. They were probably tired of my asking. I surely was. It was time to go, but I didn't want to go, and I also didn't want to ask. I'd have to walk.

Maybe I hoped I'd discover a bus that ran along my route, one that would get me within a mile or two of my place. Maybe I thought I could hitchhike. I think there was a part of me, and this was the child's hope, that thought something could still just happen. There'd be a brilliant idea or a minor miracle, some *deus ex machina* moment where some kindly acquaintance drove up, slowed down, and rolled down a window. "Justin? What are you doing out here?"

I was not a child anymore, not really. But I was no adult, either. With no one willing to take responsibility for me, myself included, I had no one to depend on. Myself included. I started walking in the failing light of the evening as the darkened sky closed up and put away the murky colors at the horizon, along roads that offered no consideration for pedestrians. I stumbled along verges, walked in gutters, stepped in puddles hidden by long grass, hurried beneath overpasses that offered barely the space for a single car to get through, and over old heaved pavements no one thought to fix because no one should be walking on them.

I got honked at. I was stared at by people in their kitchen windows, catching sight over the fence of someone skulking through the skimpy light of a streetlamp, glared at by a man standing proprietarily in his driveway. No one was glad to see someone walking through their boundaried suburban subdivisions. I was a signal of something, some lonely failure appearing at the crepuscule, some choice no one should make. I was an unwelcome reminder of what awaited anyone who ran into whatever had run into me.

But after two hours, I made it. I turned into the development, arrayed in clusters of six-unit pods arranged around parking lots that gave off from a central flabby oval, or a deflated inner tube. In the oval's middle was a field with a drainage ditch cutting through it. I walked down the short access way from the main road and I saw streetlights burning greenish white, amber spilling through the shades at kitchen windows. Twinkling humble domesticity. But not mine. I had made it, not to home, only to the end.

I was tired. My unit was on the far side of the deflated inner tube. I cut straight through the middle, through the field, down into and then out of the ditch. The last leg of a journey not meant to be undertaken by a human body. A last gesture of unwelcome from a world that didn't seem to want me. Before I reached my door, I knew something new about not being home. I don't think I had been aware of thinking much of anything at all during the walk, but somehow in the last few steps of the trip it all fell into place.

There had been self-flagellation—about how I had gotten to such a place and why I couldn't just be different. And beneath this reflex there were in fact some real and urgent questions, like really how had I gotten to such a place and seriously why couldn't I just be different. There were no easy answers. I'd never felt more lost.

And outside of the smarting questions and the wretchedness and the disorientation, a new knowledge was forming like crystals in the chilly air. I was having a little epiphany at the ragged end of my long walk. Before I'd taken the first of those 15,000 steps, I'd known that something wasn't working, but this was new: the terrible gift of pointed knowledge in place of shrugging acknowledgment. And it was knowledge imparted by the walking.

I had taken the trip many times in my rogue's gallery of automotive disasters, and it had only served to return me to a place I didn't want to be. I'd had that information already—the facts of where I lived and how on this evening I had had to get from the place I was to the place I'd rest my head, and that it wasn't great. It took the walking to make my exile a truth. The walk had placed the understanding in my body. Walking has a magic in it, in the rhythm and the repetition, like a physical catechism in which one step is always answering the last and again asking the next, a chain of responses or confirmations. The walk itself is an argument built simply by keeping our bodies upright in their precarious, ridiculous postures, on two legs and propelled forward.

I walked to arrive at a place where I knew I didn't belong and couldn't stay. All that effort expended to tour entire towns that would not want me, to arrive at a place that was just a rabbit warren of closed doors and drawn curtains. All that work to know some terrible news. It wasn't knowledge that I wanted; what I wanted was a home. I wanted to belong. Knowledge that I had no such thing was awful to have. Large, intractable, unavoidable, inescapable. And intolerable.

Mrs. Schnarr had invited me out into the world, but she had died years earlier and there was no one to tell me what to do if that world was now busy shutting itself off and turning in, if I had walked only hearing the sound of my own lonely footsteps and other people's clicking locks. The world had made its point: only I was left outside.

I knew the way back. I didn't need a noise to follow, the sound of hammers swung by family members and friends. There were no hammers, but the reason I couldn't find home now was that there wasn't one.

And now here I was, at the place where I lived. My bivouac. I don't remember opening my door or going in. It didn't matter, because I could no longer stay. But if I now had to go off in search of a home without help or guidance, and I did, that didn't mean I wanted to. But I think some things that night got left behind. I no longer hoped to be the one who was granted an exception. I no longer sat and dreamed of being in a different kind of reality. I had to find home. The walk hadn't led me there and I didn't know where it was, but I suspected it meant going to somewhere bigger. Somewhere I wasn't known and where things were more affordable. So it was in discovering that I was Theseus that I had the chance to again become Odysseus.

Of course, not all walking is a journey. Sometimes you're just placing yourself in the right aisle at the grocery store, to get within easy reach of the right jar of pickles. But in the two kinds of great journeys we are either Theseus escaping the labyrinth or Odysseus trying to get home.

As a child I had been a wee Odysseus, hopelessly and mystifyingly lost, prevented by forces from returning home until I had satisfied the goddesses that I had suffered enough. The journey home is the greater story, and it often contains within it escapes from labyrinths. My young adulthood was like a nested array of labyrinths, and escape from one was only entry into another. I needed now to find the way to the way home. But it would take some fundamental changes to even get access to a starting point where the big journey could begin.

When I started working on this essay, I'd watch my son, then eighteen, leave my house and walk to his mom's. What was it like to try to get home and especially what was it like not to be sure that home lies this way, or if it can be found at all? We said he had two homes, sixteen blocks apart, and how nice that they were close enough for him to walk between them.

As I'd watch him go, a sadness would hiss in my chest, and the breath would come in cold and sharp around my heart. But present too was a keening anxiety about being a young adult and what home meant. And that anxiety only grew during the early months of the pandemic as he made a trip that seemed pointless, going from one place where very little happened and almost no one was to another place where slightly more might happen, but still almost no one was. I was watching him walking without getting anywhere, and outgrowing a life that he couldn't get out of. Things just got more and more constricting. I could feel a cloudy unsettledness coalesce around me when I thought about his future. But I knew that it was more about memory than prediction. More about me than him.

Thinking about these two walks, I thought about him. I wondered what it felt like in his body, walking between places. Did he get the urge to keep walking, past a parent's place and on to the limits of the city and then beyond? What would the terrible knowledge be? What would the walk teach him? How would the relentless, rhythmic, slow, hypnotic message read? I don't know what he has learned, but it's a walk we all seem to take alone.

Acknowledgments

This anthology has its origins in a serendipitous encounter on the streets of Philadelphia. My eternal gratitude goes to Ken Kalfus for suggesting I apply for Swim Pony's Cross Pollination Residency back in 2015. That led to my collaborating with Adrienne Mackey, JJ Tiziou, and Sam Wend on a transformative walk around the perimeter of Philadelphia. My heartfelt thanks go to those three artists, strangers who quickly became friends, for giving me a new perspective on my city and on the act of walking itself, as well as to the Knight Foundation for supporting Adrienne's and Swim Pony's vision for shaking up artists' creative processes through interdisciplinary investigation. This book is a testament to that vision's viability.

My thanks to New Door Books, especially Doug Gordon, for responding enthusiastically to my spark of an idea for a collection of essays and agreeing to publish their first anthology. Doug and the rest of the Working Writers Group, Louis Greenstein, Mark Lyons, Vikram Paralkar, Nathaniel Popkin, David Sanders, Debra Leigh Scott, and Miriam Seidel, all helped turn that initial spark into an actual book, solid and substantive. Additional thanks to Miriam for her dynamic cover—and her abiding patience. And to Hazami Sayed for her evocative photographs of paths and pavements from around the world, incorporated into the myriad "ways" on the cover and in the interior design.

I'm grateful as well to Lise Funderburg for her generous advice on how to navigate editing an anthology, to Chris Myers for his always keen eye and attentive ear, and to Kabria Rogers for sharing her marketing savvy.

My most effusive thanks, though, are reserved for the 25 writers who shared their stories, experiences, and perspectives on walking. This is your book, fellow authors, as much as mine. Thank you for embarking on this wild adventure with me, all the more appreciated during the restrictions imposed by COVID-19. It's been slow going at times, but the many lively conversations along the way have sustained me, and, as with all pilgrimages, have generated a growing sense of fellowship. I've been delighted and honored to have you as companions on this journey.

Finally, I thank my family for their unfailing encouragement and support, from my granddaughter Nellie, who will have just taken her first steps about the time this book is in print, to my husband Joe, with whom I would walk anywhere.

Ann de Forest

About the Authors

Yasser Allaham was born in Damascus, Syria, and has made his home in the United States since 2017. He was studying finance when war broke out in his country. He currently works as a long-haul truck driver.

Liana Brent is an archaeologist and educator with a Ph.D. in Classics from Cornell University. Since she moves around so often, she believes that walking is the best way to get to know a place.

Nancy Brokaw is a Philadelphia-based writer of critical and historical texts on photography, video, installation art, and other topics. A recipient of a Pennsylvania Council on the Arts Fellowship for Arts Commentary, she is a former editor of *The Photo Review* and has contributed articles to other publications, including *Exposure, Photographers International, Art India, Wild River Review,* and others.

Justin Coffin lives and walks in Philadelphia. His latest book, *El Bunny,* is full of his words as well as paintings by Terrence Laragione.

A California native living and writing in fairly happy exile in Philadelphia for more than three decades, **Ann de Forest** writes about the urban landscape and the resonance of place. She is a contributing writer for *Hidden City Daily* and editor of *Extant Magazine.* Her poems, short stories, and essays have appeared in *Coal Hill Review, Noctua Review, Unbroken, Hotel Amerika, The Journal, PIF, Cleaver Magazine,* and *The Best Short Stories of Philadelphia* (Toho Press, 2021).

Dwight Sterling Dunston (a.k.a. Sterling Duns) is a West Philly–based hip-hop artist, musician, educator, and healer with roots in the Carolinas and deeper West Africa. He holds a B.A. in English from Dickinson College and an M.A. in Poetry from the University of East Anglia in Norwich, England.

Victoria Reynolds Farmer lives in a suburb of Atlanta with her husband. She works as a Community Manager for a market research firm. In her free time, she writes about gender, culture, and embodiment and serves as a panelist on the Christian Feminist Podcast.

A writer, thinker, and scholar dedicated to understanding both contemporary life and the Western tradition, **Mark Geanuleas** makes his home in and around southeastern Pennsylvania and is currently at work on his first two books, *The Roots of Contemporary Artistic Experience* and *Itinerant Essays on Contemporary America*.

Jay Heinrichs is the author of *Thank You for Arguing*, a *New York Times* bestseller.

Kathryn Hellerstein is a poet, translator, and scholar. Her translated and edited books include *In New York: A Selection* (Moyshe Leyb Halpern) and *Paper Bridges: Selected Poems of Kadya Molodowsky*. She is also the author of *A Question of Tradition: Women Poets in Yiddish, 1586–1987.* Now she's working on Jews and China, and on family history. She teaches Yiddish and modern Jewish literature and culture at the University of Pennsylvania.

Mickey Herr is interested in what roots us to place, whether it is blood or merely walking the same streets hundreds of years apart; her writing contemplates our connections. As a contributing writer to *Hidden City Daily*, she is most interested in elevating the hidden histories of women. She is currently working on a novel and is the co-author of *William Lewis, Esquire: Enlightened Statesman, Profound Lawyer, and Useful Citizen* (2012). She shares a "writer's photography" and other inspirations at mickeyherr.com.

Hannah Judd is a musician, scholar, and archivist whose work focuses on digitization, preservation, and exploring ideas of online communities and the sounds they make. She is a Ph.D. candidate in ethnomusicology at the University of Chicago and holds a B.A. in music and creative writing from the University of Pennsylvania.

JeeYeun Lee is an interdisciplinary artist, writer, and activist based in Chicago whose work explores dynamics of connection, power, and resistance. She holds an M.F.A. in Fiber from Cranbrook Academy of Art, an M.A. in Ethnic Studies from the University of California at Berkeley, and a B.A. in Linguistics from Stanford University.

Adrienne Mackey is a multidisciplinary artist exploring the power of performance and play both in her role as Founder of her company, Swim Pony, and as an Assistant Professor of Acting, Directing & Devising at the University of Washington's School of Drama.

Rahul Mehta is the author of a novel, *No Other World* (Harper, 2017), and a short story collection, *Quarantine* (HarperPerennial, 2011). Their collection of poems and lyric essays, *My Tarot Told Me to Quit Twitter and Other Truths*, is forthcoming from the University Press of Kentucky.

Christine Nelson served as the Drue Heinz Curator of Literary and Historical Manuscripts at the Morgan Library & Museum in New York and as co-curator of the 2017 bicentenary exhibition *This Ever New Self: Thoreau and His Journal*, a collaboration with David Wood of the Concord Museum. She is the author of *The Magic of Handwriting* (TASCHEN, 2018) and *The Brontës: A Family Writes* (Scala, 2016), and curator of major exhibitions on the life of Charlotte Brontë, the history of diary keeping, and the composition of *The Little Prince*. She lives in West Philadelphia.

Lena Popkin is a recent graduate of Tufts University. She is passionate about sustainable architecture and design, among other ways of adapting our world to new challenges.

Nathaniel Popkin is the author of seven books, including *To Reach the Spring: From Complicity to Consciousness in the Age of Eco-Crisis*, and co-editor of the anthology *Who Will Speak for America?* In his work as a writer and editor of fiction, nonfiction, film, criticism, and journalism, Nathaniel explores memory and loss, urban and historical change, architectural palimpsests, ecological grief, and the struggle for the democratic ideal.

Paula Read is a writer and translator who knew at a young age that she might want to live outside her native California. She never suspected that once she left, she would never move back. Four countries, three languages, and a second nationality later, she is pursuing a Ph.D. in Creative Writing while writing fiction and nonfiction on belonging, ecology, grief, and how our history informs our future. You can follow her at paulareadwrites.com.

Kabria Rogers was born and raised in Philadelphia, Pennsylvania. Being raised by a single mother in an intergenerational household in a major city powered her passion for self-expression through writing and her observations on social injustice. She currently lives in Philadelphia with her wife and two cats.

David Hallock Sanders is the author of the novel *Busara Road*, which was awarded a Gold Medal by the Nautilus Book Awards, was named a Finalist for both the Eric Hoffer Award Montaigne Medal and the Screencraft Cinematic Book Competition, and was shortlisted as a finalist for the William Faulkner–William Wisdom Prize for a novel-in-progress. His screenplay based on the novel was named a semifinalist in both the Rhode Island and Cinequest International Screenplay Competitions, and his short fiction, plays, essays, and poetry have been selected for a variety of publications and prizes.

Born in Morocco, **Ruth Knafo Setton** is the author of the novel *The Road to Fez*. She is a multi-genre author whose fiction, creative nonfiction, screenplays, and poetry have won many awards and appeared in numerous anthologies. She teaches Creative Writing at Lehigh University and for Semester at Sea.

Jacques-Jean "JJ" Tiziou is an artist and community organizer. His 85,000-square-foot *How Philly Moves* mural at PHL International Airport was recognized as one of the nation's best public art projects by Americans for the Arts. He also hosts house concerts, works as a licensed massage therapist, and serves as a block captain. JJ has walked the full perimeter of the city eight times (as of 2021) and devoted himself to facilitating access to this unique experience for others. So far, over three hundred Philadelphians have set out to participate in *Walk Around Philadelphia*. You can find more of his work at www.jjtiziou.net.

Sharon White's book *Vanished Gardens: Finding Nature in Philadelphia* won the Association of Writers and Writing Programs award in creative nonfiction. *Boiling Lake (On Voyage)*, a collection of short fiction, is her most recent book. New work appears in *The Rupture*, *DIAGRAM*, and *Nowhere* magazine, where her essay "Sightings" was a finalist in the Fall 2020 Travel writing contest.

Kalela Williams is the Director of Writing at Mighty Writers, a Philadelphia youth organization, and the founder of Black History Maven, a gathering community that honors an inclusive history and affirms Black culture, identity, and pride. Her writing has appeared in literary magazines including *Calyx: A Journal of Art and Literature for Women* and *Drunken Boat*, and it has been featured on a BBC Radio 4 program.

Tom Zoellner is a professor of English at Chapman University and the author of *The National Road: Dispatches from a Changing America* (Counterpoint Press, 2020).